Clean Architecture

Robert C. Martin Series

Visit **informit.com/martinseries** for a complete list of available publications.

The **Robert C. Martin Series** is directed at software developers, team-leaders, business analysts, and managers who want to increase their skills and proficiency to the level of a Master Craftsman. The series contains books that guide software professionals in the principles, patterns, and practices of programming, software project management, requirements gathering, design, analysis, testing, and others.

Make sure to connect with us!
informit.com/socialconnect

Clean Architecture

A Craftsman's Guide to Software Structure and Design

Robert C. Martin

PRENTICE
HALL

Boston • Columbus • Indianapolis • New York • San Francisco • Amsterdam • Cape Town
Dubai • London • Madrid • Milan • Munich • Paris • Montreal • Toronto • Delhi • Mexico City
São Paulo • Sydney • Hong Kong • Seoul • Singapore • Taipei • Tokyo

For information about buying this title in bulk quantities, or for special sales opportunities (which may include electronic versions; custom cover designs; and content particular to your business, training goals, marketing focus, or branding interests), please contact our corporate sales department at corpsales@pearsoned.com or (800) 382-3419.

For government sales inquiries, please contact governmentsales@pearsoned.com.

For questions about sales outside the U.S., please contact intlcs@pearson.com.

Visit us on the Web: informit.com

Library of Congress Control Number: 2017945537

ISBN-13: 978-0-13-449416-6
ISBN-10: 0-13-449416-4

3   18

This book is dedicated to my lovely wife, my four spectacular children, and their families, including my quiver full of five grandchildren—who are the dessert of my life.

Contents

FOREWORD

What do we talk about when we talk about architecture?

As with any metaphor, describing software through the lens of architecture can hide as much as it can reveal. It can both promise more than it can deliver and deliver more than it promises.

The obvious appeal of architecture is structure, and structure is something that dominates the paradigms and discussions of software development—components, classes, functions, modules, layers, and services, micro or macro. But the gross structure of so many software systems often defies either belief or understanding—Enterprise Soviet schemes destined for legacy, improbable Jenga towers reaching toward the cloud, archaeological layers buried in a big-ball-of-mud slide. It's not obvious that software structure obeys our intuition the way building structure does.

Buildings have an obvious physical structure, whether rooted in stone or concrete, whether arching high or sprawling wide, whether large or small, whether magnificent or mundane. Their structures have little choice but to respect the physics of gravity and their materials. On the other hand—except in its sense of seriousness—software has little time for gravity. And what is software made of? Unlike buildings, which may be made of bricks, concrete, wood, steel, and glass, software is made of software. Large software constructs are made from smaller software components, which are in turn made of smaller software components still, and so on. It's coding turtles all the way down.

When we talk about software architecture, software is recursive and fractal in nature, etched and sketched in code. Everything is details. Interlocking levels of detail also contribute to a building's architecture, but it doesn't make sense to talk about physical scale in software. Software has structure—many structures and many kinds of structures—but its variety eclipses the range of physical structure found in buildings. You can even argue quite convincingly that there is more design activity and focus in software than in building architecture—in this sense, it's not unreasonable to consider software architecture more architectural than building architecture!

But physical scale is something humans understand and look for in the world. Although appealing and visually obvious, the boxes on a PowerPoint diagram are not a software system's architecture. There's no doubt they represent a particular view of an architecture, but to mistake boxes for *the* big picture—for *the* architecture—is to miss the big picture and the architecture: Software architecture doesn't look like anything. A particular visualization is a choice, not a given. It is a choice founded on a further set of choices: what to include; what to exclude; what to emphasize by shape or color; what to de-emphasize through uniformity or omission. There is nothing natural or intrinsic about one view over another.

Although it might not make sense to talk about physics and physical scale in software architecture, we do appreciate and care about certain physical constraints. Processor speed and network bandwidth can deliver a harsh verdict on a system's performance. Memory and storage can limit the ambitions of any code base. Software may be such stuff as dreams are made on, but it runs in the physical world.

> *This is the monstrosity in love, lady, that the will is infinite, and the execution confined; that the desire is boundless, and the act a slave to limit.*
> —William Shakespeare

The physical world is where we and our companies and our economies live. This gives us another calibration we can understand software architecture by, other less physical forces and quantities through which we can talk and reason.

> *Architecture represents the significant design decisions that shape a system, where significant is measured by cost of change.*
>
> —Grady Booch

Time, money, and effort give us a sense of scale to sort between the large and the small, to distinguish the architectural stuff from the rest. This measure also tells us how we can determine whether an architecture is good or not: Not only does a good architecture meet the needs of its users, developers, and owners at a given point in time, but it also meets them over time.

> *If you think good architecture is expensive, try bad architecture.*
>
> —Brian Foote and Joseph Yoder

The kinds of changes a system's development typically experiences should not be the changes that are costly, that are hard to make, that take managed projects of their own rather than being folded into the daily and weekly flow of work.

That point leads us to a not-so-small physics-related problem: time travel. How do we know what those typical changes will be so that we can shape those significant decisions around them? How do we reduce future development effort and cost without crystal balls and time machines?

> *Architecture is the decisions that you wish you could get right early in a project, but that you are not necessarily more likely to get them right than any other.*
>
> —Ralph Johnson

Understanding the past is hard enough as it is; our grasp of the present is slippery at best; predicting the future is nontrivial.

This is where the road forks many ways.

Down the darkest path comes the idea that strong and stable architecture comes from authority and rigidity. If change is expensive, change is eliminated—its causes subdued or headed off into a bureaucratic ditch. The architect's mandate is total and totalitarian, with the architecture becoming a dystopia for its developers and a constant source of frustration for all.

Down another path comes a strong smell of speculative generality. A route filled with hard-coded guesswork, countless parameters, tombs of dead code, and more accidental complexity than you can shake a maintenance budget at.

The path we are most interested is the cleanest one. It recognizes the softness of software and aims to preserve it as a first-class property of the system. It recognizes that we operate with incomplete knowledge, but it also understands that, as humans, operating with incomplete knowledge is something we do, something we're good at. It plays more to our strengths than to our weaknesses. We create things and we discover things. We ask questions and we run experiments. A good architecture comes from understanding it more as a journey than as a destination, more as an ongoing process of enquiry than as a frozen artifact.

> *Architecture is a hypothesis, that needs to be proven by implementation and measurement.*
>
> —Tom Gilb

To walk this path requires care and attention, thought and observation, practice and principle. This might at first sound slow, but it's all in the way that you walk.

> *The only way to go fast, is to go well.*
>
> —Robert C. Martin

Enjoy the journey.

—Kevlin Henney
May 2017

PREFACE

The title of this book is *Clean Architecture*. That's an audacious name. Some would even call it arrogant. So why did I choose that title, and why did I write this book?

I wrote my very first line of code in 1964, at the age of 12. The year is now 2016, so I have been writing code for more than half a century. In that time, I have learned a few things about how to structure software systems—things that I believe others would likely find valuable.

I learned these things by building many systems, both large and small. I have built small embedded systems and large batch processing systems. I have built real-time systems and web systems. I have built console apps, GUI apps, process control apps, games, accounting systems, telecommunications systems, design tools, drawing apps, and many, many others.

I have built single-threaded apps, multithreaded apps, apps with few heavy-weight processes, apps with many light-weight processes, multiprocessor apps, database apps, mathematical apps, computational geometry apps, and many, many others.

I've built a lot of apps. I've built a lot of systems. And from them all, and by taking them all into consideration, I've learned something startling.

The architecture rules are the same!

This is startling because the systems that I have built have all been so radically different. Why should such different systems all share similar rules of architecture? My conclusion is that *the rules of software architecture are independent of every other variable*.

This is even more startling when you consider the change that has taken place in hardware over the same half-century. I started programming on machines the size of kitchen refrigerators that had half-megahertz cycle times, 4K of core memory, 32K of disk memory, and a 10 character per second teletype interface. I am writing this preface on a bus while touring in South Africa. I am using a MacBook with four i7 cores running at 2.8 gigahertz each. It has 16 gigabytes of RAM, a terabyte of SSD, and a 2880×1800 retina display capable of showing extremely high-definition video. The difference in computational power is staggering. Any reasonable analysis will show that this MacBook is at least 10^{22} more powerful than those early computers that I started using half a century ago.

Twenty-two orders of magnitude is a very large number. It is the number of angstroms from Earth to Alpha-Centuri. It is the number of electrons in the change in your pocket or purse. And yet that number—that number *at least*— is the computational power increase that I have experienced in my own lifetime.

And with all that vast change in computational power, what has been the effect on the software I write? It's gotten bigger certainly. I used to think 2000 lines was a big program. After all, it was a full box of cards that weighed 10 pounds. Now, however, a program isn't really big until it exceeds 100,000 lines.

The software has also gotten much more performant. We can do things today that we could scarcely dream about in the 1960s. *The Forbin Project*, *The*

Moon Is a Harsh Mistress, and *2001: A Space Odyssey* all tried to imagine our current future, but missed the mark rather significantly. They all imagined huge machines that gained sentience. What we have instead are impossibly small machines that are still ... just machines.

And there is one thing more about the software we have now, compared to the software from back then: *It's made of the same stuff*. It's made of `if` statements, assignment statements, and `while` loops.

Oh, you might object and say that we've got much better languages and superior paradigms. After all, we program in Java, or C#, or Ruby, and we use object-oriented design. True—and yet the code is still just an assemblage of sequence, selection, and iteration, just as it was back in the 1960s and 1950s.

When you really look closely at the practice of programming computers, you realize that very little has changed in 50 years. The languages have gotten a little better. The tools have gotten fantastically better. But the basic building blocks of a computer program have not changed.

If I took a computer programmer from 1966 forward in time to 2016 and put her[1] in front of my MacBook running IntelliJ and showed her Java, she might need 24 hours to recover from the shock. But then she would be able to write the code. Java just isn't that different from C, or even from Fortran.

And if I transported you back to 1966 and showed you how to write and edit PDP-8 code by punching paper tape on a 10 character per second teletype, you might need 24 hours to recover from the disappointment. But then you would be able to write the code. The code just hasn't changed that much.

That's the secret: This changelessness of the code is the reason that the rules of software architecture are so consistent across system types. The rules of software architecture are the rules of ordering and assembling the building

---

1. And she very likely would be female since, back then, women made up a large fraction of programmers.

blocks of programs. And since those building blocks are universal and haven't changed, the rules for ordering them are likewise universal and changeless.

Younger programmers might think this is nonsense. They might insist that everything is new and different nowadays, that the rules of the past are past and gone. If that is what they think, they are sadly mistaken. The rules have not changed. Despite all the new languages, and all the new frameworks, and all the paradigms, the rules are the same now as they were when Alan Turing wrote the first machine code in 1946.

But one thing has changed: Back then, we didn't know what the rules were. Consequently, we broke them, over and over again. Now, with half a century of experience behind us, we have a grasp of those rules.

And it is those rules—those timeless, changeless, rules—that this book is all about.

Register your copy of *Clean Architecture* on the InformIT site for convenient access to updates and/or corrections as they become available. To start the registration process, go to informit.com/register and log in or create an account. Enter the product ISBN (9780134494166) and click Submit. Look on the Registered Products tab for an Access Bonus Content link next to this product, and follow that link to access the bonus materials.

Acknowledgments

The people who played a part in the creation of this book—in no particular order:

Chris Guzikowski

Chris Zahn

Matt Heuser

Jeff Overbey

Micah Martin

Justin Martin

Carl Hickman

James Grenning

Simon Brown

Kevlin Henney

Jason Gorman

Doug Bradbury

Colin Jones

Grady Booch

Kent Beck

Martin Fowler

Alistair Cockburn

James O. Coplien

Tim Conrad

Richard Lloyd

Ken Finder

Kris Iyer (CK)

Mike Carew

Jerry Fitzpatrick

Jim Newkirk

Ed Thelen

Joe Mabel

Bill Degnan

And many others too numerous to name.

In my final review of this book, as I was reading the chapter on Screaming Architecture, Jim Weirich's bright-eyed smile and melodic laugh echoed through my mind. Godspeed, Jim!

ABOUT THE AUTHOR

Robert C. Martin (Uncle Bob) has been a programmer since 1970. He is the co-founder of cleancoders.com, which offers online video training for software developers, and is the founder of Uncle Bob Consulting LLC, which offers software consulting, training, and skill development services to major corporations worldwide. He served as the Master Craftsman at 8th Light, Inc., a Chicago-based software consulting firm. He has published dozens of articles in various trade journals and is a regular speaker at international conferences and trade shows. He served three years as the editor-in-chief of the *C++ Report* and served as the first chairman of the Agile Alliance.

Martin has authored and edited many books, including *The Clean Coder, Clean Code, UML for Java Programmers, Agile Software Development, Extreme Programming in Practice, More C++ Gems, Pattern Languages of Program Design 3*, and *Designing Object Oriented C++ Applications Using the Booch Method*.

INTRODUCTION

It doesn't take a huge amount of knowledge and skill to get a program working. Kids in high school do it all the time. Young men and women in college start billion-dollar businesses based on scrabbling together a few lines of PHP or Ruby. Hoards of junior programmers in cube farms around the world slog through massive requirements documents held in huge issue tracking systems to get their systems to "work" by the sheer brute force of *will*. The code they produce may not be pretty; but it works. It works because getting something to work—once—just isn't that hard.

Getting it right is another matter entirely. Getting software right is *hard*. It takes knowledge and skills that most young programmers haven't yet acquired. It requires thought and insight that most programmers don't take the time to develop. It requires a level of discipline and dedication that most programmers never dreamed they'd need. Mostly, it takes a passion for the craft and the desire to be a professional.

And when you get software right, something magical happens: You don't need hordes of programmers to keep it working. You don't need massive requirements documents and huge issue tracking systems. You don't need global cube farms and 24/7 programming.

When software is done right, it requires a fraction of the human resources to create and maintain. Changes are simple and rapid. Defects are few and far between. Effort is minimized, and functionality and flexibility are maximized.

Yes, this vision sounds a bit utopian. But I've been there; I've seen it happen. I've worked in projects where the design and architecture of the system made it easy to write and easy to maintain. I've experienced projects that required a fraction of the anticipated human resources. I've worked on systems that had extremely low defect rates. I've seen the extraordinary effect that good software architecture can have on a system, a project, and a team. I've been to the promised land.

But don't take my word for it. Look at your own experience. Have you experienced the opposite? Have you worked on systems that are so interconnected and intricately coupled that every change, regardless of how trivial, takes weeks and involves huge risks? Have you experienced the impedance of bad code and rotten design? Has the design of the systems you've worked on had a huge negative effect on the morale of the team, the trust of the customers, and the patience of the managers? Have you seen teams, departments, and even companies that have been brought down by the rotten structure of their software? Have you been to programming hell?

I have—and to some extent, most of the rest of us have, too. It is far more common to fight your way through terrible software designs than it is to enjoy the pleasure of working with a good one.

WHAT IS DESIGN AND ARCHITECTURE?

There has been a lot of confusion about design and architecture over the years. What is design? What is architecture? What are the differences between the two?

One of the goals of this book is to cut through all that confusion and to define, once and for all, what design and architecture are. For starters, I'll assert that there is no difference between them. *None at all.*

The word "architecture" is often used in the context of something at a high level that is divorced from the lower-level details, whereas "design" more often seems to imply structures and decisions at a lower level. But this usage is nonsensical when you look at what a real architect does.

Consider the architect who designed my new home. Does this home have an architecture? Of course it does. And what is that architecture? Well, it is the shape of the home, the outward appearance, the elevations, and the layout of the spaces and rooms. But as I look through the diagrams that my architect produced, I see an immense number of low-level details. I see where every outlet, light switch, and light will be placed. I see which switches control which lights. I see where the furnace is placed, and the size and placement of the water heater and the sump pump. I see detailed depictions of how the walls, roofs, and foundations will be constructed.

In short, I see all the little details that support all the high-level decisions. I also see that those low-level details and high-level decisions are part of the whole design of the house.

And so it is with software design. The low-level details and the high-level structure are all part of the same whole. They form a continuous fabric that defines the shape of the system. You can't have one without the other; indeed, no clear dividing line separates them. There is simply a continuum of decisions from the highest to the lowest levels.

THE GOAL?

And the goal of those decisions? The goal of good software design? That goal is nothing less than my utopian description:

The goal of software architecture is to minimize the human resources required to build and maintain the required system.

The measure of design quality is simply the measure of the effort required to meet the needs of the customer. If that effort is low, and stays low throughout the lifetime of the system, the design is good. If that effort grows with each new release, the design is bad. It's as simple as that.

CASE STUDY

As an example, consider the following case study. It includes real data from a real company that wishes to remain anonymous.

First, let's look at the growth of the engineering staff. I'm sure you'll agree that this trend is very encouraging. Growth like that shown in Figure 1.1 must be an indication of significant success!

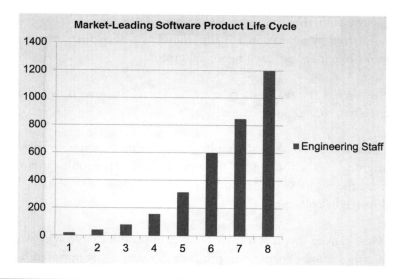

Figure 1.1 Growth of the engineering staff

Reproduced with permission from a slide presentation by Jason Gorman

Now let's look at the company's productivity over the same time period, as measured by simple lines of code (Figure 1.2).

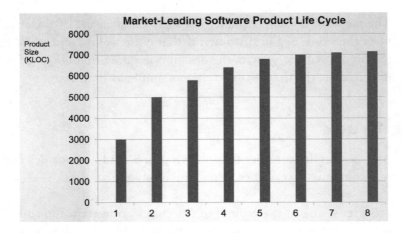

Figure 1.2 Productivity over the same period of time

Clearly something is going wrong here. Even though every release is supported by an ever-increasing number of developers, the growth of the code looks like it is approaching an asymptote.

Now here's the really scary graph: Figure 1.3 shows how the cost per line of code has changed over time.

These trends aren't sustainable. It doesn't matter how profitable the company might be at the moment: Those curves will catastrophically drain the profit from the business model and drive the company into a stall, if not into a downright collapse.

What caused this remarkable change in productivity? Why was the code 40 times more expensive to produce in release 8 as opposed to release 1?

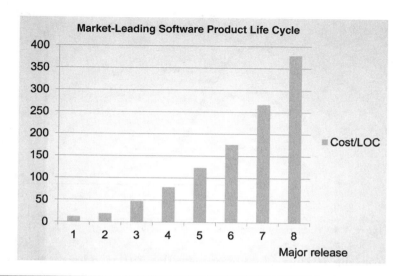

Figure 1.3 Cost per line of code over time

THE SIGNATURE OF A MESS

What you are looking at is the signature of a mess. When systems are thrown together in a hurry, when the sheer number of programmers is the sole driver of output, and when little or no thought is given to the cleanliness of the code or the structure of the design, then you can bank on riding this curve to its ugly end.

Figure 1.4 shows what this curve looks like to the developers. They started out at nearly 100% productivity, but with each release their productivity declined. By the fourth release, it was clear that their productivity was going to bottom out in an asymptotic approach to zero.

Figure 1.4 Productivity by release

From the developers' point of view, this is tremendously frustrating, because everyone is working *hard*. Nobody has decreased their effort.

And yet, despite all their heroics, overtime, and dedication, they simply aren't getting much of anything done anymore. All their effort has been diverted away from features and is now consumed with managing the mess. Their job, such as it is, has changed into moving the mess from one place to the next, and the next, and the next, so that they can add one more meager little feature.

THE EXECUTIVE VIEW

If you think *that's* bad, imagine what this picture looks like to the executives! Consider Figure 1.5, which depicts monthly development payroll for the same period.

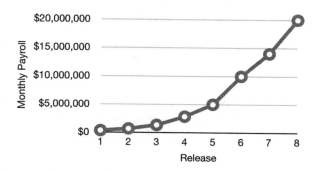

Figure 1.5 Monthly development payroll by release

Release 1 was delivered with a monthly payroll of a few hundred thousand dollars. The second release cost a few hundred thousand more. By the eighth release monthly payroll was $20 million, and climbing.

Just this chart alone is scary. Clearly something startling is happening. One hopes that revenues are outpacing costs and therefore justifying the expense. But no matter how you look at this curve, it's cause for concern.

But now compare the curve in Figure 1.5 with the lines of code written per release in Figure 1.2. That initial few hundred thousand dollars per month bought a lot of functionality—but the final $20 million bought almost nothing! Any CFO would look at these two graphs and know that immediate action is necessary to stave off disaster.

But which action can be taken? What has gone wrong? What has caused this incredible decline in productivity? What can executives do, other than to stamp their feet and rage at the developers?

WHAT WENT WRONG?

Nearly 2600 years ago, Aesop told the story of the Tortoise and the Hare. The moral of that story has been stated many times in many different ways:

- "Slow and steady wins the race."
- "The race is not to the swift, nor the battle to the strong."
- "The more haste, the less speed."

The story itself illustrates the foolishness of overconfidence. The Hare, so confident in its intrinsic speed, does not take the race seriously, and so naps while the Tortoise crosses the finish line.

Modern developers are in a similar race, and exhibit a similar overconfidence. Oh, they don't sleep—far from it. Most modern developers work their butts off. But a part of their brain *does* sleep—the part that knows that good, clean, well-designed code *matters*.

These developers buy into a familiar lie: "We can clean it up later; we just have to get to market first!" Of course, things never do get cleaned up later, because market pressures never abate. Getting to market first simply means that you've now got a horde of competitors on your tail, and you have to stay ahead of them by running as fast as you can.

And so the developers never switch modes. They can't go back and clean things up because they've got to get the next feature done, and the next, and the next, and the next. And so the mess builds, and productivity continues its asymptotic approach toward zero.

Just as the Hare was overconfident in its speed, so the developers are overconfident in their ability to remain productive. But the creeping mess of code that saps their productivity never sleeps and never relents. If given its way, it will reduce productivity to zero in a matter of months.

The bigger lie that developers buy into is the notion that writing messy code makes them go fast in the short term, and just slows them down in the long term. Developers who accept this lie exhibit the hare's overconfidence in their ability to switch modes from making messes to cleaning up messes sometime in the future, but they also make a simple error of fact. The fact is that *making messes is always slower than staying clean*, no matter which time scale you are using.

Consider the results of a remarkable experiment performed by Jason Gorman depicted in Figure 1.6. Jason conducted this test over a period of six days. Each day he completed a simple program to convert integers into Roman numerals. He knew his work was complete when his predefined set of acceptance tests passed. Each day the task took a little less than 30 minutes. Jason used a well-known cleanliness discipline named test-driven development (TDD) on the first, third, and fifth days. On the other three days, he wrote the code without that discipline.

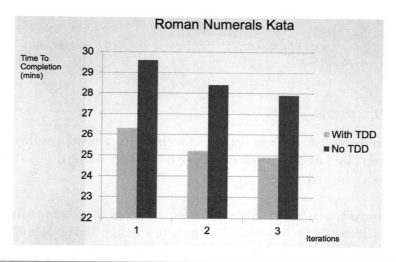

Figure 1.6 Time to completion by iterations and use/non-use of TDD

First, notice the learning curve apparent in Figure 1.6. Work on the latter days is completed more quickly than the former days. Notice also that work on the TDD days proceeded approximately 10% faster than work on the non-TDD days, and that even the slowest TDD day was faster than the fastest non-TDD day.

Some folks might look at that result and think it's a remarkable outcome. But to those who haven't been deluded by the Hare's overconfidence, the result is expected, because they know this simple truth of software development:

The only way to go fast, is to go well.

And that's the answer to the executive's dilemma. The only way to reverse the decline in productivity and the increase in cost is to get the developers to stop thinking like the overconfident Hare and start taking responsibility for the mess that they've made.

The developers may think that the answer is to start over from scratch and redesign the whole system—but that's just the Hare talking again. The same overconfidence that led to the mess is now telling them that they can build it better if only they can start the race over. The reality is less rosy:

> *Their overconfidence will drive the redesign into the same mess as the original project.*

CONCLUSION

In every case, the best option is for the development organization to recognize and avoid its own overconfidence and to start taking the quality of its software architecture seriously.

To take software architecture seriously, you need to know what good software architecture is. To build a system with a design and an architecture that minimize effort and maximize productivity, you need to know which attributes of system architecture lead to that end.

That's what this book is about. It describes what good clean architectures and designs look like, so that software developers can build systems that will have long profitable lifetimes.

A Tale of Two Values

2

Every software system provides two different values to the stakeholders: behavior and structure. Software developers are responsible for ensuring that both those values remain high. Unfortunately, they often focus on one to the exclusion of the other. Even more unfortunately, they often focus on the lesser of the two values, leaving the software system eventually valueless.

BEHAVIOR

The first value of software is its behavior. Programmers are hired to make machines behave in a way that makes or saves money for the stakeholders. We do this by helping the stakeholders develop a functional specification, or requirements document. Then we write the code that causes the stakeholder's machines to satisfy those requirements.

When the machine violates those requirements, programmers get their debuggers out and fix the problem.

Many programmers believe that is the entirety of their job. They believe their job is to make the machine implement the requirements and to fix any bugs. They are sadly mistaken.

ARCHITECTURE

The second value of software has to do with the word "software"—a compound word composed of "soft" and "ware." The word "ware" means "product"; the word "soft"... Well, that's where the second value lies.

Software was invented to be "soft." It was intended to be a way to easily change the behavior of machines. If we'd wanted the behavior of machines to be hard to change, we would have called it *hard*ware.

To fulfill its purpose, software must be soft—that is, it must be easy to change. When the stakeholders change their minds about a feature, that change should be simple and easy to make. The difficulty in making such a change should be proportional only to the scope of the change, and not to the *shape* of the change.

It is this difference between scope and shape that often drives the growth in software development costs. It is the reason that costs grow out of proportion to the size of the requested changes. It is the reason that the first year of development is much cheaper than the second, and the second year is much cheaper than the third.

From the stakeholders' point of view, they are simply providing a stream of changes of roughly similar scope. From the developers' point of view, the stakeholders are giving them a stream of jigsaw puzzle pieces that they must fit into a puzzle of ever-increasing complexity. Each new request is harder to fit than the last, because the shape of the system does not match the shape of the request.

I'm using the word "shape" here in a unconventional way, but I think the metaphor is apt. Software developers often feel as if they are forced to jam square pegs into round holes.

The problem, of course, is the architecture of the system. The more this architecture prefers one shape over another, the more likely new features will be harder and harder to fit into that structure. Therefore architectures should be as shape agnostic are practical.

THE GREATER VALUE

Function or architecture? Which of these two provides the greater value? Is it more important for the software system to work, or is it more important for the software system to be easy to change?

If you ask the business managers, they'll often say that it's more important for the software system to work. Developers, in turn, often go along with this attitude. *But it's the wrong attitude.* I can prove that it is wrong with the simple logical tool of examining the extremes.

- *If you give me a program that works perfectly but is impossible to change, then it won't work when the requirements change, and I won't be able to make it work. Therefore the program will become useless.*
- *If you give me a program that does not work but is easy to change, then I can make it work, and keep it working as requirements change. Therefore the program will remain continually useful.*

You may not find this argument convincing. After all, there's no such thing as a program that is impossible to change. However, there are systems that are *practically* impossible to change, because the cost of change exceeds the benefit of change. Many systems reach that point in some of their features or configurations.

If you ask the business managers if they want to be able to make changes, they'll say that of course they do, but may then qualify their answer by noting that the current functionality is more important than any later flexibility. In contrast, if the business managers ask you for a change, and your estimated costs for that change are unaffordably high, the business managers will likely be furious that you allowed the system to get to the point where the change was impractical.

EISENHOWER'S MATRIX

Consider President Dwight D. Eisenhower's matrix of importance versus urgency (Figure 2.1). Of this matrix, Eisenhower said:

> *I have two kinds of problems, the urgent and the important. The urgent are not important, and the important are never urgent.*[1]

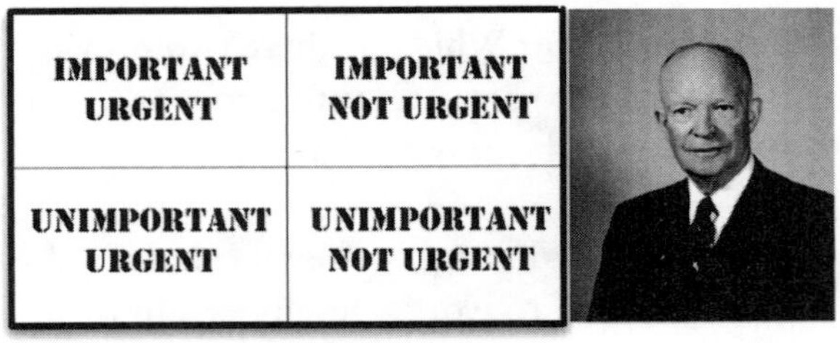

IMPORTANT URGENT	IMPORTANT NOT URGENT
UNIMPORTANT URGENT	UNIMPORTANT NOT URGENT

Figure 2.1 Eisenhower matrix

---

1. From a speech at Northwestern University in 1954.

There is a great deal of truth to this old adage. Those things that are urgent are rarely of great importance, and those things that are important are seldom of great urgency.

The first value of software—behavior—is urgent but not always particularly important.

The second value of software—architecture—is important but never particularly urgent.

Of course, some things are both urgent and important. Other things are not urgent and not important. Ultimately, we can arrange these four couplets into priorities:

1. Urgent and important
2. Not urgent and important
3. Urgent and not important
4. Not urgent and not important

Note that the architecture of the code—the important stuff—is in the top two positions of this list, whereas the behavior of the code occupies the first and *third* positions.

The mistake that business managers and developers often make is to elevate items in position 3 to position 1. In other words, they fail to separate those features that are urgent but not important from those features that truly are urgent and important. This failure then leads to ignoring the important architecture of the system in favor of the unimportant features of the system.

The dilemma for software developers is that business managers are not equipped to evaluate the importance of architecture. *That's what software developers were hired to do.* Therefore it is the responsibility of the software development team to assert the importance of architecture over the urgency of features.

FIGHT FOR THE ARCHITECTURE

Fulfilling this responsibility means wading into a fight—or perhaps a better word is "struggle." Frankly, that's always the way these things are done. The development team has to struggle for what they believe to be best for the company, and so do the management team, and the marketing team, and the sales team, and the operations team. *It's always a struggle.*

Effective software development teams tackle that struggle head on. They unabashedly squabble with all the other stakeholders as equals. Remember, as a software developer, *you are a stakeholder.* You have a stake in the software that you need to safeguard. That's part of your role, and part of your duty. And it's a big part of why you were hired.

This challenge is doubly important if you are a software architect. Software architects are, by virtue of their job description, more focused on the structure of the system than on its features and functions. Architects create an architecture that allows those features and functions to be easily developed, easily modified, and easily extended.

Just remember: If architecture comes last, then the system will become ever more costly to develop, and eventually change will become practically impossible for part or all of the system. If that is allowed to happen, it means the software development team did not fight hard enough for what they knew was necessary.

STARTING WITH THE BRICKS: PROGRAMMING PARADIGMS

Software architecture begins with the code—and so we will begin our discussion of architecture by looking at what we've learned about code since code was first written.

In 1938, Alan Turing laid the foundations of what was to become computer programming. He was not the first to conceive of a programmable machine, but he was the first to understand that programs were simply data. By 1945, Turing was writing real programs on real computers in code that we would recognize (if we squinted enough). Those programs used loops, branches, assignment, subroutines, stacks, and other familiar structures. Turing's language was binary.

Since those days, a number of revolutions in programming have occurred. One revolution with which we are all very familiar is the revolution of languages. First, in the late 1940s, came assemblers. These "languages" relieved the programmers of the drudgery of translating their programs into binary. In 1951, Grace Hopper invented A0, the first compiler. In fact, she coined the term *compiler*. Fortran was invented in 1953 (the year after I was born). What followed was an unceasing flood of new programming languages—COBOL, PL/1, SNOBOL, C, Pascal, C++, Java, ad infinitum.

Another, probably more significant, revolution was in programming *paradigms*. Paradigms are ways of programming, relatively unrelated to languages. A paradigm tells you which programming structures to use, and when to use them. To date, there have been three such paradigms. For reasons we shall discuss later, there are unlikely to be any others.

PARADIGM 3 OVERVIEW

KOHNKE

The three paradigms included in this overview chapter are structured programming, object-orient programming, and functional programming.

STRUCTURED PROGRAMMING

The first paradigm to be adopted (but not the first to be invented) was structured programming, which was discovered by Edsger Wybe Dijkstra in 1968. Dijkstra showed that the use of unrestrained jumps (`goto` statements) is harmful to program structure. As we'll see in the chapters that follow, he replaced those jumps with the more familiar `if/then/else` and `do/while/until` constructs.

We can summarize the structured programming paradigm as follows:

Structured programming imposes discipline on direct transfer of control.

OBJECT-ORIENTED PROGRAMMING

The second paradigm to be adopted was actually discovered two years earlier, in 1966, by Ole Johan Dahl and Kristen Nygaard. These two programmers noticed that the function call stack frame in the `ALGOL` language could be moved to a heap, thereby allowing local variables declared by a function to exist long after the function returned. The function became a constructor for a class, the local variables became instance variables, and the nested functions became methods. This led inevitably to the discovery of polymorphism through the disciplined use of function pointers.

We can summarize the object-oriented programming paradigm as follows:

Object-oriented programming imposes discipline on indirect transfer of control.

FUNCTIONAL PROGRAMMING

The third paradigm, which has only recently begun to be adopted, was the first to be invented. Indeed, its invention predates computer programming itself. Functional programming is the direct result of the work of Alonzo Church, who in 1936 invented λ-calculus while pursuing the same mathematical problem that was motivating Alan Turing at the same time. His λ-calculus is the foundation of the LISP language, invented in 1958 by John McCarthy. A foundational notion of λ-calculus is immutability—that is, the notion that the values of symbols do not change. This effectively means that a functional language has no assignment statement. Most functional languages do, in fact, have some means to alter the value of a variable, but only under very strict discipline.

We can summarize the functional programming paradigm as follows:

> *Functional programming imposes discipline upon assignment.*

FOOD FOR THOUGHT

Notice the pattern that I've quite deliberately set up in introducing these three programming paradigms: Each of the paradigms *removes* capabilities from the programmer. None of them adds new capabilities. Each imposes some kind of extra discipline that is *negative* in its intent. The paradigms tell us what *not* to do, more than they tell us what *to* do.

Another way to look at this issue is to recognize that each paradigm takes something away from us. The three paradigms together remove `goto` statements, function pointers, and assignment. Is there anything left to take away?

Probably not. Thus these three paradigms are likely to be the only three we will see—at least the only three that are negative. Further evidence that there are no more such paradigms is that they were all discovered within the ten years between 1958 and 1968. In the many decades that have followed, no new paradigms have been added.

CONCLUSION

What does this history lesson on paradigms have to do with architecture? Everything. We use polymorphism as the mechanism to cross architectural boundaries; we use functional programming to impose discipline on the location of and access to data; and we use structured programming as the algorithmic foundation of our modules.

Notice how well those three align with the three big concerns of architecture: function, separation of components, and data management.

STRUCTURED PROGRAMMING

Edsger Wybe Dijkstra was born in Rotterdam in 1930. He survived the bombing of Rotterdam during World War II, along with the German occupation of the Netherlands, and in 1948 graduated from high school with the highest possible marks in math, physics, chemistry, and biology. In March 1952, at the age of 21 (and just 9 months before I was born), Dijkstra took a job with the Mathematical Center of Amsterdam as the Netherlands' very first programmer.

In 1955, having been a programmer for three years, and while still a student, Dijkstra concluded that the intellectual challenge of programming was greater than the intellectual challenge of theoretical physics. As a result, he chose programming as his long-term career.

In 1957, Dijkstra married Maria Debets. At the time, you had to state your profession as part of the marriage rites in the Netherlands. The Dutch authorities were unwilling to accept "programmer" as Dijkstra's profession; they had never heard of such a profession. To satisfy them, Dijkstra settled for "theoretical physicist" as his job title.

As part of deciding to make programming his career, Dijkstra conferred with his boss, Adriaan van Wijngaarden. Dijkstra was concerned that no one had identified a discipline, or science, of programming, and that he would therefore not be taken seriously. His boss replied that Dijkstra might very well be one of the people who would discover such disciplines, thereby evolving software into a science.

Dijkstra started his career in the era of vacuum tubes, when computers were huge, fragile, slow, unreliable, and (by today's standards) extremely limited. In those early years, programs were written in binary, or in very crude assembly language. Input took the physical form of paper tape or punched cards. The edit/compile/test loop was hours—if not days—long.

It was in this primitive environment that Dijkstra made his great discoveries.

PROOF

The problem that Dijkstra recognized, early on, was that programming is *hard*, and that programmers don't do it very well. A program of any complexity contains too many details for a human brain to manage without help. Overlooking just one small detail results in programs that may *seem* to work, but fail in surprising ways.

Dijkstra's solution was to apply the mathematical discipline of *proof*. His vision was the construction of a Euclidian hierarchy of postulates, theorems, corollaries, and lemmas. Dijkstra thought that programmers could use that hierarchy the way mathematicians do. In other words, programmers would use proven structures, and tie them together with code that they would then prove correct themselves.

Of course, to get this going, Dijkstra realized that he would have to demonstrate the technique for writing basic proofs of simple algorithms. This he found to be quite challenging.

During his investigation, Dijkstra discovered that certain uses of `goto` statements prevent modules from being decomposed recursively into smaller and smaller units, thereby preventing use of the divide-and-conquer approach necessary for reasonable proofs.

Other uses of `goto`, however, did not have this problem. Dijkstra realized that these "good" uses of `goto` corresponded to simple selection and iteration control structures such as `if/then/else` and `do/while`. Modules that used only those kinds of control structures *could* be recursively subdivided into provable units.

Dijkstra knew that those control structures, when combined with sequential execution, were special. They had been identified two years before by Böhm and Jacopini, who proved that all programs can be constructed from just three structures: sequence, selection, and iteration.

This discovery was remarkable: The very control structures that made a module provable were the same minimum set of control structures from which all programs can be built. Thus structured programming was born.

Dijkstra showed that sequential statements could be proved correct through simple enumeration. The technique mathematically traced the inputs of the sequence to the outputs of the sequence. This approach was no different from any normal mathematical proof.

Dijkstra tackled selection through reapplication of enumeration. Each path through the selection was enumerated. If both paths eventually produced appropriate mathematical results, then the proof was solid.

Iteration was a bit different. To prove an iteration correct, Dijkstra had to use *induction*. He proved the case for 1 by enumeration. Then he proved the case that if N was assumed correct, $N + 1$ was correct, again by enumeration. He also proved the starting and ending criteria of the iteration by enumeration.

Such proofs were laborious and complex—but they were proofs. With their development, the idea that a Euclidean hierarchy of theorems could be constructed seemed reachable.

A HARMFUL PROCLAMATION

In 1968, Dijkstra wrote a letter to the editor of *CACM*, which was published in the March issue. The title of this letter was "Go To Statement Considered Harmful." The article outlined his position on the three control structures.

And the programming world caught fire. Back then we didn't have an Internet, so people couldn't post nasty memes of Dijkstra, and they couldn't flame him online. But they could, and they did, write letters to the editors of many published journals.

Those letters weren't necessarily all polite. Some were intensely negative; others voiced strong support for his position. And so the battle was joined, ultimately to last about a decade.

Eventually the argument petered out. The reason was simple: Dijkstra had won. As computer languages evolved, the `goto` statement moved ever rearward, until it all but disappeared. Most modern languages do not have a `goto` statement—and, of course, LISP *never* did.

Nowadays we are all structured programmers, though not necessarily by choice. It's just that our languages don't give us the option to use undisciplined direct transfer of control.

Some may point to named `breaks` in Java or exceptions as `goto` analogs. In fact, these structures are not the utterly unrestricted transfers of control that older languages like Fortran or COBOL once had. Indeed, even languages that still support the `goto` keyword often restrict the target to within the scope of the current function.

FUNCTIONAL DECOMPOSITION

Structured programming allows modules to be recursively decomposed into provable units, which in turn means that modules can be functionally decomposed. That is, you can take a large-scale problem statement and decompose it into high-level functions. Each of those functions can then be decomposed into lower-level functions, ad infinitum. Moreover, each of those decomposed functions can be represented using the restricted control structures of structured programming.

Building on this foundation, disciplines such as structured analysis and structured design became popular in the late 1970s and throughout the 1980s. Men like Ed Yourdon, Larry Constantine, Tom DeMarco, and Meilir Page-Jones promoted and popularized these techniques throughout that period. By following these disciplines, programmers could break down large proposed systems into modules and components that could be further broken down into tiny provable functions.

NO FORMAL PROOFS

But the proofs never came. The Euclidean hierarchy of theorems was never built. And programmers at large never saw the benefits of working through the laborious process of formally proving each and every little function correct. In the end, Dijkstra's dream faded and died. Few of today's programmers believe that formal proofs are an appropriate way to produce high-quality software.

Of course, formal, Euclidian style, mathematical proofs are not the only strategy for proving something correct. Another highly successful strategy is the *scientific method*.

SCIENCE TO THE RESCUE

Science is fundamentally different from mathematics, in that scientific theories and laws cannot be proven correct. I cannot prove to you that Newton's second law of motion, $F = ma$, or law of gravity, $F = Gm_1m_2/r^2$, are correct. I can demonstrate these laws to you, and I can make measurements that show them correct to many decimal places, but I cannot prove them in the sense of a mathematical proof. No matter how many experiments I conduct or how much empirical evidence I gather, there is always the chance that some experiment will show that those laws of motion and gravity are incorrect.

That is the nature of scientific theories and laws: They are *falsifiable* but not provable.

And yet we bet our lives on these laws every day. Every time you get into a car, you bet your life that $F = ma$ is a reliable description of the way the world works. Every time you take a step, you bet your health and safety that $F = Gm_1m_2/r^2$ is correct.

Science does not work by proving statements true, but rather by *proving statements false*. Those statements that we cannot prove false, after much effort, we deem to be true enough for our purposes.

Of course, not all statements are provable. The statement "This is a lie" is neither true nor false. It is one of the simplest examples of a statement that is not provable.

Ultimately, we can say that mathematics is the discipline of proving provable statements true. Science, in contrast, is the discipline of proving provable statements false.

TESTS

Dijkstra once said, "Testing shows the presence, not the absence, of bugs." In other words, a program can be proven incorrect by a test, but it cannot be proven correct. All that tests can do, after sufficient testing effort, is allow us to deem a program to be correct enough for our purposes.

The implications of this fact are stunning. Software development is not a mathematical endeavor, even though it seems to manipulate mathematical constructs. Rather, software is like a science. We show correctness by failing to prove incorrectness, despite our best efforts.

Such proofs of incorrectness can be applied only to *provable* programs. A program that is not provable—due to unrestrained use of goto, for example—cannot be deemed correct no matter how many tests are applied to it.

Structured programming forces us to recursively decompose a program into a set of small provable functions. We can then use tests to try to prove those small provable functions incorrect. If such tests fail to prove incorrectness, then we deem the functions to be correct enough for our purposes.

CONCLUSION

It is this ability to create falsifiable units of programming that makes structured programming valuable today. This is the reason that modern languages do not typically support unrestrained goto statements. Moreover, at the architectural level, this is why we still consider *functional decomposition* to be one of our best practices.

At every level, from the smallest function to the largest component, software is like a science and, therefore, is driven by falsifiability. Software architects strive to define modules, components, and services that are easily falsifiable (testable). To do so, they employ restrictive disciplines similar to structured programming, albeit at a much higher level.

It is those restrictive disciplines that we will study in some detail in the chapters to come.

OBJECT-ORIENTED PROGRAMMING

As we will see, the basis of a good architecture is the understanding and application of the principles of object-oriented design (OO). But just what is OO?

One answer to this question is "The combination of data and function." Although often cited, this is a very unsatisfying answer because it implies that o.f() is somehow different from f(o). This is absurd. Programmers were passing data structures into functions long before 1966, when Dahl and Nygaard moved the function call stack frame to the heap and invented OO.

Another common answer to this question is "A way to model the real world." This is an evasive answer at best. What does "modeling the real world" actually mean, and why is it something we would want to do? Perhaps this statement is intended to imply that OO makes software easier to understand because it has a closer relationship to the real world—but even that statement is evasive and too loosely defined. It does not tell us what OO is.

Some folks fall back on three magic words to explain the nature of OO: *encapsulation*, *inheritance*, and *polymorphism*. The implication is that OO is the proper admixture of these three things, or at least that an OO language must support these three things.

Let's examine each of these concepts in turn.

ENCAPSULATION?

The reason encapsulation is cited as part of the definition of OO is that OO languages provide easy and effective encapsulation of data and function. As a result, a line can be drawn around a cohesive set of data and functions. Outside of that line, the data is hidden and only some of the functions are known. We see this concept in action as the private data members and the public member functions of a class.

This idea is certainly not unique to OO. Indeed, we had perfect encapsulation in C. Consider this simple C program:

point.h

```
struct Point;
struct Point* makePoint(double x, double y);
double distance (struct Point *p1, struct Point *p2);
```

point.c

```
#include "point.h"
#include <stdlib.h>
#include <math.h>

struct Point {
  double x,y;
};

struct Point* makepoint(double x, double y) {
  struct Point* p = malloc(sizeof(struct Point));
  p->x = x;
  p->y = y;
  return p;
}

double distance(struct Point* p1, struct Point* p2) {
  double dx = p1->x - p2->x;
  double dy = p1->y - p2->y;
  return sqrt(dx*dx+dy*dy);
}
```

The users of point.h have no access whatsoever to the members of struct Point. They can call the makePoint() function, and the distance() function, but they have absolutely no knowledge of the implementation of either the Point data structure or the functions.

This is perfect encapsulation—in a non-OO language. C programmers used to do this kind of thing all the time. We would forward declare data structures and functions in header files, and then implement them in implementation files. Our users never had access to the elements in those implementation files.

But then came OO in the form of C++—and the perfect encapsulation of C was broken.

The C++ compiler, for technical reasons,[1] needed the member variables of a class to be declared in the header file of that class. So our `Point` program changed to look like this:

point.h

```
class Point {
public:
  Point(double x, double y);
  double distance(const Point& p) const;

private:
  double x;
  double y;
};
```

point.cc

```
#include "point.h"
#include <math.h>

Point::Point(double x, double y)
: x(x), y(y)
{}

double Point::distance(const Point& p) const {
  double dx = x-p.x;
  double dy = y-p.y;
  return sqrt(dx*dx + dy*dy);
}
```

---

1. The C++ compiler needs to know the size of the instances of each class.

Clients of the header file `point.h` know about the member variables x and y! The compiler will prevent access to them, but the client still knows they exist. For example, if those member names are changed, the `point.cc` file must be recompiled! Encapsulation has been broken.

Indeed, the way encapsulation is partially repaired is by introducing the `public`, `private`, and `protected` keywords into the language. This, however, was a *hack* necessitated by the technical need for the compiler to see those variables in the header file.

Java and C# simply abolished the header/implementation split altogether, thereby weakening encapsulation even more. In these languages, it is impossible to separate the declaration and definition of a class.

For these reasons, it is difficult to accept that OO depends on strong encapsulation. Indeed, many OO languages[2] have little or no enforced encapsulation.

OO certainly does depend on the idea that programmers are well-behaved enough to not circumvent encapsulated data. Even so, the languages that claim to provide OO have only weakened the once perfect encapsulation we enjoyed with C.

INHERITANCE?

If OO languages did not give us better encapsulation, then they certainly gave us inheritance.

Well—sort of. Inheritance is simply the redeclaration of a group of variables and functions within an enclosing scope. This is something C programmers[3] were able to do manually long before there was an OO language.

---

2. For example, Smalltalk, Python, JavaScript, Lua, and Ruby.

3. Not just C programmers: Most languages of that era had the capability to masquerade one data structure as another.

Consider this addition to our original point.h C program:

namedPoint.h
_____

```
struct NamedPoint;

struct NamedPoint* makeNamedPoint(double x, double y, char* name);
void setName(struct NamedPoint* np, char* name);
char* getName(struct NamedPoint* np);
```

namedPoint.c
_____

```
#include "namedPoint.h"
#include <stdlib.h>

struct NamedPoint {
  double x,y;
  char* name;
};

struct NamedPoint* makeNamedPoint(double x, double y, char* name) {
  struct NamedPoint* p = malloc(sizeof(struct NamedPoint));
  p->x = x;
  p->y = y;
  p->name = name;
  return p;
}

void setName(struct NamedPoint* np, char* name) {
  np->name = name;
}

char* getName(struct NamedPoint* np) {
  return np->name;
}
```

main.c

```c
#include "point.h"
#include "namedPoint.h"
#include <stdio.h>

int main(int ac, char** av) {
  struct NamedPoint* origin = makeNamedPoint(0.0, 0.0, "origin");
  struct NamedPoint* upperRight = makeNamedPoint
    (1.0, 1.0, "upperRight");
  printf("distance=%f\n",
    distance(
            (struct Point*) origin,
            (struct Point*) upperRight));
}
```

If you look carefully at the main program, you'll see that the NamedPoint data structure acts as though it is a derivative of the Point data structure. This is because the order of the first two fields in NamedPoint is the same as Point. In short, NamedPoint can masquerade as Point because NamedPoint is a pure superset of Point and maintains the ordering of the members that correspond to Point.

This kind of trickery was a common practice[4] of programmers prior to the advent of OO. In fact, such trickery is how C++ implements single inheritance.

Thus we might say that we had a kind of inheritance long before OO languages were invented. That statement wouldn't quite be true, though. We had a trick, but it's not nearly as convenient as true inheritance. Moreover, multiple inheritance is a considerably more difficult to achieve by such trickery.

---

4. Indeed it still is.

Note also that in main.c, I was forced to cast the NamedPoint arguments to Point. In a real OO language, such upcasting would be implicit.

It's fair to say that while OO languages did not give us something completely brand new, it did make the masquerading of data structures significantly more convenient.

To recap: We can award no point to OO for encapsulation, and perhaps a half-point for inheritance. So far, that's not such a great score.

But there's one more attribute to consider.

POLYMORPHISM?

Did we have polymorphic behavior before OO languages? Of course we did. Consider this simple C copy program.

```
#include <stdio.h>

void copy() {
  int c;
  while ((c=getchar()) != EOF)
    putchar(c);
}
```

The function getchar() reads from STDIN. But which device is STDIN? The putchar() function writes to STDOUT. But which device is that? These functions are *polymorphic*—their behavior depends on the type of STDIN and STDOUT.

It's as though STDIN and STDOUT are Java-style interfaces that have implementations for each device. Of course, there are no interfaces in the example C program—so how does the call to getchar() actually get delivered to the device driver that reads the character?

The answer to that question is pretty straightforward. The UNIX operating system requires that every IO device driver provide five standard functions:[5] open, close, read, write, and seek. The signatures of those functions must be identical for every IO driver.

The FILE data structure contains five pointers to functions. In our example, it might look like this:

```
struct FILE {
  void (*open)(char* name, int mode);
  void (*close)();
  int  (*read)();
  void (*write)(char);
  void (*seek)(long index, int mode);
};
```

The IO driver for the console will define those functions and load up a FILE data structure with their addresses—something like this:

```
#include "file.h"

void open(char* name, int mode) {/*...*/}
void close() {/*...*/};
int read() {int c;/*...*/ return c;}
void write(char c) {/*...*/}
void seek(long index, int mode) {/*...*/}

struct FILE console = {open, close, read, write, seek};
```

Now if STDIN is defined as a FILE*, and if it points to the console data structure, then getchar() might be implemented this way:

---

5. UNIX systems vary; this is just an example.

```
extern struct FILE* STDIN;

int getchar() {
  return STDIN->read();
}
```

In other words, `getchar()` simply calls the function pointed to by the `read` pointer of the `FILE` data structure pointed to by `STDIN`.

This simple trick is the basis for all polymorphism in OO. In C++, for example, every virtual function within a class has a pointer in a table called a `vtable`, and all calls to virtual functions go through that table. Constructors of derivatives simply load their versions of those functions into the `vtable` of the object being created.

The bottom line is that polymorphism is an application of pointers to functions. Programmers have been using pointers to functions to achieve polymorphic behavior since Von Neumann architectures were first implemented in the late 1940s. In other words, OO has provided nothing new.

Ah, but that's not quite correct. OO languages may not have given us polymorphism, but they have made it much safer and much more convenient.

The problem with explicitly using pointers to functions to create polymorphic behavior is that pointers to functions are *dangerous*. Such use is driven by a set of manual conventions. You have to remember to follow the convention to initialize those pointers. You have to remember to follow the convention to call all your functions through those pointers. If any programmer fails to remember these conventions, the resulting bug can be devilishly hard to track down and eliminate.

OO languages eliminate these conventions and, therefore, these dangers. Using an OO language makes polymorphism trivial. That fact provides an enormous power that old C programmers could only dream of. On this basis, we can conclude that OO imposes discipline on indirect transfer of control.

THE POWER OF POLYMORPHISM

What's so great about polymorphism? To better appreciate its charms, let's reconsider the example copy program. What happens to that program if a new IO device is created? Suppose we want to use the copy program to copy data from a handwriting recognition device to a speech synthesizer device: How do we need to change the copy program to get it to work with those new devices?

We don't need any changes at all! Indeed, we don't even need to recompile the copy program. Why? Because the source code of the copy program does not depend on the source code of the IO drivers. As long as those IO drivers implement the five standard functions defined by FILE, the copy program will be happy to use them.

In short, the IO devices have become plugins to the copy program.

Why did the UNIX operating system make IO devices plugins? Because we learned, in the late 1950s, that our programs should be *device independent*. Why? Because we wrote lots of programs that were device *dependent*, only to discover that we really wanted those programs to do the same job but use a different device.

For example, we often wrote programs that read input data from decks of cards,[6] and then punched new decks of cards as output. Later, our customers stopped giving us decks of cards and started giving us reels of magnetic tape. This was very inconvenient, because it meant rewriting large portions of the original program. It would be very convenient if the same program worked interchangeably with cards or tape.

---

6. Punched cards—IBM Hollerith cards, 80 columns wide. I'm sure many of you have never even seen one of these, but they were commonplace in the 1950s, 1960s, and even 1970s.

The plugin architecture was invented to support this kind of IO device independence, and has been implemented in almost every operating system since its introduction. Even so, most programmers did not extend the idea to their own programs, because using pointers to functions was dangerous.

OO allows the plugin architecture to be used anywhere, for anything.

DEPENDENCY INVERSION

Imagine what software was like before a safe and convenient mechanism for polymorphism was available. In the typical calling tree, main functions called high-level functions, which called mid-level functions, which called low-level functions. In that calling tree, however, source code dependencies inexorably followed the flow of control (Figure 5.1).

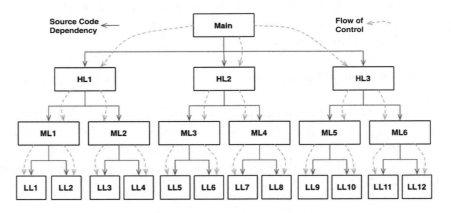

Figure 5.1 Source code dependencies versus flow of control

For `main` to call one of the high-level functions, it had to mention the name of the module that contained that function In C, this was a `#include`. In Java, it was an `import` statement. In C#, it was a `using` statement. Indeed, every caller was forced to mention the name of the module that contained the callee.

This requirement presented the software architect with few, if any, options. The flow of control was dictated by the behavior of the system, and the source code dependencies were dictated by that flow of control.

When polymorphism is brought into play, however, something very different can happen (Figure 5.2).

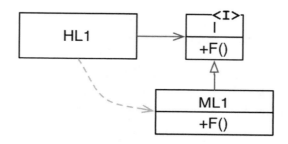

Figure 5.2 Dependency inversion

In Figure 5.2, module `HL1` calls the `F()` function in module `ML1`. The fact that it calls this function through an interface is a source code contrivance. At runtime, the interface doesn't exist. `HL1` simply calls `F()` within `ML1`.[7]

Note, however, that the source code dependency (the inheritance relationship) between `ML1` and the interface `I` points in the opposite direction compared to the flow of control. This is called *dependency inversion*, and its implications for the software architect are profound.

The fact that OO languages provide safe and convenient polymorphism means that *any source code dependency, no matter where it is, can be inverted.*

Now look back at that calling tree in Figure 5.1, and its many source code dependencies. Any of those source code dependencies can be turned around by inserting an interface between them.

---

7. Albeit indirectly.

With this approach, software architects working in systems written in OO languages have *absolute control* over the direction of all source code dependencies in the system. They are not constrained to align those dependencies with the flow of control. No matter which module does the calling and which module is called, the software architect can point the source code dependency in either direction.

That is power! That is the power that OO provides. That's what OO is really all about—at least from the architect's point of view.

What can you do with that power? As an example, you can rearrange the source code dependencies of your system so that the database and the user interface (UI) depend on the business rules (Figure 5.3), rather than the other way around.

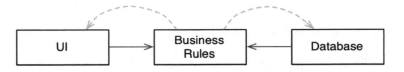

Figure 5.3 The database and the user interface depend on the business rules

This means that the UI and the database can be plugins to the business rules. It means that the source code of the business rules never mentions the UI or the database.

As a consequence, the business rules, the UI, and the database can be compiled into three separate components or deployment units (e.g., jar files, DLLs, or Gem files) that have the same dependencies as the source code. The component containing the business rules will not depend on the components containing the UI and database.

In turn, the business rules can be *deployed independently* of the UI and the database. Changes to the UI or the database need not have any effect on the business rules. Those components can be deployed separately and independently.

In short, when the source code in a component changes, only that component needs to be redeployed. This is *independent deployability*.

If the modules in your system can be deployed independently, then they can be developed independently by different teams. That's *independent developability*.

CONCLUSION

What is OO? There are many opinions and many answers to this question. To the software architect, however, the answer is clear: OO is the ability, through the use of polymorphism, to gain absolute control over every source code dependency in the system. It allows the architect to create a plugin architecture, in which modules that contain high-level policies are independent of modules that contain low-level details. The low-level details are relegated to plugin modules that can be deployed and developed independently from the modules that contain high-level policies.

6 FUNCTIONAL PROGRAMMING

In many ways, the concepts of functional programming predate programming itself. This paradigm is strongly based on the λ-calculus invented by Alonzo Church in the 1930s.

SQUARES OF INTEGERS

To explain what functional programming is, it's best to examine some examples. Let's investigate a simple problem: printing the squares of the first 25 integers.

In a language like Java, we might write the following:

```
public class Squint {
  public static void main(String args[]) {
    for (int i=0; i<25; i++)
      System.out.println(i*i);
  }
}
```

In a language like Clojure, which is a derivative of Lisp, and is functional, we might implement this same program as follows:

```
(println (take 25 (map (fn [x] (* x x)) (range))))
```

If you don't know Lisp, then this might look a little strange. So let me reformat it a bit and add some comments.

```
(println ;_____ Print
  (take 25 ;_____ the first 25
    (map (fn [x] (* x x)) ;__ squares
      (range)))) ;_____ of Integers
```

It should be clear that `println`, `take`, `map`, and `range` are all functions. In Lisp, you call a function by putting it in parentheses. For example, `(range)` calls the range function.

The expression `(fn [x] (* x x))` is an anonymous function that calls the multiply function, passing its input argument in twice. In other words, it computes the square of its input.

Looking at the whole thing again, it's best to start with the innermost function call.

- The `range` function returns a never-ending list of integers starting with 0.
- This list is passed into the `map` function, which calls the anonymous squaring function on each element, producing a new never-ending list of all the squares.
- The list of squares is passed into the `take` function, which returns a new list with only the first 25 elements.
- The `println` function prints its input, which is a list of the first 25 squares of integers.

If you find yourself terrified by the concept of never-ending lists, don't worry. Only the first 25 elements of those never-ending lists are actually created. That's because no element of a never-ending list is evaluated until it is accessed.

If you found all of that confusing, then you can look forward to a glorious time learning all about Clojure and functional programming. It is not my goal to teach you about these topics here.

Instead, my goal here is to point out something very dramatic about the difference between the Clojure and Java programs. The Java program uses a *mutable variable*—a variable that changes state during the execution of the program. That variable is `i`—the loop control variable. No such mutable variable exists in the Clojure program. In the Clojure program, variables like `x` are initialized, but they are never modified.

This leads us to a surprising statement: Variables in functional languages *do not vary*.

IMMUTABILITY AND ARCHITECTURE

Why is this point important as an architectural consideration? Why would an architect be concerned with the mutability of variables? The answer is absurdly simple: All race conditions, deadlock conditions, and concurrent update problems are due to mutable variables. You cannot have a race condition or a concurrent update problem if no variable is ever updated. You cannot have deadlocks without mutable locks.

In other words, all the problems that we face in concurrent applications—all the problems we face in applications that require multiple threads, and multiple processors—cannot happen if there are no mutable variables.

As an architect, you should be very interested in issues of concurrency. You want to make sure that the systems you design will be robust in the presence of multiple threads and processors. The question you must be asking yourself, then, is whether immutability is practicable.

The answer to that question is affirmative, if you have infinite storage and infinite processor speed. Lacking those infinite resources, the answer is a bit more nuanced. Yes, immutability can be practicable, if certain compromises are made.

Let's look at some of those compromises.

SEGREGATION OF MUTABILITY

One of the most common compromises in regard to immutability is to segregate the application, or the services within the application, into mutable and immutable components. The immutable components perform their tasks in a purely functional way, without using any mutable variables. The immutable components communicate with one or more other components that are not purely functional, and allow for the state of variables to be mutated (Figure 6.1).

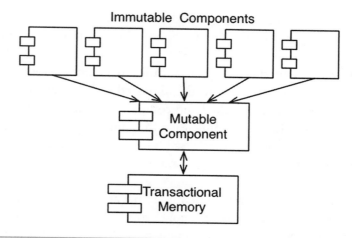

Figure 6.1 Mutating state and transactional memory

Since mutating state exposes those components to all the problems of concurrency, it is common practice to use some kind of *transactional memory* to protect the mutable variables from concurrent updates and race conditions.

Transactional memory simply treats variables in memory the same way a database treats records on disk.[1] It protects those variables with a transaction- or retry-based scheme.

A simple example of this approach is Clojure's `atom` facility:

```
(def counter (atom 0)) ; initialize counter to 0
(swap! counter inc)    ; safely increment counter.
```

In this code, the `counter` variable is defined as an `atom`. In Clojure, an `atom` is a special kind of variable whose value is allowed to mutate under very disciplined conditions that are enforced by the `swap!` function.

The `swap!` function, shown in the preceding code, takes two arguments: the `atom` to be mutated, and a function that computes the new value to be stored

---

1. I know... What's a disk?

in the `atom`. In our example code, the `counter atom` will be changed to the value computed by the `inc` function, which simply increments its argument.

The strategy used by `swap!` is a traditional *compare and swap* algorithm. The value of `counter` is read and passed to `inc`. When `inc` returns, the value of `counter` is locked and compared to the value that was passed to `inc`. If the value is the same, then the value returned by `inc` is stored in `counter` and the lock is released. Otherwise, the lock is released, and the strategy is retried from the beginning.

The `atom` facility is adequate for simple applications. Unfortunately, it cannot completely safeguard against concurrent updates and deadlocks when multiple dependent variables come into play. In those instances, more elaborate facilities can be used.

The point is that well-structured applications will be segregated into those components that do not mutate variables and those that do. This kind of segregation is supported by the use of appropriate disciplines to protect those mutated variables.

Architects would be wise to push as much processing as possible into the immutable components, and to drive as much code as possible out of those components that must allow mutation.

EVENT SOURCING

The limits of storage and processing power have been rapidly receding from view. Nowadays it is common for processors to execute billions of instructions per second and to have billions of bytes of RAM. The more memory we have, and the faster our machines are, the less we need mutable state.

As a simple example, imagine a banking application that maintains the account balances of its customers. It mutates those balances when deposit and withdrawal transactions are executed.

Now imagine that instead of storing the account balances, we store only the transactions. Whenever anyone wants to know the balance of an account, we simply add up all the transactions for that account, from the beginning of time. This scheme requires no mutable variables.

Obviously, this approach sounds absurd. Over time, the number of transactions would grow without bound, and the processing power required to compute the totals would become intolerable. To make this scheme work forever, we would need infinite storage and infinite processing power.

But perhaps we don't have to make the scheme work forever. And perhaps we have enough storage and enough processing power to make the scheme work for the reasonable lifetime of the application.

This is the idea behind *event sourcing*.[2] Event sourcing is a strategy wherein we store the transactions, but not the state. When state is required, we simply apply all the transactions from the beginning of time.

Of course, we can take shortcuts. For example, we can compute and save the state every midnight. Then, when the state information is required, we need compute only the transactions since midnight.

Now consider the data storage required for this scheme: We would need a lot of it. Realistically, offline data storage has been growing so fast that we now consider trillions of bytes to be small—so we have a lot of it.

More importantly, nothing ever gets deleted or updated from such a data store. As a consequence, our applications are not CRUD; they are just CR. Also, because neither updates nor deletions occur in the data store, there cannot be any concurrent update issues.

If we have enough storage and enough processor power, we can make our applications entirely immutable—and, therefore, *entirely functional*.

If this still sounds absurd, it might help if you remembered that this is precisely the way your source code control system works.

---

2. Thanks to Greg Young for teaching me about this concept.

CONCLUSION

To summarize:

- Structured programming is discipline imposed upon direct transfer of control.
- Object-oriented programming is discipline imposed upon indirect transfer of control.
- Functional programming is discipline imposed upon variable assignment.

Each of these three paradigms has taken something away from us. Each restricts some aspect of the way we write code. None of them has added to our power or our capabilities.

What we have learned over the last half-century is *what not to do*.

With that realization, we have to face an unwelcome fact: Software is not a rapidly advancing technology. The rules of software are the same today as they were in 1946, when Alan Turing wrote the very first code that would execute in an electronic computer. The tools have changed, and the hardware has changed, but the essence of software remains the same.

Software—the stuff of computer programs—is composed of sequence, selection, iteration, and indirection. Nothing more. Nothing less.

III

DESIGN PRINCIPLES

Good software systems begin with clean code. On the one hand, if the bricks aren't well made, the architecture of the building doesn't matter much. On the other hand, you can make a substantial mess with well-made bricks. This is where the SOLID principles come in.

The SOLID principles tell us how to arrange our functions and data structures into classes, and how those classes should be interconnected. The use of the word "class" does not imply that these principles are applicable only to object-oriented software. A class is simply a coupled grouping of functions and data. Every software system has such groupings, whether they are called classes or not. The SOLID principles apply to those groupings.

The goal of the principles is the creation of mid-level software structures that:

- Tolerate change,
- Are easy to understand, and
- Are the basis of components that can be used in many software systems.

The term "mid-level" refers to the fact that these principles are applied by programmers working at the module level. They are applied just above the level of the code and help to define the kinds of software structures used within modules and components.

Just as it is possible to create a substantial mess with well-made bricks, so it is also possible to create a system-wide mess with well-designed mid-level components. For this reason, once we have covered the SOLID principles, we will move on to their counterparts in the component world, and then to the principles of high-level architecture.

The history of the SOLID principles is long. I began to assemble them in the late 1980s while debating software design principles with others on USENET (an early kind of Facebook). Over the years, the principles have shifted and changed. Some were deleted. Others were merged. Still others were added. The final grouping stabilized in the early 2000s, although I presented them in a different order.

In 2004 or thereabouts, Michael Feathers sent me an email saying that if I rearranged the principles, their first words would spell the word SOLID—and thus the SOLID principles were born.

The chapters that follow describe each principle more thoroughly. Here is the executive summary:

- **SRP:** The Single Responsibility Principle

  An active corollary to Conway's law: The best structure for a software system is heavily influenced by the social structure of the organization that uses it so that each software module has one, and only one, reason to change.

- **OCP:** The Open-Closed Principle

  Bertrand Meyer made this principle famous in the 1980s. The gist is that for software systems to be easy to change, they must be designed to allow the behavior of those systems to be changed by adding new code, rather than changing existing code.

- **LSP:** The Liskov Substitution Principle

  Barbara Liskov's famous definition of subtypes, from 1988. In short, this principle says that to build software systems from interchangeable parts, those parts must adhere to a contract that allows those parts to be substituted one for another.

- **ISP:** The Interface Segregation Principle

  This principle advises software designers to avoid depending on things that they don't use.

- **DIP:** The Dependency Inversion Principle

  The code that implements high-level policy should not depend on the code that implements low-level details. Rather, details should depend on policies.

These principles have been described in detail in many different publications[1] over the years. The chapters that follow will focus on the architectural implications of these principles instead of repeating those detailed discussions. If you are not already familiar with these principles, what follows is insufficient to understand them in detail and you would be well advised to study them in the footnoted documents.

---

1. For example, *Agile Software Development, Principles, Patterns, and Practices*, Robert C. Martin, Prentice Hall, 2002, http://www.butunclebob.com/ArticleS.UncleBob.PrinciplesOfOod, and https://en.wikipedia.org/wiki/SOLID_(object-oriented_design) (or just google SOLID).

SRP: The Single Responsibility Principle

KOHNKE

Of all the SOLID principles, the Single Responsibility Principle (SRP) might be the least well understood. That's likely because it has a particularly inappropriate name. It is too easy for programmers to hear the name and then assume that it means that every module should do just one thing.

Make no mistake, there *is* a principle like that. A *function* should do one, and only one, thing. We use that principle when we are refactoring large functions into smaller functions; we use it at the lowest levels. But it is not one of the SOLID principles—it is not the SRP.

Historically, the SRP has been described this way:

> *A module should have one, and only one, reason to change.*

Software systems are changed to satisfy users and stakeholders; those users and stakeholders *are* the "reason to change" that the principle is talking about. Indeed, we can rephrase the principle to say this:

> *A module should be responsible to one, and only one, user or stakeholder.*

Unfortunately, the words "user" and "stakeholder" aren't really the right words to use here. There will likely be more than one user or stakeholder who wants the system changed in the same way. Instead, we're really referring to a group—one or more people who require that change. We'll refer to that group as an *actor.*

Thus the final version of the SRP is:

> *A module should be responsible to one, and only one, actor.*

Now, what do we mean by the word "module"? The simplest definition is just a source file. Most of the time that definition works fine. Some languages and development environments, though, don't use source files to contain their code. In those cases a module is just a cohesive set of functions and data structures.

That word "cohesive" implies the SRP. Cohesion is the force that binds together the code responsible to a single actor.

Perhaps the best way to understand this principle is by looking at the symptoms of violating it.

SYMPTOM 1: ACCIDENTAL DUPLICATION

My favorite example is the `Employee` class from a payroll application. It has three methods: `calculatePay()`, `reportHours()`, and `save()` (Figure 7.1).

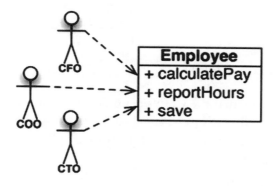

Figure 7.1 The `Employee` class

This class violates the SRP because those three methods are responsible to three very different actors.

- The `calculatePay()` method is specified by the accounting department, which reports to the CFO.
- The `reportHours()` method is specified and used by the human resources department, which reports to the COO.
- The `save()` method is specified by the database administrators (DBAs), who report to the CTO.

By putting the source code for these three methods into a single `Employee` class, the developers have coupled each of these actors to the others. This coupling can cause the actions of the CFO's team to affect something that the COO's team depends on.

For example, suppose that the `calculatePay()` function and the `reportHours()` function share a common algorithm for calculating non-overtime hours. Suppose also that the developers, who are careful not to duplicate code, put that algorithm into a function named `regularHours()` (Figure 7.2).

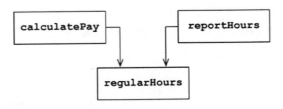

Figure 7.2 Shared algorithm

Now suppose that the CFO's team decides that the way non-overtime hours are calculated needs to be tweaked. In contrast, the COO's team in HR does not want that particular tweak because they use non-overtime hours for a different purpose.

A developer is tasked to make the change, and sees the convenient `regularHours()` function called by the `calculatePay()` method. Unfortunately, that developer does not notice that the function is also called by the `reportHours()` function.

The developer makes the required change and carefully tests it. The CFO's team validates that the new function works as desired, and the system is deployed.

Of course, the COO's team doesn't know that this is happening. The HR personnel continue to use the reports generated by the `reportHours()` function—but now they contain incorrect numbers. Eventually the problem is discovered, and the COO is livid because the bad data has cost his budget millions of dollars.

We've all seen things like this happen. These problems occur because we put code that different actors depend on into close proximity. The SRP says to *separate the code that different actors depend on.*

Symptom 2: Merges

It's not hard to imagine that merges will be common in source files that contain many different methods. This situation is especially likely if those methods are responsible to different actors.

For example, suppose that the CTO's team of DBAs decides that there should be a simple schema change to the `Employee` table of the database. Suppose also that the COO's team of HR clerks decides that they need a change in the format of the hours report.

Two different developers, possibly from two different teams, check out the `Employee` class and begin to make changes. Unfortunately their changes collide. The result is a merge.

I probably don't need to tell you that merges are risky affairs. Our tools are pretty good nowadays, but no tool can deal with every merge case. In the end, there is always risk.

In our example, the merge puts both the CTO and the COO at risk. It's not inconceivable that the CFO could be affected as well.

There are many other symptoms that we could investigate, but they all involve multiple people changing the same source file for different reasons.

Once again, the way to avoid this problem is to *separate code that supports different actors.*

SOLUTIONS

There are many different solutions to this problem. Each moves the functions into different classes.

Perhaps the most obvious way to solve the problem is to separate the data from the functions. The three classes share access to EmployeeData, which is a simple data structure with no methods (Figure 7.3). Each class holds only the source code necessary for its particular function. The three classes are not allowed to know about each other. Thus any accidental duplication is avoided.

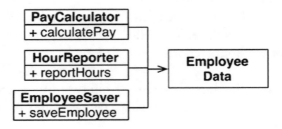

Figure 7.3 The three classes do not know about each other

The downside of this solution is that the developers now have three classes that they have to instantiate and track. A common solution to this dilemma is to use the *Facade* pattern (Figure 7.4).

Figure 7.4 The Facade pattern

The EmployeeFacade contains very little code. It is responsible for instantiating and delegating to the classes with the functions.

Some developers prefer to keep the most important business rules closer to the data. This can be done by keeping the most important method in the original `Employee` class and then using that class as a *Facade* for the lesser functions (Figure 7.5).

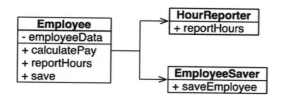

Figure 7.5 The most important method is kept in the original `Employee` class and used as a *Facade* for the lesser functions

You might object to these solutions on the basis that every class would contain just one function. This is hardly the case. The number of functions required to calculate pay, generate a report, or save the data is likely to be large in each case. Each of those classes would have many *private* methods in them.

Each of the classes that contain such a family of methods is a scope. Outside of that scope, no one knows that the private members of the family exist.

CONCLUSION

The Single Responsibility Principle is about functions and classes—but it reappears in a different form at two more levels. At the level of components, it becomes the Common Closure Principle. At the architectural level, it becomes the Axis of Change responsible for the creation of Architectural Boundaries. We'll be studying all of these ideas in the chapters to come.

OCP: The Open-Closed Principle

The Open-Closed Principle (OCP) was coined in 1988 by Bertrand Meyer.[1] It says:

> A *software artifact should be open for extension but closed for modification.*

In other words, the behavior of a software artifact ought to be extendible, without having to modify that artifact.

This, of course, is the most fundamental reason that we study software architecture. Clearly, if simple extensions to the requirements force massive changes to the software, then the architects of that software system have engaged in a spectacular failure.

Most students of software design recognize the OCP as a principle that guides them in the design of classes and modules. But the principle takes on even greater significance when we consider the level of architectural components.

A thought experiment will make this clear.

A THOUGHT EXPERIMENT

Imagine, for a moment, that we have a system that displays a financial summary on a web page. The data on the page is scrollable, and negative numbers are rendered in red.

Now imagine that the stakeholders ask that this same information be turned into a report to be printed on a black-and-white printer. The report should be properly paginated, with appropriate page headers, page footers, and column labels. Negative numbers should be surrounded by parentheses.

Clearly, some new code must be written. But how much old code will have to change?

---

1. Bertrand Meyer. *Object Oriented Software Construction*, Prentice Hall, 1988, p. 23.

A good software architecture would reduce the amount of changed code to the barest minimum. Ideally, zero.

How? By properly separating the things that change for different reasons (the Single Responsibility Principle), and then organizing the dependencies between those things properly (the Dependency Inversion Principle).

By applying the SRP, we might come up with the data-flow view shown in Figure 8.1. Some analysis procedure inspects the financial data and produces reportable data, which is then formatted appropriately by the two reporter processes.

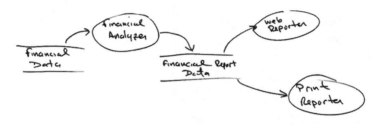

Figure 8.1 Applying the SRP

The essential insight here is that generating the report involves two separate responsibilities: the calculation of the reported data, and the presentation of that data into a web- and printer-friendly form.

Having made this separation, we need to organize the source code dependencies to ensure that changes to one of those responsibilities do not cause changes in the other. Also, the new organization should ensure that the behavior can be extended without undo modification.

We accomplish this by partitioning the processes into classes, and separating those classes into components, as shown by the double lines in the diagram in Figure 8.2. In this figure, the component at the upper left is the *Controller*. At the upper right, we have the *Interactor*. At the lower right, there is the *Database*. Finally, at the lower left, there are four components that represent the *Presenters* and the *Views*.

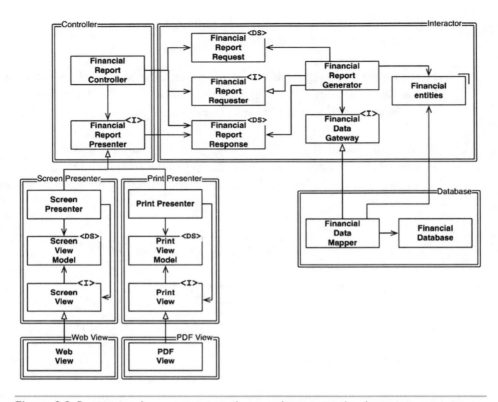

Figure 8.2 Partitioning the processes into classes and separating the classes into components

Classes marked with <I> are interfaces; those marked with <DS> are data structures. Open arrowheads are *using* relationships. Closed arrowheads are *implements* or *inheritance* relationships.

The first thing to notice is that all the dependencies are *source code* dependencies. An arrow pointing from class A to class B means that the source code of class A mentions the name of class B, but class B mentions nothing about class A. Thus, in Figure 8.2, `FinancialDataMapper` knows about `FinancialDataGateway` through an *implements* relationship, but `FinancialDataGateway` knows nothing at all about `FinancialDataMapper`.

The next thing to notice is that each double line is crossed *in one direction only*. This means that all component relationships are unidirectional, as shown in the component graph in Figure 8.3. These arrows point toward the components that we want to protect from change.

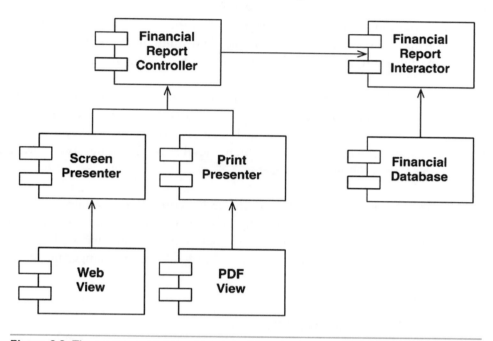

Figure 8.3 The component relationships are unidirectional

Let me say that again: If component A should be protected from changes in component B, then component B should depend on component A.

We want to protect the *Controller* from changes in the *Presenters*. We want to protect the *Presenters* from changes in the *Views*. We want to protect the *Interactor* from changes in—well, *anything*.

The *Interactor* is in the position that best conforms to the OCP. Changes to the *Database*, or the *Controller*, or the *Presenters*, or the *Views*, will have no impact on the *Interactor*.

Why should the *Interactor* hold such a privileged position? Because it contains the business rules. The *Interactor* contains the highest-level policies of the application. All the other components are dealing with peripheral concerns. The *Interactor* deals with the central concern.

Even though the *Controller* is peripheral to the *Interactor*, it is nevertheless central to the *Presenters* and *Views*. And while the *Presenters* might be peripheral to the *Controller*, they are central to the *Views*.

Notice how this creates a hierarchy of protection based on the notion of "level." *Interactors* are the highest-level concept, so they are the most protected. *Views* are among the lowest-level concepts, so they are the least protected. *Presenters* are higher level than *Views*, but lower level than the *Controller* or the *Interactor*.

This is how the OCP works at the architectural level. Architects separate functionality based on how, why, and when it changes, and then organize that separated functionality into a hierarchy of components. Higher-level components in that hierarchy are protected from the changes made to lower-level components.

DIRECTIONAL CONTROL

If you recoiled in horror from the class design shown earlier, look again. Much of the complexity in that diagram was intended to make sure that the dependencies between the components pointed in the correct direction.

For example, the `FinancialDataGateway` interface between the `FinancialReportGenerator` and the `FinancialDataMapper` exists to invert the dependency that would otherwise have pointed from the *Interactor* component to the *Database* component. The same is true of the `FinancialReportPresenter` interface, and the two *View* interfaces.

INFORMATION HIDING

The `FinancialReportRequester` interface serves a different purpose. It is there to protect the `FinancialReportController` from knowing too much about the internals of the *Interactor*. If that interface were not there, then the *Controller* would have transitive dependencies on the `FinancialEntities`.

Transitive dependencies are a violation of the general principle that software entities should not depend on things they don't directly use. We'll encounter that principle again when we talk about the Interface Segregation Principle and the Common Reuse Principle.

So, even though our first priority is to protect the *Interactor* from changes to the *Controller*, we also want to protect the *Controller* from changes to the *Interactor* by hiding the internals of the *Interactor*.

CONCLUSION

The OCP is one of the driving forces behind the architecture of systems. The goal is to make the system easy to extend without incurring a high impact of change. This goal is accomplished by partitioning the system into components, and arranging those components into a dependency hierarchy that protects higher-level components from changes in lower-level components.

LSP: The Liskov Substitution Principle

In 1988, Barbara Liskov wrote the following as a way of defining subtypes.

> *What is wanted here is something like the following substitution property: If for each object o1 of type S there is an object o2 of type T such that for all programs P defined in terms of T, the behavior of P is unchanged when o1 is substituted for o2 then S is a subtype of T.*[1]

To understand this idea, which is known as the Liskov Substitution Principle (LSP), let's look at some examples.

GUIDING THE USE OF INHERITANCE

Imagine that we have a class named License, as shown in Figure 9.1. This class has a method named calcFee(), which is called by the Billing application. There are two "subtypes" of License: PersonalLicense and BusinessLicense. They use different algorithms to calculate the license fee.

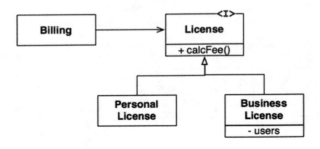

Figure 9.1 License, and its derivatives, conform to LSP

This design conforms to the LSP because the behavior of the Billing application does not depend, in any way, on which of the two subtypes it uses. Both of the subtypes are substitutable for the License type.

1. Barbara Liskov, "Data Abstraction and Hierarchy," *SIGPLAN Notices* 23, 5 (May 1988).

THE SQUARE/RECTANGLE PROBLEM

The canonical example of a violation of the LSP is the famed (or infamous, depending on your perspective) square/rectangle problem (Figure 9.2).

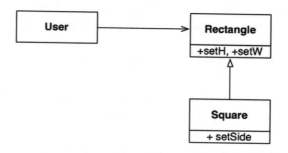

Figure 9.2 The infamous square/rectangle problem

In this example, Square is not a proper subtype of Rectangle because the height and width of the Rectangle are independently mutable; in contrast, the height and width of the Square must change together. Since the User believes it is communicating with a Rectangle, it could easily get confused. The following code shows why:

```
Rectangle r = …
r.setW(5);
r.setH(2);
assert(r.area() == 10);
```

If the … code produced a Square, then the assertion would fail.

The only way to defend against this kind of LSP violation is to add mechanisms to the User (such as an if statement) that detects whether the Rectangle is, in fact, a Square. Since the behavior of the User depends on the types it uses, those types are not substitutable.

LSP AND ARCHITECTURE

In the early years of the object-oriented revolution, we thought of the LSP as a way to guide the use of inheritance, as shown in the previous sections. However, over the years the LSP has morphed into a broader principle of software design that pertains to interfaces and implementations.

The interfaces in question can be of many forms. We might have a Java-style interface, implemented by several classes. Or we might have several Ruby classes that share the same method signatures. Or we might have a set of services that all respond to the same REST interface.

In all of these situations, and more, the LSP is applicable because there are users who depend on well-defined interfaces, and on the substitutability of the implementations of those interfaces.

The best way to understand the LSP from an architectural viewpoint is to look at what happens to the architecture of a system when the principle is violated.

EXAMPLE LSP VIOLATION

Assume that we are building an aggregator for many taxi dispatch services. Customers use our website to find the most appropriate taxi to use, regardless of taxi company. Once the customer makes a decision, our system dispatches the chosen taxi by using a restful service.

Now assume that the URI for the restful dispatch service is part of the information contained in the driver database. Once our system has chosen a driver appropriate for the customer, it gets that URI from the driver record and then uses it to dispatch the driver.

Suppose Driver Bob has a dispatch URI that looks like this:

```
purplecab.com/driver/Bob
```

Our system will append the dispatch information onto this URI and send it with a PUT, as follows:

```
purplecab.com/driver/Bob
        /pickupAddress/24 Maple St.
        /pickupTime/153
        /destination/ORD
```

Clearly, this means that all the dispatch services, for all the different companies, must conform to the same REST interface. They must treat the `pickupAddress`, `pickupTime`, and `destination` fields identically.

Now suppose the Acme taxi company hired some programmers who didn't read the spec very carefully. They abbreviated the destination field to just `dest`. Acme is the largest taxi company in our area, and Acme's CEO's ex-wife is our CEO's new wife, and … Well, you get the picture. What would happen to the architecture of our system?

Obviously, we would need to add a special case. The dispatch request for any Acme driver would have to be constructed using a different set of rules from all the other drivers.

The simplest way to accomplish this goal would be to add an `if` statement to the module that constructed the dispatch command:

```
if (driver.getDispatchUri().startsWith("acme.com"))…
```

But, of course, no architect worth his or her salt would allow such a construction to exist in the system. Putting the word "acme" into the code itself creates an opportunity for all kinds of horrible and mysterious errors, not to mention security breaches.

For example, what if Acme became even more successful and bought the Purple Taxi company. What if the merged company maintained the separate brands and the separate websites, but unified all of the original companies' systems? Would we have to add another if statement for "purple"?

Our architect would have to insulate the system from bugs like this by creating some kind of dispatch command creation module that was driven by a configuration database keyed by the dispatch URI. The configuration data might look something like this:

URI	Dispatch Format
Acme.com	/pickupAddress/%s/pickupTime/%s/dest/%s
.	/pickupAddress/%s/pickupTime/%s/destination/%s

And so our architect has had to add a significant and complex mechanism to deal with the fact that the interfaces of the restful services are not all substitutable.

CONCLUSION

The LSP can, and should, be extended to the level of architecture. A simple violation of substitutability, can cause a system's architecture to be polluted with a significant amount of extra mechanisms.

ISP: The Interface Segregation Principle

The Interface Segregation Principle (ISP) derives its name from the diagram shown in Figure 10.1.

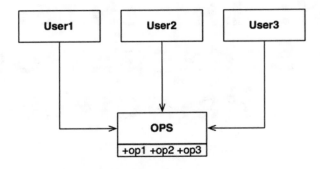

Figure 10.1 The Interface Segregation Principle

In the situation illustrated in Figure 10.1, there are several users who use the operations of the OPS class. Let's assume that User1 uses only op1, User2 uses only op2, and User3 uses only op3.

Now imagine that OPS is a class written in a language like Java. Clearly, in that case, the source code of User1 will inadvertently depend on op2 and op3, even though it doesn't call them. This dependence means that a change to the source code of op2 in OPS will force User1 to be recompiled and redeployed, even though nothing that it cared about has actually changed.

This problem can be resolved by segregating the operations into interfaces as shown in Figure 10.2.

Again, if we imagine that this is implemented in a statically typed language like Java, then the source code of User1 will depend on U1Ops, and op1, but will not depend on OPS. Thus a change to OPS that User1 does not care about will not cause User1 to be recompiled and redeployed.

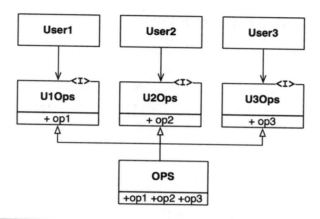

Figure 10.2 Segregated operations

ISP AND LANGUAGE

Clearly, the previously given description depends critically on language type. Statically typed languages like Java force programmers to create declarations that users must `import`, or `use`, or otherwise `include`. It is these `included` declarations in source code that create the source code dependencies that force recompilation and redeployment.

In dynamically typed languages like Ruby and Python, such declarations don't exist in source code. Instead, they are inferred at runtime. Thus there are no source code dependencies to force recompilation and redeployment. This is the primary reason that dynamically typed languages create systems that are more flexible and less tightly coupled than statically typed languages.

This fact could lead you to conclude that the ISP is a language issue, rather than an architecture issue.

ISP AND ARCHITECTURE

If you take a step back and look at the root motivations of the ISP, you can see a deeper concern lurking there. In general, it is harmful to depend on modules that contain more than you need. This is obviously true for source code dependencies that can force unnecessary recompilation and redeployment—but it is also true at a much higher, architectural level.

Consider, for example, an architect working on a system, S. He wants to include a certain framework, F, into the system. Now suppose that the authors of F have bound it to a particular database, D. So S depends on F. which depends on D (Figure 10.3).

Figure 10.3 A problematic architecture

Now suppose that D contains features that F does not use and, therefore, that S does not care about. Changes to those features within D may well force the redeployment of F and, therefore, the redeployment of S. Even worse, a failure of one of the features within D may cause failures in F and S.

CONCLUSION

The lesson here is that depending on something that carries baggage that you don't need can cause you troubles that you didn't expect.

We'll explore this idea in more detail when we discuss the Common Reuse Principle in Chapter 13, "Component Cohesion."

DIP: THE DEPENDENCY INVERSION PRINCIPLE

The Dependency Inversion Principle (DIP) tells us that the most flexible systems are those in which source code dependencies refer only to abstractions, not to concretions.

In a statically typed language, like Java, this means that the use, import, and include statements should refer only to source modules containing interfaces, abstract classes, or some other kind of abstract declaration. Nothing concrete should be depended on.

The same rule applies for dynamically typed languages, like Ruby and Python. Source code dependencies should not refer to concrete modules. However, in these languages it is a bit harder to define what a concrete module is. In particular, it is any module in which the functions being called are implemented.

Clearly, treating this idea as a rule is unrealistic, because software systems must depend on many concrete facilities. For example, the `String` class in Java is concrete, and it would be unrealistic to try to force it to be abstract. The source code dependency on the concrete `java.lang.string` cannot, and should not, be avoided.

By comparison, the `String` class is very stable. Changes to that class are very rare and tightly controlled. Programmers and architects do not have to worry about frequent and capricious changes to `String`.

For these reasons, we tend to ignore the stable background of operating system and platform facilities when it comes to DIP. We tolerate those concrete dependencies because we know we can rely on them not to change.

It is the *volatile* concrete elements of our system that we want to avoid depending on. Those are the modules that we are actively developing, and that are undergoing frequent change.

STABLE ABSTRACTIONS

Every change to an abstract interface corresponds to a change to its concrete implementations. Conversely, changes to concrete implementations do not always, or even usually, require changes to the interfaces that they implement. Therefore interfaces are less volatile than implementations.

Indeed, good software designers and architects work hard to reduce the volatility of interfaces. They try to find ways to add functionality to implementations without making changes to the interfaces. This is Software Design 101.

The implication, then, is that stable software architectures are those that avoid depending on volatile concretions, and that favor the use of stable abstract interfaces. This implication boils down to a set of very specific coding practices:

- **Don't refer to volatile concrete classes.** Refer to abstract interfaces instead. This rule applies in all languages, whether statically or dynamically typed. It also puts severe constraints on the creation of objects and generally enforces the use of *Abstract Factories*.
- **Don't derive from volatile concrete classes.** This is a corollary to the previous rule, but it bears special mention. In statically typed languages, inheritance is the strongest, and most rigid, of all the source code relationships; consequently, it should be used with great care. In dynamically typed languages, inheritance is less of a problem, but it is still a dependency—and caution is always the wisest choice.
- **Don't override concrete functions.** Concrete functions often require source code dependencies. When you override those functions, you do not eliminate those dependencies—indeed, you *inherit* them. To manage those dependencies, you should make the function abstract and create multiple implementations.
- **Never mention the name of anything concrete and volatile.** This is really just a restatement of the principle itself.

FACTORIES

To comply with these rules, the creation of volatile concrete objects requires special handling. This caution is warranted because, in virtually all languages, the creation of an object requires a source code dependency on the concrete definition of that object.

In most object-oriented languages, such as Java, we would use an *Abstract Factory* to manage this undesirable dependency.

The diagram in Figure 11.1 shows the structure. The `Application` uses the `ConcreteImpl` through the `Service` interface. However, the `Application` must somehow create instances of the `ConcreteImpl`. To achieve this without creating a source code dependency on the `ConcreteImpl`, the `Application` calls the `makeSvc` method of the `ServiceFactory` interface. This method is implemented by the `ServiceFactoryImpl` class, which derives from `ServiceFactory`. That implementation instantiates the `ConcreteImpl` and returns it as a `Service`.

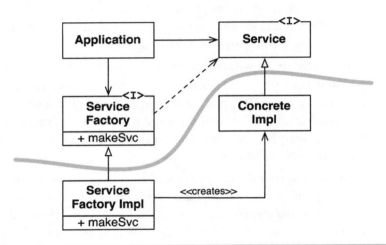

Figure 11.1 Use of the *Abstract Factory* pattern to manage the dependency

The curved line in Figure 11.1 is an architectural boundary. It separates the abstract from the concrete. All source code dependencies cross that curved line pointing in the same direction, toward the abstract side.

The curved line divides the system into two components: one abstract and the other concrete. The abstract component contains all the high-level business rules of the application. The concrete component contains all the implementation details that those business rules manipulate.

Note that the flow of control crosses the curved line in the opposite direction of the source code dependencies. The source code dependencies are inverted against the flow of control—which is why we refer to this principle as Dependency Inversion.

CONCRETE COMPONENTS

The concrete component in Figure 11.1 contains a single dependency, so it violates the DIP. This is typical. DIP violations cannot be entirely removed, but they can be gathered into a small number of concrete components and kept separate from the rest of the system.

Most systems will contain at least one such concrete component—often called `main` because it contains the `main`[1] function. In the case illustrated in Figure 11.1, the `main` function would instantiate the `ServiceFactoryImpl` and place that instance in a global variable of type `ServiceFactory`. The `Application` would then access the factory through that global variable.

CONCLUSION

As we move forward in this book and cover higher-level architectural principles, the DIP will show up again and again. It will be the most visible organizing principle in our architecture diagrams. The curved line in Figure 11.1 will become the architectural boundaries in later chapters. The way the dependencies cross that curved line in one direction, and toward more abstract entities, will become a new rule that we will call the *Dependency Rule*.

---

1. In other words, the function that is invoked by the operating system when the application is first started up.

COMPONENT PRINCIPLES

If the SOLID principles tell us how to arrange the bricks into walls and rooms, then the component principles tell us how to arrange the rooms into buildings. Large software systems, like large buildings, are built out of smaller components.

In Part IV, we will discuss what software components are, which elements should compose them, and how they should be composed together into systems.

COMPONENTS 12

Components are the units of deployment. They are the smallest entities that can be deployed as part of a system. In Java, they are jar files. In Ruby, they are gem files. In .Net, they are DLLs. In compiled languages, they are aggregations of binary files. In interpreted languages, they are aggregations of source files. In all languages, they are the granule of deployment.

Components can be linked together into a single executable. Or they can be aggregated together into a single archive, such as a .war file. Or they can be independently deployed as separate dynamically loaded plugins, such as .jar or .dll or .exe files. Regardless of how they are eventually deployed, well-designed components always retain the ability to be independently deployable and, therefore, independently developable.

A BRIEF HISTORY OF COMPONENTS

In the early years of software development, programmers controlled the memory location and layout of their programs. One of the first lines of code in a program would be the *origin* statement, which declared the address at which the program was to be loaded.

Consider the following simple PDP-8 program. It consists of a subroutine named GETSTR that inputs a string from the keyboard and saves it in a buffer. It also has a little unit test program to exercise GETSTR.

```
            *200
            TLS
START,      CLA
            TAD BUFR
            JMS GETSTR
            CLA
            TAD BUFR
            JMS PUTSTR
            JMP START
```

```
        BUFR,       3000

        GETSTR,     0
                    DCA PTR
        NXTCH,      KSF
                    JMP -1
                    KRB
                    DCA I PTR
                    TAD I PTR
                    AND K177
                    ISZ PTR
                    TAD MCR
                    SZA
                    JMP NXTCH


    K177,           177
    MCR,            -15
```

Note the *200 command at the start of this program. It tells the compiler to generate code that will be loaded at address 200$_8$.

This kind of programming is a foreign concept for most programmers today. They rarely have to think about where a program is loaded in the memory of the computer. But in the early days, this was one of the first decisions a programmer needed to make. In those days, programs were not relocatable.

How did you access a library function in those olden days? The preceding code illustrates the approach used. Programmers included the source code of the library functions with their application code, and compiled them all as a single program.[1] Libraries were kept in source, not in binary.

---

1. My first employer kept several dozen decks of the subroutine library source code on a shelf. When you wrote a new program, you simply grabbed one of those decks and slapped it onto the end of your deck.

The problem with this approach was that, during this era, devices were slow and memory was expensive and, therefore, limited. Compilers needed to make several passes over the source code, but memory was too limited to keep all the source code resident. Consequently, the compiler had to read in the source code several times using the slow devices.

This took a long time—and the larger your function library, the longer the compiler took. Compiling a large program could take hours.

To shorten the compile times, programmers separated the source code of the function library from the applications. They compiled the function library separately and loaded the binary at a known address—say, 2000_8. They created a symbol table for the function library and compiled that with their application code. When they wanted to run an application, they would load the binary function library,[2] and then load the application. Memory looked like the layout shown in Figure 12.1.

	x000-x177	x200-x377	x400-x577	x600-x777
0000-0777		Application		
1000-1777				
2000-2777				
3000-3777		Function Library		
4000-4777				
5000-5777				
6000-6777				
7000-7777				

Figure 12.1 Early memory layout

This worked fine so long as the application could fit between addresses 0000_8 and 1777_8. But soon applications grew to be larger than the space allotted

---

2. Actually, most of those old machines used core memory, which did not get erased when you powered the computer down. We often left the function library loaded for days at a time.

for them. At that point, programmers had to split their applications into two address segments, jumping around the function library (Figure 12.2).

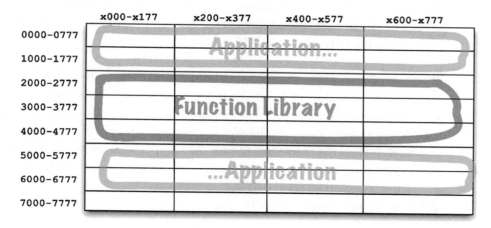

Figure 12.2 Splitting the application into two address segments

Obviously, this was not a sustainable situation. As programmers added more functions to the function library, it exceeded its bounds, and they had to allocate more space for it (in this example, near 7000_8). This fragmentation of programs and libraries necessarily continued as computer memory grew.

Clearly, something had to be done.

RELOCATABILITY

The solution was relocatable binaries. The idea behind them was very simple. The compiler was changed to output binary code that could be relocated in memory by a smart loader. The loader would be told where to load the relocatable code. The relocatable code was instrumented with flags that told the loader which parts of the loaded data had to be altered to be loaded at the selected address. Usually this just meant adding the starting address to any memory reference addresses in the binary.

Now the programmer could tell the loader where to load the function library, and where to load the application. In fact, the loader would accept several binary inputs and simply load them in memory one right after the other, relocating them as it loaded them. This allowed programmers to load only those functions that they needed.

The compiler was also changed to emit the names of the functions as metadata in the relocatable binary. If a program called a library function, the compiler would emit that name as an *external reference*. If a program defined a library function, the compiler would emit that name as an *external definition*. Then the loader could *link* the external references to the external definitions once it had determined where it had loaded those definitions.

And the linking loader was born.

LINKERS

The linking loader allowed programmers to divide their programs up onto separately compilable and loadable segments. This worked well when relatively small programs were being linked with relatively small libraries. However, in the late 1960s and early 1970s, programmers got more ambitious, and their programs got a lot bigger.

Eventually, the linking loaders were too slow to tolerate. Function libraries were stored on slow devices such a magnetic tape. Even the disks, back then, were quite slow. Using these relatively slow devices, the linking loaders had to read dozens, if not hundreds, of binary libraries to resolve the external references. As programs grew larger and larger, and more library functions accumulated in libraries, a linking loader could take more than an hour just to load the program.

Eventually, the loading and the linking were separated into two phases. Programmers took the slow part—the part that did that linking—and put it into a separate application called the *linker*. The output of the linker was a linked relocatable that a relocating loader could load very quickly. This allowed programmers to prepare an executable using the slow linker, but then they could load it quickly, at any time.

Then came the 1980s. Programmers were working in C or some other high-level language. As their ambitions grew, so did their programs. Programs that numbered hundreds of thousands of lines of code were not unusual.

Source modules were compiled from .c files into .o files, and then fed into the linker to create executable files that could be quickly loaded. Compiling each individual module was relatively fast, but compiling *all* the modules took a bit of time. The linker would then take even more time. Turnaround had again grown to an hour or more in many cases.

It seemed as if programmers were doomed to endlessly chase their tails. Throughout the 1960s, 1970s, and 1980s, all the changes made to speed up workflow were thwarted by programmers' ambitions, and the size of the programs they wrote. They could not seem to escape from the hour-long turnaround times. Loading time remained fast, but compile-link times were the bottleneck.

We were, of course, experiencing Murphy's law of program size:

Programs will grow to fill all available compile and link time.

But Murphy was not the only contender in town. Along came Moore,[3] and in the late 1980s, the two battled it out. Moore won that battle. Disks started to shrink and got significantly faster. Computer memory started to get so ridiculously cheap that much of the data on disk could be cached in RAM. Computer clock rates increased from 1 MHz to 100 MHz.

By the mid-1990s, the time spent linking had begun to shrink faster than our ambitions could make programs grow. In many cases, link time decreased to a matter of *seconds*. For small jobs, the idea of a linking loader became feasible again.

---

3. Moore's law: Computer speed, memory, and density double every 18 months. This law held from the 1950s to 2000, but then, at least for clock rates, stopped cold.

This was the era of Active-X, shared libraries, and the beginnings of .jar files. Computers and devices had gotten so fast that we could, once again, do the linking at load time. We could link together several .jar files, or several shared libraries in a matter of seconds, and execute the resulting program. And so the component plugin architecture was born.

Today we routinely ship .jar files or DLLs or shared libraries as plugins to existing applications. If you want to create a mod to *Minecraft*, for example, you simply include your custom .jar files in a certain folder. If you want to plug *Resharper* into *Visual Studio*, you simply include the appropriate DLLs.

CONCLUSION

These dynamically linked files, which can be plugged together at runtime, are the software components of our architectures. It has taken 50 years, but we have arrived at a place where component plugin architecture can be the casual default as opposed to the herculean effort it once was.

13 COMPONENT COHESION

KOHNKE

Which classes belong in which components? This is an important decision, and requires guidance from good software engineering principles. Unfortunately, over the years, this decision has been made in an ad hoc manner based almost entirely on context.

In this chapter we will discuss the three principles of component cohesion:

- **REP:** The Reuse/Release Equivalence Principle
- **CCP:** The Common Closure Principle
- **CRP:** The Common Reuse Principle

THE REUSE/RELEASE EQUIVALENCE PRINCIPLE

The granule of reuse is the granule of release.

The last decade has seen the rise of a menagerie of module management tools, such as Maven, Leiningen, and RVM. These tools have grown in importance because, during that time, a vast number of reusable components and component libraries have been created. We are now living in the age of software reuse—a fulfillment of one of the oldest promises of the object-oriented model.

The Reuse/Release Equivalence Principle (REP) is a principle that seems obvious, at least in hindsight. People who want to reuse software components cannot, and will not, do so unless those components are tracked through a release process and are given release numbers.

This is not simply because, without release numbers, there would be no way to ensure that all the reused components are compatible with each other. Rather, it also reflects the fact that software developers need to know when new releases are coming, and which changes those new releases will bring.

It is not uncommon for developers to be alerted about a new release and decide, based on the changes made in that release, to continue to use the old release instead. Therefore the release process must produce the appropriate notifications and release documentation so that users can make informed decisions about when and whether to integrate the new release.

From a software design and architecture point of view, this principle means that the classes and modules that are formed into a component must belong to a cohesive group. The component cannot simply consist of a random hodgepodge of classes and modules; instead, there must be some overarching theme or purpose that those modules all share.

Of course, this should be obvious. However, there is another way to look at this issue that is perhaps not quite so obvious. Classes and modules that are grouped together into a component should be *releasable* together. The fact that they share the same version number and the same release tracking, and are included under the same release documentation, should make sense both to the author and to the users.

This is weak advice: Saying that something should "make sense" is just a way of waving your hands in the air and trying to sound authoritative. The advice is weak because it is hard to precisely explain the glue that holds the classes and modules together into a single component. Weak though the advice may be, the principle itself is important, because violations are easy to detect— they don't "make sense." If you violate the REP, your users will know, and they won't be impressed with your architectural skills.

The weakness of this principle is more than compensated for by the strength of the next two principles. Indeed, the CCP and the CRP strongly define the this principle, but in a negative sense.

THE COMMON CLOSURE PRINCIPLE

Gather into components those classes that change for the same reasons and at the same times. Separate into different components those classes that change at different times and for different reasons.

This is the Single Responsibility Principle restated for components. Just as the SRP says that a *class* should not contain multiples reasons to change, so the Common Closure Principle (CCP) says that a *component* should not have multiple reasons to change.

For most applications, maintainability is more important than reusability. If the code in an application must change, you would rather that all of the changes occur in one component, rather than being distributed across many components.[1] If changes are confined to a single component, then we need to redeploy only the one changed component. Other components that don't depend on the changed component do not need to be revalidated or redeployed.

The CCP prompts us to gather together in one place all the classes that are likely change for the same reasons. If two classes are so tightly bound, either physically or conceptually, that they always change together, then they belong in the same component. This minimizes the workload related to releasing, revalidating, and redeploying the software.

This principle is closely associated with the Open Closed Principle (OCP). Indeed, it is "closure" in the OCP sense of the word that the CCP addresses. The OCP states that classes should be closed for modification but open for extension. Because 100% closure is not attainable, closure must be strategic. We design our classes such that they are closed to the most common kinds of changes that we expect or have experienced.

The CCP amplifies this lesson by gathering together into the same component those classes that are closed to the same types of changes. Thus, when a change in requirements comes along, that change has a good chance of being restricted to a minimal number of components.

---

1. See the section on "The Kitty Problem" in Chapter 27, "Services: Great and Small."

SIMILARITY WITH SRP

As stated earlier, the CCP is the component form of the SRP. The SRP tells us to separate methods into different classes, if they change for different reasons. The CCP tells us to separate classes into different components, if they change for different reasons. Both principles can be summarized by the following sound bite:

> *Gather together those things that change at the same times and for the same reasons. Separate those things that change at different times or for different reasons.*

THE COMMON REUSE PRINCIPLE

> *Don't force users of a component to depend on things they don't need.*

The Common Reuse Principle (CRP) is yet another principle that helps us to decide which classes and modules should be placed into a component. It states that classes and modules that tend to be reused together belong in the same component.

Classes are seldom reused in isolation. More typically, reusable classes collaborate with other classes that are part of the reusable abstraction. The CRP states that these classes belong together in the same component. In such a component we would expect to see classes that have lots of dependencies on each other.

A simple example might be a container class and its associated iterators. These classes are reused together because they are tightly coupled to each other. Thus they ought to be in the same component.

But the CRP tells us more than just which classes to put together into a component: It also tells us which classes *not* to keep together in a component. When one component uses another, a dependency is created between the components. Perhaps the *using* component uses only one class within the *used* component—but that still doesn't weaken the dependency. The *using* component still depends on the *used* component.

Because of that dependency, every time the *used* component is changed, the *using* component will likely need corresponding changes. Even if no changes are necessary to the *using* component, it will likely still need to be recompiled, revalidated, and redeployed. This is true even if the *using* component doesn't care about the change made in the *used* component.

Thus when we depend on a component, we want to make sure we depend on every class in that component. Put another way, we want to make sure that the classes that we put into a component are inseparable—that it is impossible to depend on some and not on the others. Otherwise, we will be redeploying more components than is necessary, and wasting significant effort.

Therefore the CRP tells us more about which classes *shouldn't* be together than about which classes *should* be together. The CRP says that classes that are not tightly bound to each other should not be in the same component.

RELATION TO ISP

The CRP is the generic version of the ISP. The ISP advises us not to depend on classes that have methods we don't use. The CRP advises us not to depend on components that have classes we don't use.

All of this advice can be reduced to a single sound bite:

> *Don't depend on things you don't need.*

THE TENSION DIAGRAM FOR COMPONENT COHESION

You may have already realized that the three cohesion principles tend to fight each other. The REP and CCP are *inclusive* principles: Both tend to make components larger. The CRP is an *exclusive* principle, driving components to be smaller. It is the tension between these principles that good architects seek to resolve.

Figure 13.1 is a tension diagram[2] that shows how the three principles of cohesion interact with each other. The edges of the diagram describe the *cost* of abandoning the principle on the opposite vertex.

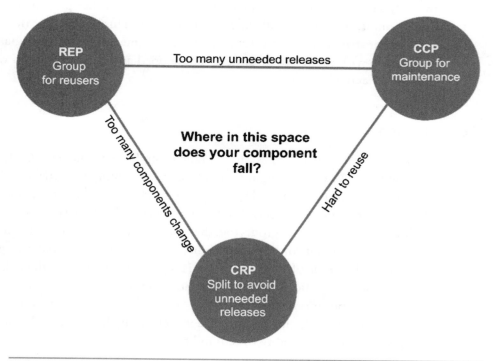

Figure 13.1 Cohesion principles tension diagram

An architect who focuses on just the REP and CRP will find that too many components are impacted when simple changes are made. In contrast, an architect who focuses too strongly on the CCP and REP will cause too many unneeded releases to be generated.

---

2. Thanks to Tim Ottinger for this idea.

A good architect finds a position in that tension triangle that meets the *current* concerns of the development team, but is also aware that those concerns will change over time. For example, early in the development of a project, the CCP is much more important than the REP, because develop-ability is more important than reuse.

Generally, projects tend to start on the right hand side of the triangle, where the only sacrifice is reuse. As the project matures, and other projects begin to draw from it, the project will slide over to the left. This means that the component structure of a project can vary with time and maturity. It has more to do with the way that project is developed and used, than with what the project actually does.

CONCLUSION

In the past, our view of cohesion was much simpler than the REP, CCP, and CRP implied. We once thought that cohesion was simply the attribute that a module performs one, and only one, function. However, the three principles of component cohesion describe a much more complex variety of cohesion. In choosing the classes to group together into components, we must consider the opposing forces involved in reusability and develop-ability. Balancing these forces with the needs of the application is nontrivial. Moreover, the balance is almost always dynamic. That is, the partitioning that is appropriate today might not be appropriate next year. As a consequence, the composition of the components will likely jitter and evolve with time as the focus of the project changes from develop-ability to reusability.

14 COMPONENT COUPLING

KOHNKE

The next three principles deal with the relationships between components. Here again we will run into the tension between develop-ability and logical design. The forces that impinge upon the architecture of a component structure are technical, political, and volatile.

THE ACYCLIC DEPENDENCIES PRINCIPLE

Allow no cycles in the component dependency graph.

Have you ever worked all day, gotten some stuff working, and then gone home, only to arrive the next morning to find that your stuff no longer works? Why doesn't it work? Because somebody stayed later than you and changed something you depend on! I call this "the morning after syndrome."

The "morning after syndrome" occurs in development environments where many developers are modifying the same source files. In relatively small projects with just a few developers, it isn't too big a problem. But as the size of the project and the development team grow, the mornings after can get pretty nightmarish. It is not uncommon for weeks to go by without the team being able to build a stable version of the project. Instead, everyone keeps on changing and changing their code trying to make it work with the last changes that someone else made.

Over the last several decades, two solutions to this problem have evolved, both of which came from the telecommunications industry. The first is "the weekly build," and the second is the Acyclic Dependencies Principle (ADP).

THE WEEKLY BUILD

The weekly build used to be common in medium-sized projects. It works like this: All the developers ignore each other for the first four days of the week. They all work on private copies of the code, and don't worry about integrating their work on a collective basis. Then, on Friday, they integrate all their changes and build the system.

This approach has the wonderful advantage of allowing the developers to live in an isolated world for four days out of five. The disadvantage, of course, is the large integration penalty that is paid on Friday.

Unfortunately, as the project grows, it becomes less feasible to finish integrating the project on Friday. The integration burden grows until it starts to overflow into Saturday. A few such Saturdays are enough to convince the developers that integration should really begin on Thursday—and so the start of integration slowly creeps toward the middle of the week.

As the duty cycle of development versus integration decreases, the efficiency of the team decreases, too. Eventually this situation becomes so frustrating that the developers, or the project managers, declare that the schedule should be changed to a biweekly build. This suffices for a time, but the integration time continues to grow with project size.

Eventually, this scenario leads to a crisis. To maintain efficiency, the build schedule has to be continually lengthened—but lengthening the build schedule increases project risks. Integration and testing become increasingly harder to do, and the team loses the benefit of rapid feedback.

ELIMINATING DEPENDENCY CYCLES

The solution to this problem is to partition the development environment into releasable components. The components become units of work that can be the responsibility of a single developer, or a team of developers. When developers get a component working, they release it for use by the other developers. They give it a release number and move it into a directory for other teams to use. They then continue to modify their component in their own private areas. Everyone else uses the released version.

As new releases of a component are made available, other teams can decide whether they will immediately adopt the new release. If they decide not to, they simply continue using the old release. Once they decide that they are ready, they begin to use the new release.

Thus no team is at the mercy of the others. Changes made to one component do not need to have an immediate affect on other teams. Each team can decide for itself when to adapt its own components to new releases of the components. Moreover, integration happens in small increments. There is no single point in time when all developers must come together and integrate everything they are doing.

This is a very simple and rational process, and it is widely used. To make it work successfully, however, you must *manage* the dependency structure of the components. *There can be no cycles.* If there are cycles in the dependency structure, then the "morning after syndrome" cannot be avoided.

Consider the component diagram in Figure 14.1. It shows a rather typical structure of components assembled into an application. The function of this application is unimportant for the purpose of this example. What *is* important is the dependency structure of the components. Notice that this structure is a *directed graph*. The components are the *nodes*, and the dependency relationships are the *directed edges*.

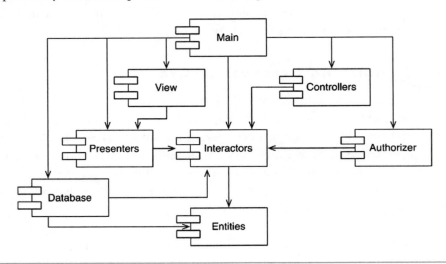

Figure 14.1 Typical component diagram

Notice one more thing: Regardless of which component you begin at, it is impossible to follow the dependency relationships and wind up back at that component. This structure has no cycles. It is a *directed acyclic graph* (DAG).

Now consider what happens when the team responsible for Presenters makes a new release of their component. It is easy to find out who is affected by this release; you just follow the dependency arrows backward. Thus View and Main will both be affected. The developers currently working on those components will have to decide when they should integrate their work with the new release of Presenters.

Notice also that when Main is released, it has utterly no effect on any of the other components in the system. They don't know about Main, and they don't care when it changes. This is nice. It means that the impact of releasing Main is relatively small.

When the developers working on the Presenters component would like to run a test of that component, they just need to build their version of Presenters with the versions of the Interactors and Entities components that they are currently using. None of the other components in the system need be involved. This is nice. It means that the developers working on Presenters have relatively little work to do to set up a test, and that they have relatively few variables to consider.

When it is time to release the whole system, the process proceeds from the bottom up. First the Entities component is compiled, tested, and released. Then the same is done for Database and Interactors. These components are followed by Presenters, View, Controllers, and then Authorizer. Main goes last. This process is very clear and easy to deal with. We know how to build the system because we understand the dependencies between its parts.

THE EFFECT OF A CYCLE IN THE COMPONENT DEPENDENCY GRAPH

Suppose that a new requirement forces us to change one of the classes in Entities such that it makes use of a class in Authorizer. For example, let's say that the User class in Entities uses the Permissions class in Authorizer. This creates a dependency cycle, as shown in Figure 14.2.

This cycle creates some immediate problems. For example, the developers working on the Database component know that to release it, the component must be compatible with Entities. However, with the cycle in place, the Database component must now *also* be compatible with Authorizer. But Authorizer depends on Interactors. This makes Database much more difficult to release. Entities, Authorizer, and Interactors have, in effect, become one large component—which means that all of the developers working on any of those components will experience the dreaded "morning after syndrome." They will be stepping all over one another because they must all use exactly the same release of one another's components.

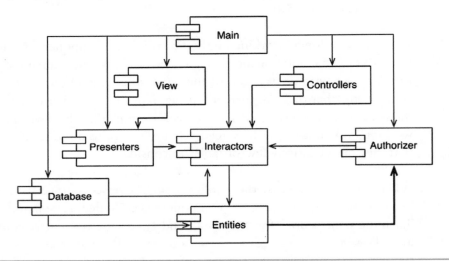

Figure 14.2 A dependency cycle

But this is just part of the trouble. Consider what happens when we want to test the Entities component. To our chagrin, we find that we must build and integrate with Authorizer and Interactors. This level of coupling between components is troubling, if not intolerable.

You may have wondered why you have to include so many different libraries, and so much of everybody else's stuff, just to run a simple unit test of one of your classes. If you investigate the matter a bit, you will probably discover that there are cycles in the dependency graph. Such cycles make it very difficult to isolate components. Unit testing and releasing become very difficult and error prone. In addition, build issues grow geometrically with the number of modules.

Moreover, when there are cycles in the dependency graph, it can be very difficult to work out the order in which you must build the components. Indeed, there probably is no correct order. This can lead to some very nasty problems in languages like Java that read their declarations from compiled binary files.

BREAKING THE CYCLE

It is always possible to break a cycle of components and reinstate the dependency graph as a DAG. There are two primary mechanisms for doing so:

1. Apply the Dependency Inversion Principle (DIP). In the case in Figure 14.3, we could create an interface that has the methods that User needs. We could then put that interface into Entities and inherit it into Authorizer. This inverts the dependency between Entities and Authorizer, thereby breaking the cycle.

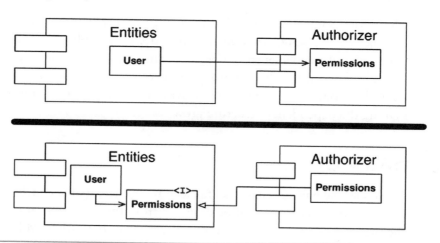

Figure 14.3 Inverting the dependency between Entities and Authorizer

2. Create a new component that both Entities and Authorizer depend on. Move the class(es) that they both depend on into that new component (Figure 14.4).

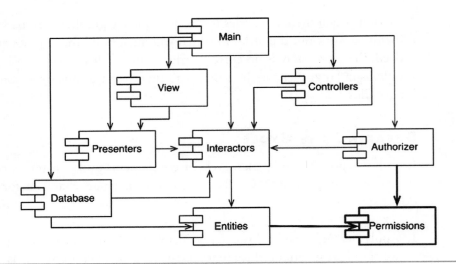

Figure 14.4 The new component that both `Entities` and `Authorizer` depend on

THE "JITTERS"

The second solution implies that the component structure is volatile in the presence of changing requirements. Indeed, as the application grows, the component dependency structure jitters and grows. Thus the dependency structure must always be monitored for cycles. When cycles occur, they must be broken somehow. Sometimes this will mean creating new components, making the dependency structure grow.

TOP-DOWN DESIGN

The issues we have discussed so far lead to an inescapable conclusion: The component structure cannot be designed from the top down. It is not one of the first things about the system that is designed, but rather evolves as the system grows and changes.

Some readers may find this point to be counterintuitive. We have come to expect that large-grained decompositions, like components, will also be high-level *functional* decompositions.

When we see a large-grained grouping such as a component dependency structure, we believe that the components ought to somehow represent the functions of the system. Yet this does not seem to be an attribute of component dependency diagrams.

In fact, component dependency diagrams have very little do to with describing the function of the application. Instead, they are a map to the *buildability* and *maintainability* of the application. This is why they aren't designed at the beginning of the project. There is no software to build or maintain, so there is no need for a build and maintenance map. But as more and more modules accumulate in the early stages of implementation and design, there is a growing need to manage the dependencies so that the project can be developed without the "morning after syndrome." Moreover, we want to keep changes as localized as possible, so we start paying attention to the SRP and CCP and collocate classes that are likely to change together.

One of the overriding concerns with this dependency structure is the isolation of volatility. We don't want components that change frequently and for capricious reasons to affect components that otherwise ought to be stable. For example, we don't want cosmetic changes to the GUI to have an impact on our business rules. We don't want the addition or modification of reports to have an impact on our highest-level policies. Consequently, the component dependency graph is created and molded by architects to protect stable high-value components from volatile components.

As the application continues to grow, we start to become concerned about creating reusable elements. At this point, the CRP begins to influence the composition of the components. Finally, as cycles appear, the ADP is applied and the component dependency graph jitters and grows.

If we tried to design the component dependency structure before we designed any classes, we would likely fail rather badly. We would not know much about common closure, we would be unaware of any reusable elements, and we would almost certainly create components that produced dependency cycles. Thus the component dependency structure grows and evolves with the logical design of the system.

THE STABLE DEPENDENCIES PRINCIPLE

Depend in the direction of stability.

Designs cannot be completely static. Some volatility is necessary if the design is to be maintained. By conforming to the Common Closure Principle (CCP), we create components that are sensitive to certain kinds of changes but immune to others. Some of these components are *designed* to be volatile. We *expect* them to change.

Any component that we expect to be volatile should not be depended on by a component that is difficult to change. Otherwise, the volatile component will also be difficult to change.

It is the perversity of software that a module that you have designed to be easy to change can be made difficult to change by someone else who simply hangs a dependency on it. Not a line of source code in your module need change, yet your module will suddenly become more challenging to change. By conforming to the Stable Dependencies Principle (SDP), we ensure that modules that are intended to be easy to change are not depended on by modules that are harder to change.

STABILITY

What is meant by "stability"? Stand a penny on its side. Is it stable in that position? You would likely say "no." However, unless disturbed, it will remain in that position for a very long time. Thus stability has nothing directly to do with frequency of change. The penny is not changing, but it is difficult to think of it as stable.

Webster's Dictionary says that something is stable if it is "not easily moved." Stability is related to the amount of work required to make a change. On the one hand, the standing penny is not stable because it requires very little work to topple it. On the other hand, a table is very stable because it takes a considerable amount of effort to turn it over.

How does this relate to software? Many factors may make a software component hard to change—for example, its size, complexity, and clarity, among other characteristics. We will ignore all those factors and focus on something different here. One sure way to make a software component difficult to change, is to make lots of other software components depend on it. A component with lots of incoming dependencies is very stable because it requires a great deal of work to reconcile any changes with all the dependent components.

The diagram in Figure 14.5 shows X, which is a stable component. Three components depend on X, so it has three good reasons not to change. We say that X is *responsible* to those three components. Conversely, X depends on nothing, so it has no external influence to make it change. We say it is *independent*.

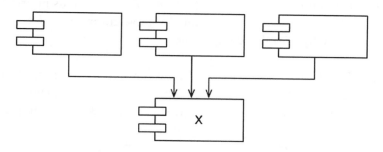

Figure 14.5 X: a stable component

Figure 14.6 shows Y, which is a very unstable component. No other components depend on Y, so we say that it is irresponsible. Y also has three components that it depends on, so changes may come from three external sources. We say that Y is dependent.

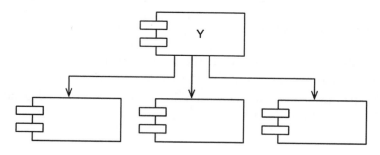

Figure 14.6 Y: a very unstable component

STABILITY METRICS

How can we measure the stability of a component? One way is to count the number of dependencies that enter and leave that component. These counts will allow us to calculate the *positional* stability of the component.

- *Fan-in*: Incoming dependencies. This metric identifies the number of classes outside this component that depend on classes within the component.
- *Fan-out*: Outgoing dependencies. This metric identifies the number of classes inside this component that depend on classes outside the component.
- *I*: Instability: $I = Fan\text{-}out \div (Fan\text{-}in + Fan\text{-}out)$. This metric has the range [0, 1]. $I = 0$ indicates a maximally stable component. $I = 1$ indicates a maximally unstable component.

The *Fan-in* and *Fan-out* metrics[1] are calculated by counting the number of *classes* outside the component in question that have dependencies with the classes inside the component in question. Consider the example in Figure 14.7.

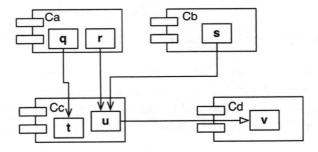

Figure 14.7 Our example

Let's say we want to calculate the stability of the component Cc. We find that there are three classes outside Cc that depend on classes in Cc. Thus, *Fan-in* = 3. Moreover, there is one class outside Cc that classes in Cc depend on. Thus, *Fan-out* = 1 and $I = 1/4$.

---

1. In previous publications, I used the names *Efferent* and *Afferent* couplings (Ce and Ca) for *Fan-out* and *Fan-in*, respectively. That was just hubris on my part: I liked the metaphor of the central nervous system.

In C++, these dependencies are typically represented by `#include` statements. Indeed, the I metric is easiest to calculate when you have organized your source code such that there is one class in each source file. In Java, the I metric can be calculated by counting `import` statements and qualified names.

When the I metric is equal to 1, it means that no other component depends on this component (*Fan-in* $= 0$), and this component depends on other components (*Fan-out* > 0). This situation is as unstable as a component can get; it is irresponsible and dependent. Its lack of dependents gives the component no reason not to change, and the components that it depends on may give it ample reason to change.

In contrast, when the I metric is equal to 0, it means that the component is depended on by other components (*Fan-in* > 0), but does not itself depend on any other components (*Fan-out* $= 0$). Such a component is *responsible* and *independent*. It is as stable as it can get. Its dependents make it hard to change the component, and its has no dependencies that might force it to change.

The SDP says that the I metric of a component should be larger than the I metrics of the components that it depends on. That is, I metrics should *decrease* in the direction of dependency.

NOT ALL COMPONENTS SHOULD BE STABLE

If all the components in a system were maximally stable, the system would be unchangeable. This is not a desirable situation. Indeed, we want to design our component structure so that some components are unstable and some are stable. The diagram in Figure 14.8 shows an ideal configuration for a system with three components.

The changeable components are on top and depend on the stable component at the bottom. Putting the unstable components at the top of the diagram is a useful convention because any arrow that points *up* is violating the SDP (and, as we shall see later, the ADP).

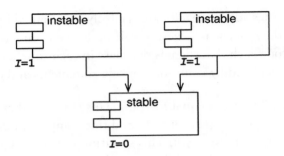

Figure 14.8 An ideal configuration for a system with three components

The diagram in Figure 14.9 shows how the SDP can be violated.

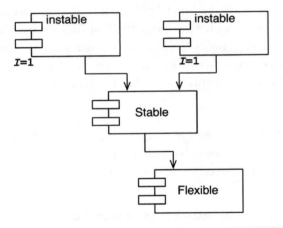

Figure 14.9 SDP violation

`Flexible` is a component that we have designed to be easy to change. We want `Flexible` to be unstable. However, some developer, working in the component named `Stable`, has hung a dependency on `Flexible`. This violates the SDP because the *I* metric for `Stable` is much smaller than the *I* metric for `Flexible`. As a result, `Flexible` will no longer be easy to change. A change to `Flexible` will force us to deal with `Stable` and all its dependents.

To fix this problem, we somehow have to break the dependence of `Stable` on `Flexible`. Why does this dependency exist? Let's assume that there is a class C within `Flexible` that another class U within `Stable` needs to use (Figure 14.10).

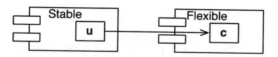

Figure 14.10 U within `Stable` uses C within `Flexible`

We can fix this by employing the DIP. We create an interface class called US and put it in a component named `UServer`. We make sure that this interface declares all the methods that U needs to use. We then make C implement this interface as shown in Figure 14.11. This breaks the dependency of `Stable` on `Flexible`, and forces both components to depend on `UServer`. `UServer` is very stable ($I = 0$), and `Flexible` retains its necessary instability ($I = 1$). All the dependencies now flow in the direction of *decreasing I*.

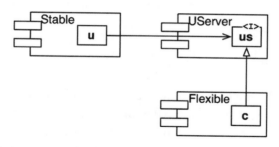

Figure 14.11 C implements the interface class US

Abstract Components

You may find it strange that we would create a component—in this example, `UService`—that contains nothing but an interface. Such a component contains no executable code! It turns out, however, that this is a very common, and necessary, tactic when using statically typed languages like Java and C#. These abstract components are very stable and, therefore, are ideal targets for less stable components to depend on.

When using dynamically typed languages like Ruby and Python, these abstract components don't exist at all, nor do the dependencies that would have targeted them. Dependency structures in these languages are much simpler because dependency inversion does not require either the declaration or the inheritance of interfaces.

THE STABLE ABSTRACTIONS PRINCIPLE

A component should be as abstract as it is stable.

WHERE DO WE PUT THE HIGH-LEVEL POLICY?

Some software in the system should not change very often. This software represents high-level architecture and policy decisions. We don't want these business and architectural decisions to be volatile. Thus the software that encapsulates the high-level policies of the system should be placed into stable components $(I = 0)$. Unstable components $(I = 1)$ should contain only the software that is volatile—software that we want to be able to quickly and easily change.

However, if the high-level policies are placed into stable components, then the source code that represents those policies will be difficult to change. This could make the overall architecture inflexible. How can a component that is maximally stable $(I = 0)$ be flexible enough to withstand change? The answer is found in the OCP. This principle tells us that it is possible and desirable to create classes that are flexible enough to be extended without requiring modification. Which kind of classes conform to this principle? *Abstract* classes.

INTRODUCING THE STABLE ABSTRACTIONS PRINCIPLE

The Stable Abstractions Principle (SAP) sets up a relationship between stability and abstractness. On the one hand, it says that a stable component should also be abstract so that its stability does not prevent it from being extended. On the other hand, it says that an unstable component should be concrete since its instability allows the concrete code within it to be easily changed.

Thus, if a component is to be stable, it should consist of interfaces and abstract classes so that it can be extended. Stable components that are extensible are flexible and do not overly constrain the architecture.

The SAP and the SDP combined amount to the DIP for components. This is true because the SDP says that dependencies should run in the direction of stability, and the SAP says that stability implies abstraction. Thus *dependencies run in the direction of abstraction.*

The DIP, however, is a principle that deals with classes—and with classes there are no shades of gray. Either a class is abstract or it is not. The combination of the SDP and the SAP deals with components, and allows that a component can be partially abstract and partially stable.

MEASURING ABSTRACTION

The *A* metric is a measure of the abstractness of a component. Its value is simply the ratio of interfaces and abstract classes in a component to the total number of classes in the component.

- *Nc:* The number of classes in the component.
- *Na:* The number of abstract classes and interfaces in the component.
- *A:* Abstractness. $A = Na \div Nc$.

The *A* metric ranges from 0 to 1. A value of 0 implies that the component has no abstract classes at all. A value of 1 implies that the component contains nothing but abstract classes.

THE MAIN SEQUENCE

We are now in a position to define the relationship between stability (*I*) and abstractness (*A*). To do so, we create a graph with *A* on the vertical axis and *I* on the horizontal axis (Figure 14.12). If we plot the two "good" kinds of components on this graph, we will find the components that are maximally stable and abstract at the upper left at (0, 1). The components that are maximally unstable and concrete are at the lower right at (1, 0).

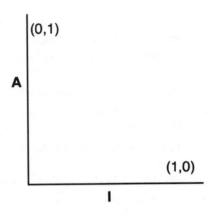

Figure 14.12 The I/A graph

Not all components fall into one of these two positions, because components often have *degrees* of abstraction and stability. For example, it is very common for one abstract class to derive from another abstract class. The derivative is an abstraction that has a dependency. Thus, though it is maximally abstract, it will not be maximally stable. Its dependency will decrease its stability.

Since we cannot enforce a rule that all components sit at either (0, 1) or (1, 0), we must assume that there is a locus of points on the *A/I* graph that defines reasonable positions for components. We can infer what that locus is by finding the areas where components should *not* be—in other words, by determining the zones of *exclusion* (Figure 14.13).

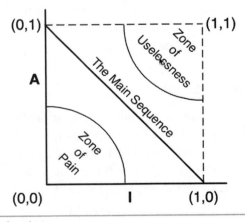

Figure 14.13 Zones of exclusion

The Zone of Pain

Consider a component in the area of (0, 0). This is a highly stable and concrete component. Such a component is not desirable because it is rigid. It cannot be extended because it is not abstract, and it is very difficult to change because of its stability. Thus we do not normally expect to see well-designed components sitting near (0, 0). The area around (0, 0) is a zone of exclusion called the *Zone of Pain*.

Some software entities do, in fact, fall within the Zone of Pain. An example would be a database schema. Database schemas are notoriously volatile, extremely concrete, and highly depended on. This is one reason why the interface between OO applications and databases is so difficult to manage, and why schema updates are generally painful.

Another example of software that sits near the area of (0, 0) is a concrete utility library. Although such a library has an *I* metric of 1, it may actually be nonvolatile. Consider the `String` component, for example. Even though all the classes within it are concrete, it is so commonly used that changing it would create chaos. Therefore `String` is nonvolatile.

Nonvolatile components are harmless in the (0, 0) zone since they are not likely to be changed. For that reason, it is only volatile software components that are problematic in the Zone of Pain. The more volatile a component in the Zone of Pain, the more "painful" it is. Indeed, we might consider volatility to be a third axis of the graph. With this understanding, Figure 14.13 shows only the most painful plane, where volatility = 1.

The Zone of Uselessness

Consider a component near (1, 1). This location is undesirable because it is maximally abstract, yet has no dependents. Such components are useless. Thus this area is called the *Zone of Uselessness*.

The software entities that inhabit this region are a kind of detritus. They are often leftover abstract classes that no one ever implemented. We find them in systems from time to time, sitting in the code base, unused.

A component that has a position deep within the Zone of Uselessness must contain a significant fraction of such entities. Clearly, the presence of such useless entities is undesirable.

AVOIDING THE ZONES OF EXCLUSION

It seems clear that our most volatile components should be kept as far from both zones of exclusion as possible. The locus of points that are maximally distant from each zone is the line that connects (1, 0) and (0, 1). I call this line the *Main Sequence*.[2]

A component that sits on the Main Sequence is not "too abstract" for its stability, nor is it "too unstable" for its abstractness. It is neither useless nor particularly painful. It is depended on to the extent that it is abstract, and it depends on others to the extent that it is concrete.

The most desirable position for a component is at one of the two endpoints of the Main Sequence. Good architects strive to position the majority of their components at those endpoints. However, in my experience, some small fraction of the components in a large system are neither perfectly abstract nor perfectly stable. Those components have the best characteristics if they are on, *or close*, to the Main Sequence.

DISTANCE FROM THE MAIN SEQUENCE

This leads us to our last metric. If it is desirable for components to be on, or close, to the Main Sequence, then we can create a metric that measures how far away a component is from this ideal.

- D^3: Distance. $D = |A+I-1|$. The range of this metric is [0, 1]. A value of 0 indicates that the component is directly on the Main Sequence. A value of 1 indicates that the component is as far away as possible from the Main Sequence.

---

2. The author begs the reader's indulgence for the arrogance of borrowing such an important term from astronomy.

3. In previous publications, I called this metric D'. I see no reason to continue that practice.

Given this metric, a design can be analyzed for its overall conformance to the Main Sequence. The D metric for each component can be calculated. Any component that has a D value that is not near zero can be reexamined and restructured.

Statistical analysis of a design is also possible. We can calculate the mean and variance of all the D metrics for the components within a design. We would expect a conforming design to have a mean and variance that are close to zero. The variance can be used to establish "control limits" so as to identify components that are "exceptional" in comparison to all the others.

In the scatterplot in Figure 14.14, we see that the bulk of the components lie along the Main Sequence, but some of them are more than one standard deviation ($Z = 1$) away from the mean. These aberrant components are worth examining more closely. For some reason, they are either very abstract with few dependents or very concrete with many dependents.

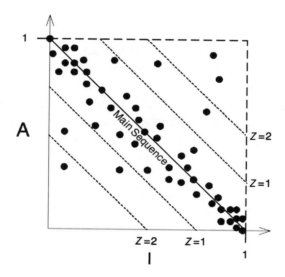

Figure 14.14 Scatterplot of the components

Another way to use the metrics is to plot the D metric of each component over time. The graph in Figure 14.15 is a mock-up of such a plot. You can see that some strange dependencies have been creeping into the `Payroll` component over the last few releases. The plot shows a control threshold at $D = 0.1$. The R2.1 point has exceeded this control limit, so it would be worth our while to find out why this component is so far from the main sequence.

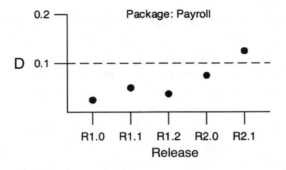

Figure 14.15 Plot of D for a single component over time

CONCLUSION

The *dependency management metrics* described in this chapter measure the conformance of a design to a pattern of dependency and abstraction that I think is a "good" pattern. Experience has shown that certain dependencies are good and others are bad. This pattern reflects that experience. However, a metric is not a god; it is merely a measurement against an arbitrary standard. These metrics are imperfect, at best, but it is my hope that you find them useful.

ARCHITECTURE V

Chapter 15

What Is Architecture?

The word "architecture" conjures visions of power and mystery. It makes us think of weighty decisions and deep technical prowess. Software architecture is at the pinnacle of technical achievement. When we think of a software architect, we think of someone who has power, and who commands respect. What young aspiring software developer has not dreamed of one day becoming a software architect?

But what is software architecture? What does a software architect do, and when does he or she do it?

First of all, a software architect is a programmer; and continues to be a programmer. Never fall for the lie that suggests that software architects pull back from code to focus on higher-level issues. They do not! Software architects are the best programmers, and they continue to take programming tasks, while they also guide the rest of the team toward a design that maximizes productivity. Software architects may not write as much code as other programmers do, but they continue to engage in programming tasks. They do this because they cannot do their jobs properly if they are not experiencing the problems that they are creating for the rest of the programmers.

The architecture of a software system is the shape given to that system by those who build it. The form of that shape is in the division of that system into components, the arrangement of those components, and the ways in which those components communicate with each other.

The purpose of that shape is to facilitate the development, deployment, operation, and maintenance of the software system contained within it.

> *The strategy behind that facilitation is to leave as many options open as possible, for as long as possible.*

Perhaps this statement has surprised you. Perhaps you thought that the goal of software architecture was to make the system work properly. Certainly we want the system to work properly, and certainly the architecture of the system must support that as one of its highest priorities.

However, the architecture of a system has very little bearing on whether that system works. There are many systems out there, with terrible architectures, that work just fine. Their troubles do not lie in their operation; rather, they occur in their deployment, maintenance, and ongoing development.

This is not to say that architecture plays no role in supporting the proper behavior of the system. It certainly does, and that role is critical. But the role is passive and cosmetic, not active or essential. There are few, if any, *behavioral* options that the architecture of a system can leave open.

The primary purpose of architecture is to support the life cycle of the system. Good architecture makes the system easy to understand, easy to develop, easy to maintain, and easy to deploy. The ultimate goal is to minimize the lifetime cost of the system and to maximize programmer productivity.

DEVELOPMENT

A software system that is hard to develop is not likely to have a long and healthy lifetime. So the architecture of a system should make that system easy to develop, for the team(s) who develop it.

Different team structures imply different architectural decisions. On the one hand, a small team of five developers can quite effectively work together to develop a monolithic system without well-defined components or interfaces. In fact, such a team would likely find the strictures of an architecture something of an impediment during the early days of development. This is likely the reason why so many systems lack good architecture: They were begun with none, because the team was small and did not want the impediment of a superstructure.

On the other hand, a system being developed by five different teams, each of which includes seven developers, cannot make progress unless the system is divided into well-defined components with reliably stable interfaces. If no other factors are considered, the architecture of that system will likely evolve into five components—one for each team.

Such a component-per-team architecture is not likely to be the best architecture for deployment, operation, and maintenance of the system. Nevertheless, it is the architecture that a group of teams will gravitate toward if they are driven solely by development schedule.

DEPLOYMENT

To be effective, a software system must be deployable. The higher the cost of deployment, the less useful the system is. A goal of a software architecture, then, should be to make a system that can be easily deployed *with a single action*.

Unfortunately, deployment strategy is seldom considered during initial development. This leads to architectures that may make the system easy to develop, but leave it very difficult to deploy.

For example, in the early development of a system, the developers may decide to use a "micro-service architecture." They may find that this approach makes the system very easy to develop since the component boundaries are very firm and the interfaces relatively stable. However, when it comes time to deploy the system, they may discover that the number of micro-services has become daunting; configuring the connections between them, and the timing of their initiation, may also turn out to be a huge source of errors.

Had the architects considered deployment issues early on, they might have decided on fewer services, a hybrid of services and in-process components, and a more integrated means of managing the interconnections.

OPERATION

The impact of architecture on system operation tends to be less dramatic than the impact of architecture on development, deployment, and maintenance. Almost any operational difficulty can be resolved by throwing more hardware at the system without drastically impacting the software architecture.

Indeed, we have seen this happen over and over again. Software systems that have inefficient architectures can often be made to work effectively simply by adding more storage and more servers. The fact that hardware is cheap and people are expensive means that architectures that impede operation are not as costly as architectures that impede development, deployment, and maintenance.

This is not to say that an architecture that is well tuned to the operation of the system is not desirable. It is! It's just that the cost equation leans more toward development, deployment, and maintenance.

Having said that, there is another role that architecture plays in the operation of the system: A good software architecture communicates the operational needs of the system.

Perhaps a better way to say this is that the architecture of a system makes the operation of the system readily apparent to the developers. Architecture should reveal operation. The architecture of the system should elevate the use cases, the features, and the required behaviors of the system to first-class entities that are visible landmarks for the developers. This simplifies the understanding of the system and, therefore, greatly aids in development and maintenance.

MAINTENANCE

Of all the aspects of a software system, maintenance is the most costly. The never-ending parade of new features and the inevitable trail of defects and corrections consume vast amounts of human resources.

The primary cost of maintenance is in *spelunking* and risk. Spelunking is the cost of digging through the existing software, trying to determine the best place and the best strategy to add a new feature or to repair a defect. While making such changes, the likelihood of creating inadvertent defects is always there, adding to the cost of risk.

A carefully thought-through architecture vastly mitigates these costs. By separating the system into components, and isolating those components through stable interfaces, it is possible to illuminate the pathways for future features and greatly reduce the risk of inadvertent breakage.

KEEPING OPTIONS OPEN

As we described in an earlier chapter, software has two types of value: the value of its behavior and the value of its structure. The second of these is the greater of the two because it is this value that makes software *soft*.

Software was invented because we needed a way to quickly and easily change the behavior of machines. But that flexibility depends critically on the shape of the system, the arrangement of its components, and the way those components are interconnected.

The way you keep software soft is to leave as many options open as possible, for as long as possible. What are the options that we need to leave open? *They are the details that don't matter.*

All software systems can be decomposed into two major elements: policy and details. The policy element embodies all the business rules and procedures. The policy is where the true value of the system lives.

The details are those things that are necessary to enable humans, other systems, and programmers to communicate with the policy, but that do not impact the behavior of the policy at all. They include IO devices, databases, web systems, servers, frameworks, communication protocols, and so forth.

The goal of the architect is to create a shape for the system that recognizes policy as the most essential element of the system while making the details *irrelevant* to that policy. This allows decisions about those details to be *delayed* and *deferred*.

For example:

- It is not necessary to choose a database system in the early days of development, because the high-level policy should not care which kind of database will be used. Indeed, if the architect is careful, the high-level policy will not care if the database is relational, distributed, hierarchical, or just plain flat files.
- It is not necessary to choose a web server early in development, because the high-level policy should not know that it is being delivered over the web. If the high-level policy is unaware of HTML, AJAX, JSP, JSF, or any of the rest of the alphabet soup of web development, then you don't need to decide which web system to use until much later in the project. Indeed, *you don't even have to decide if the system will be delivered over the web.*
- It is not necessary to adopt REST early in development, because the high-level policy should be agnostic about the interface to the outside world. Nor is it necessary to adopt a micro-services framework, or a SOA framework. Again, the high-level policy should not care about these things.
- It is not necessary to adopt a dependency injection framework early in development, because the high-level policy should not care how dependencies are resolved.

I think you get the point. If you can develop the high-level policy without committing to the details that surround it, you can delay and defer decisions about those details for a long time. And the longer you wait to make those decisions, *the more information you have with which to make them properly.*

This also leaves you the option to try different experiments. If you have a portion of the high-level policy working, and it is agnostic about the database, you could try connecting it to several different databases to check applicability and performance. The same is true with web systems, web frameworks, or even the web itself.

The longer you leave options open, the more experiments you can run, the more things you can try, and the more information you will have when you reach the point at which those decisions can no longer be deferred.

What if the decisions have already been made by someone else? What if your company has made a commitment to a certain database, or a certain web server, or a certain framework? *A good architect pretends that the decision has not been made*, and shapes the system such that those decisions can still be deferred or changed for as long as possible.

A good architect maximizes the number of decisions not made.

DEVICE INDEPENDENCE

As an example of this kind of thinking, let's take a trip back to the 1960s, when computers were teenagers and most programmers were mathematicians or engineers from other disciplines (and-one third or more were women).

In those days we made a lot of mistakes. We didn't know they were mistakes at the time, of course. How could we?

One of those mistakes was to bind our code directly to the IO devices. If we needed to print something on a printer, we wrote code that used the IO instructions that would control the printer. Our code was *device dependent*.

For example, when I wrote PDP-8 programs that printed on the teleprinter, I used a set of machine instructions that looked like this:

```
PRTCHR, 0
        TSF
        JMP  .-1
        TLS
        JMP  I PRTCHR
```

PRTCHR is a subroutine that prints one character on the teleprinter. The beginning zero was used as the storage for the return address. (Don't ask.) The TSF instruction skipped the next instruction if the teleprinter was ready to print a character. If the teleprinter was busy, then TSF just fell through to the JMP .-1 instruction, which just jumped back to the TSF instruction. If the teleprinter was ready, then TSF would skip to the TLS instruction, which sent the character in the A register to the teleprinter. Then the JMP I PRTCHR instruction returned to the caller.

At first this strategy worked fine. If we needed to read cards from the card reader, we used code that talked directly to the card reader. If we needed to punch cards, we wrote code that directly manipulated the punch. The programs worked perfectly. How could we know this was a mistake?

But big batches of punched cards are difficult to manage. They can be lost, mutilated, spindled, shuffled, or dropped. Individual cards can be lost and extra cards can be inserted. So data integrity became a significant problem.

Magnetic tape was the solution. We could move the card images to tape. If you drop a magnetic tape, the records don't get shuffled. You can't accidentally lose a record, or insert a blank record simply by handing the tape. The tape is much more secure. It's also faster to read and write, and it is very easy to make backup copies.

Unfortunately, all our software was written to manipulate card readers and card punches. Those programs had to be rewritten to use magnetic tape. That was a big job.

By the late 1960s, we had learned our lesson—and we invented *device independence*. The operating systems of the day abstracted the IO devices into software functions that handled unit records that looked like cards. The programs would invoke operating system services that dealt with abstract unit-record devices. Operators could tell the operating system whether those abstract services should be connected to card readers, magnetic tape, or any other unit-record device.

Now the same program could read and write cards, or read and write tape, *without any change*. The Open–Closed Principle was born (but not yet named).

JUNK MAIL

In the late 1960s, I worked for a company that printed junk mail for clients. The clients would send us magnetic tapes with unit records containing the names and addresses of their customers, and we would write programs that printed nice personalized advertisements.

You know the kind:

Hello Mr. Martin,

Congratulations!

We chose YOU from everyone else who lives on Witchwood Lane to participate in our new fantastic one-time-only offering...

The clients would send us huge rolls of form letters with all the words except the name and address, and any other element they wanted us to print. We wrote programs that extracted the names, addresses, and other elements from the magnetic tape, and printed those elements exactly where they needed to appear on the forms.

These rolls of form letters weighed 500 pounds and contained thousands of letters. Clients would send us hundreds of these rolls. We would print each one individually.

At first, we had an IBM 360 doing the printing on its sole line printer. We could print a few thousand letters per shift. Unfortunately, this tied up a very expensive machine for a very long time. In those days, IBM 360s rented for tens of thousands of dollars per month.

So we told the operating system to use magnetic tape instead of the line printer. Our programs didn't care, because they had been written to use the IO abstractions of the operating system.

The 360 could pump out a full tape in 10 minutes or so—enough to print several rolls of form letters. The tapes were taken outside of the computer room and mounted on tape drives connected to offline printers. We had five of them, and we ran those five printers 24 hours per day, seven days per week, printing hundreds of thousands of pieces of junk mail every week.

The value of device independence was enormous! We could write our programs without knowing or caring which device would be used. We could test those programs using the local line printer connected to the computer. Then we could tell the operating system to "print" to magnetic tape and run off hundreds of thousands of forms.

Our programs had a shape. That shape disconnected policy from detail. The policy was the formatting of the name and address records. The detail was the device. We deferred the decision about which device we would use.

PHYSICAL ADDRESSING

In the early 1970s, I worked on a large accounting system for a local truckers union. We had a 25MB disk drive on which we stored records for Agents, Employers, and Members. The different records had different sizes, so we formatted the first few cylinders of the disk so that each sector was just the size of an Agent record. The next few cylinders were formatted to have sectors that fit the Employer records. The last few cylinders were formatted to fit the Member records.

We wrote our software to know the detailed structure of the disk. It knew that the disk had 200 cylinders and 10 heads, and that each cylinder had several dozen sectors per head. It knew which cylinders held the Agents, Employers, and Members. All this was hard-wired into the code.

We kept an index on the disk that allowed us to look up each of the Agents, Employers, and Members. This index was in yet another specially formatted set of cylinders on the disk. The Agent index was composed of records that contained the ID of an agent, and the cylinder number, head number, and sector number of that Agent record. Employers and Members had similar indices. Members were also kept in a doubly linked list on the disk. Each

`Member` record held the cylinder, head, and sector number of the next `Member` record, and of the previous `Member` record.

What would happen if we needed to upgrade to a new disk drive—one with more heads, or one with more cylinders, or one with more sectors per cylinder? We had to write a special program to read in the old data from the old disk, and then write it out to the new disk, translating all of the cylinder/head/sector numbers. We also had to change all the hard-wiring in our code—and that hard-wiring was *everywhere*! All the business rules knew the cylinder/head/sector scheme in detail.

One day a more experienced programmer joined our ranks. When he saw what we had done, the blood drained from his face, and he stared aghast at us, as if we were aliens of some kind. Then he gently advised us to change our addressing scheme to use relative addresses.

Our wiser colleague suggested that we consider the disk to be one huge linear array of sectors, each addressable by a sequential integer. Then we could write a little conversion routine that knew the physical structure of the disk, and could translate the relative address to a cylinder/head/sector number on the fly.

Fortunately for us, we took his advice. We changed the high-level policy of the system to be agnostic about the physical structure of the disk. That allowed us to decouple the decision about disk drive structure from the application.

CONCLUSION

The two stories in this chapter are examples, in the small, of a principle that architects employ in the large. Good architects carefully separate details from policy, and then decouple the policy from the details so thoroughly that the policy has no knowledge of the details and does not depend on the details in any way. Good architects design the policy so that decisions about the details can be delayed and deferred for as long as possible.

16 INDEPENDENCE

As we previously stated, a good architecture must support:

- The use cases and operation of the system.
- The maintenance of the system.
- The development of the system.
- The deployment of the system.

USE CASES

The first bullet—use cases—means that the architecture of the system must support the intent of the system. If the system is a shopping cart application, then the architecture must support shopping cart use cases. Indeed, this is the first concern of the architect, and the first priority of the architecture. The architecture must support the use cases.

However, as we discussed previously, architecture does not wield much influence over the behavior of the system. There are very few behavioral options that the architecture can leave open. But influence isn't everything. The most important thing a good architecture can do to support behavior is to clarify and expose that behavior so that the intent of the system is visible at the architectural level.

A shopping cart application with a good architecture will *look* like a shopping cart application. The use cases of that system will be plainly visible within the structure of that system. Developers will not have to hunt for behaviors, because those behaviors will be first-class elements visible at the top level of the system. Those elements will be classes or functions or modules that have prominent positions within the architecture, and they will have names that clearly describe their function.

Chapter 21, "Screaming Architecture," will make this point much clearer.

OPERATION

Architecture plays a more substantial, and less cosmetic, role in supporting the operation of the system. If the system must handle 100,000 customers per second, the architecture must support that kind of throughput and response time for each use case that demands it. If the system must query big data cubes in milliseconds, then the architecture must be structured to allow this kind of operation.

For some systems, this will mean arranging the processing elements of the system into an array of little services can be run in parallel on many different servers. For other systems, it will mean a plethora of little lightweight threads sharing the address space of a single process within a single processor. Still other systems will need just a few processes running in isolated address spaces. And some systems can even survive as simple monolithic programs running in a single process.

As strange as it may seem, this decision is one of the options that a good architect leaves open. A system that is written as a monolith, and that depends on that monolithic structure, cannot easily be upgraded to multiple processes, multiple threads, or micro-services should the need arise. By comparison, an architecture that maintains the proper isolation of its components, and does not assume the means of communication between those components, will be much easier to transition through the spectrum of threads, processes, and services as the operational needs of the system change over time.

DEVELOPMENT

Architecture plays a significant role in supporting the development environment. This is where Conway's law comes into play. Conway's law says:

> *Any organization that designs a system will produce a design whose structure is a copy of the organization's communication structure.*

A system that must be developed by an organization with many teams and many concerns must have an architecture that facilitates independent actions by those teams, so that the teams do not interfere with each other during development. This is accomplished by properly partitioning the system into well-isolated, independently developable components. Those components can then be allocated to teams that can work independently of each other.

DEPLOYMENT

The architecture also plays a huge role in determining the ease with which the system is deployed. The goal is "immediate deployment." A good architecture does not rely on dozens of little configuration scripts and property file tweaks. It does not require manual creation of directories or files that must be arranged just so. A good architecture helps the system to be immediately deployable after build.

Again, this is achieved through the proper partitioning and isolation of the components of the system, including those master components that tie the whole system together and ensure that each component is properly started, integrated, and supervised.

LEAVING OPTIONS OPEN

A good architecture balances all of these concerns with a component structure that mutually satisfies them all. Sounds easy, right? Well, it's easy for me to write that.

The reality is that achieving this balance is pretty hard. The problem is that most of the time we don't know what all the use cases are, nor do we know the operational constraints, the team structure, or the deployment requirements. Worse, even if we did know them, they will inevitably change as the system moves through its life cycle. In short, the goals we must meet are indistinct and inconstant. Welcome to the real world.

But all is not lost: Some principles of architecture are relatively inexpensive to implement and can help balance those concerns, even when you don't have a clear picture of the targets you have to hit. Those principles help us partition our systems into well-isolated components that allow us to leave as many options open as possible, for as long as possible.

A good architecture makes the system easy to change, in all the ways that it must change, by leaving options open.

DECOUPLING LAYERS

Consider the use cases. The architect wants the structure of the system to support all the necessary use cases, but does not know what all those use cases are. However, the architect *does* know the basic intent of the system. It's a shopping cart system, or it's a bill of materials system, or it's an order processing system. So the architect can employ the Single Responsibility Principle and the Common Closure Principle to separate those things that change for different reasons, and to collect those things that change for the same reasons—given the context of the intent of the system.

What changes for different reasons? There are some obvious things. User interfaces change for reasons that have nothing to do with business rules. Use cases have elements of both. Clearly, then, a good architect will want to separate the UI portions of a use case from the business rule portions in such a way that they can be changed independently of each other, while keeping those use cases visible and clear.

Business rules themselves may be closely tied to the application, or they may be more general. For example, the validation of input fields is a business rule that is closely tied to the application itself. In contrast, the calculation of interest on an account and the counting of inventory are business rules that are more closely associated with the domain. These two different kinds of rules will change at different rates, and for different reasons—so they should be separated so that they can be independently changed.

The database, the query language, and even the schema are technical details that have nothing to do with the business rules or the UI. They will change at rates, and for reasons, that are independent of other aspects of the system. Consequently, the architecture should separate them from the rest of the system so that they can be independently changed.

Thus we find the system divided into decoupled horizontal layers—the UI, application-specific business rules, application-independent business rules, and the database, just to mention a few.

DECOUPLING USE CASES

What else changes for different reasons? The use cases themselves! The use case for adding an order to an order entry system almost certainly will change at a different rate, and for different reasons, than the use case that deletes an order from the system. Use cases are a very natural way to divide the system.

At the same time, use cases are narrow vertical slices that cut through the horizontal layers of the system. Each use case uses some UI, some application-specific business rules, some application-independent business rules, and some database functionality. Thus, as we are dividing the system in to horizontal layers, we are also dividing the system into thin vertical use cases that cut through those layers.

To achieve this decoupling, we separate the UI of the add-order use case from the UI of the delete-order use case. We do the same with the business rules, and with the database. We keep the use cases separate down the vertical height of the system.

You can see the pattern here. If you decouple the elements of the system that change for different reasons, then you can continue to add new use cases without interfering with old ones. If you also group the UI and database in support of those use cases, so that each use case uses a different aspect of the UI and database, then adding new use cases will be unlikely to affect older ones.

DECOUPLING MODE

Now think of what all that decoupling means for the second bullet: operations. If the different aspects of the use cases are separated, then those that must run at a high throughput are likely already separated from those that must run at a low throughput. If the UI and the database have been separated from the business rules, then they can run in different servers. Those that require higher bandwidth can be replicated in many servers.

In short, the decoupling that we did for the sake of the use cases also helps with operations. However, to take advantage of the operational benefit, the decoupling must have the appropriate mode. To run in separate servers, the separated components cannot depend on being together in the same address space of a processor. They must be independent services, which communicate over a network of some kind.

Many architects call such components "services" or "micro-services," depending upon some vague notion of line count. Indeed, an architecture based on services is often called a service-oriented architecture.

If that nomenclature set off some alarm bells in your mind, don't worry. I'm not going to tell you that SoA is the best possible architecture, or that micro-services are the wave of the future. The point being made here is that sometimes we have to separate our components all the way to the service level.

Remember, a good architecture leaves options open. *The decoupling mode is one of those options.*

Before we explore that topic further, let's look to the other two bullets.

INDEPENDENT DEVELOP-ABILITY

The third bullet was development. Clearly when components are strongly decoupled, the interference between teams is mitigated. If the business rules don't know about the UI, then a team that focuses on the UI cannot much affect a team that focuses on the business rules. If the use cases themselves are decoupled from one another, then a team that focuses on the addOrder use case is not likely to interfere with a team that focuses on the deleteOrder use case.

So long as the layers and use cases are decoupled, the architecture of the system will support the organization of the teams, irrespective of whether they are organized as feature teams, component teams, layer teams, or some other variation.

INDEPENDENT DEPLOYABILITY

The decoupling of the use cases and layers also affords a high degree of flexibility in deployment. Indeed, if the decoupling is done well, then it should be possible to hot-swap layers and use cases in running systems. Adding a new use case could be a simple as adding a few new jar files or services to the system while leaving the rest alone.

DUPLICATION

Architects often fall into a trap—a trap that hinges on their fear of duplication.

Duplication is generally a bad thing in software. We don't like duplicated code. When code is truly duplicated, we are honor-bound as professionals to reduce and eliminate it.

But there are different kinds of duplication. There is true duplication, in which every change to one instance necessitates the same change to every duplicate of that instance. Then there is false or accidental duplication. If two apparently duplicated sections of code evolve along different paths—if they change at different rates, and for different reasons—*then they are not true duplicates.* Return to them in a few years, and you'll find that they are very different from each other.

Now imagine two use cases that have very similar screen structures. The architects will likely be strongly tempted to share the code for that structure. But should they? Is that true duplication? Or it is accidental?

Most likely it is accidental. As time goes by, the odds are that those two screens will diverge and eventually look very different. For this reason, care must be taken to avoid unifying them. Otherwise, separating them later will be a challenge.

When you are vertically separating use cases from one another, you will run into this issue, and your temptation will be to couple the use cases because they have similar screen structures, or similar algorithms, or similar database queries and/or schemas. Be careful. Resist the temptation to commit the sin of knee-jerk elimination of duplication. Make sure the duplication is real.

By the same token, when you are separating layers horizontally, you might notice that the data structure of a particular database record is very similar to the data structure of a particular screen view. You may be tempted to simply pass the database record up to the UI, rather than to create a view model that looks the same and copy the elements across. Be careful: This duplication is almost certainly accidental. Creating the separate view model is not a lot of effort, and it will help you keep the layers properly decoupled.

DECOUPLING MODES (AGAIN)

Back to modes. There are many ways to decouple layers and use cases. They can be decoupled at the source code level, at the binary code (deployment) level, and at the execution unit (service) level.

- **Source level.** We can control the dependencies between source code modules so that changes to one module do not force changes or recompilation of others (e.g., Ruby Gems).

In this decoupling mode the components all execute in the same address space, and communicate with each other using simple function calls. There is a single executable loaded into computer memory. People often call this a monolithic structure.

- **Deployment level.** We can control the dependencies between deployable units such as jar files, DLLs, or shared libraries, so that changes to the source code in one module do not force others to be rebuilt and redeployed.

  Many of the components may still live in the same address space, and communicate through function calls. Other components may live in other processes in the same processor, and communicate through interprocess communications, sockets, or shared memory. The important thing here is that the decoupled components are partitioned into independently deployable units such as jar files, Gem files, or DLLs.

- **Service level.** We can reduce the dependencies down to the level of data structures, and communicate solely through network packets such that every execution unit is entirely independent of source and binary changes to others (e.g., services or micro-services).

What is the best mode to use?

The answer is that it's hard to know which mode is best during the early phases of a project. Indeed, as the project matures, the optimal mode may change.

For example, it's not difficult to imagine that a system that runs comfortably on one server right now might grow to the point where some of its components ought to run on separate servers. While the system runs on a single server, the source-level decoupling might be sufficient. Later, however, it might require decoupling into deployable units, or even services.

One solution (which seems to be popular at the moment) is to simply decouple at the service level by default. A problem with this approach is that it is expensive and encourages coarse-grained decoupling. No matter how "micro" the micro-services get, the decoupling is not likely to be fine-grained enough.

Another problem with service-level decoupling is that it is expensive, both in development time and in system resources. Dealing with service boundaries where none are needed is a waste of effort, memory, and cycles. And, yes, I know that the last two are cheap—but the first is not.

My preference is to push the decoupling to the point where a service *could* be formed. should it become necessary; but then to leave the components in the same address space as long as possible. This leaves the option for a service open.

With this approach, initially the components are separated at the source code level. That may be good enough for the duration of the project's lifetime. If, however, deployment or development issues arise, driving some of the decoupling to a deployment level may be sufficient—at least for a while.

As the development, deployment, and operational issues increase, I carefully choose which deployable units to turn into services, and gradually shift the system in that direction.

Over time, the operational needs of the system may decline. What once required decoupling at the service level may now require only deployment-level or even source-level decoupling.

A good architecture will allow a system to be born as a monolith, deployed in a single file, but then to grow into a set of independently deployable units, and then all the way to independent services and/or micro-services. Later, as things change, it should allow for reversing that progression and sliding all the way back down into a monolith.

A good architecture protects the majority of the source code from those changes. It leaves the decoupling mode open as an option so that large deployments can use one mode, whereas small deployments can use another.

CONCLUSION

Yes, this is tricky. And I'm not saying that the change of decoupling modes should be a trivial configuration option (though sometimes that *is* appropriate). What I'm saying is that the decoupling mode of a system is one of those things that is likely to change with time, and a good architect foresees and *appropriately* facilitates those changes.

BOUNDARIES: DRAWING LINES

Software architecture is the art of drawing lines that I call *boundaries*. Those boundaries separate software elements from one another, and restrict those on one side from knowing about those on the other. Some of those lines are drawn very early in a project's life—even before any code is written. Others are drawn much later. Those that are drawn early are drawn for the purposes of deferring decisions for as long as possible, and of keeping those decisions from polluting the core business logic.

Recall that the goal of an architect is to minimize the human resources required to build and maintain the required system. What it is that saps this kind of people-power? *Coupling*—and especially coupling to premature decisions.

Which kinds of decisions are premature? Decisions that have nothing to do with the business requirements—the use cases—of the system. These include decisions about frameworks, databases, web servers, utility libraries, dependency injection, and the like. A good system architecture is one in which decisions like these are rendered ancillary and deferrable. A good system architecture does not depend on those decisions. A good system architecture allows those decisions to be made at the latest possible moment, without significant impact.

A COUPLE OF SAD STORIES

Here's the sad story of company P, which serves as a warning about making premature decisions. In the 1980s the founders of P wrote a simple monolithic desktop application. They enjoyed a great deal of success and grew the product through the 1990s into a popular and successful desktop GUI application.

But then, in the late 1990s, the web emerged as a force. Suddenly everybody had to have a web solution, and P was no exception. P's customers clamored for a version of the product on the web. To meet this demand, the company hired a bunch of hotshot twenty-something Java programmers and embarked upon a project to webify their product.

The Java guys had dreams of server farms dancing in their heads, so they adopted a rich three-tiered "architecture"[1] that they could distribute through such farms. There would be servers for the GUI, servers for the middleware, and servers for the database. Of course.

The programmers decided, very early on, that all domain objects would have three instantiations: one in the GUI tier, one in the middleware tier, and one in the database tier. Since these instantiations lived on different machines, a rich system of interprocessor and inter-tier communications was set up. Method invocations between tiers were converted to objects, serialized, and marshaled across the wire.

Now imagine what it took to implement a simple feature like adding a new field to an existing record. That field had to be added to the classes in all three tiers, and to several of the inter-tier messages. Since data traveled in both directions, four message protocols needed to be designed. Each protocol had a sending and receiving side, so eight protocol handlers were required. Three executables had to be built, each with three updated business objects, four new messages, and eight new handlers.

And think of what those executables had to do to implement the simplest of features. Think of all the object instantiations, all the serializations, all the marshaling and de-marshaling, all the building and parsing of messages, all the socket communications, timeout managers, retry scenarios, and all the other extra stuff that you have to do just to get one simple thing done.

Of course, during development the programmers did not have a server farm. Indeed, they simply ran all three executables in three different processes on a single machine. They developed this way for several years. But they were convinced that their architecture was right. And so, even though they were executing in a single machine, they continued all the object instantiations, all the serializations, all the marshaling and de-marshaling, all the building and parsing of messages, all the socket communications, and all the extra stuff in a single machine.

---

1. The word "architecture" appears in quotes here because three-tier is not an architecture; it's a topology. It's exactly the kind of decision that a good architecture strives to defer.

The irony is that company P never sold a system that required a server farm. Every system they ever deployed was a single server. And in that single server all three executables continued all the object instantiations, all the serializations, all the marshaling and de-marshaling, all the building and parsing of messages, all the socket communications, and all the extra stuff, in anticipation of a server farm that never existed, and never would.

The tragedy is that the architects, by making a premature decision, multiplied the development effort enormously.

The story of P is not isolated. I've seen it many times and in many places. Indeed, P is a superposition of all those places.

But there are worse fates than P.

Consider W, a local business that manages fleets of company cars. They recently hired an "Architect" to get their rag-tag software effort under control. And, let me tell you, control was this guy's middle name. He quickly realized that what this little operation needed was a full-blown, *enterprise-scale*, **service-oriented "ARCHITECTURE."** He created a huge domain model of all the different "objects" in the business, designed a suite of services to manage these domain objects, and put all the developers on a path to *Hell*. As a simple example, suppose you wanted to add the name, address, and phone number of a contact person to a sales record. You had to go to the `ServiceRegistry` and ask for the service ID of the `ContactService`. Then you had to send a `CreateContact` message to the `ContactService`. Of course, this message had dozens of fields that all had to have valid data in them—data to which the programmer had no access, since all the programmer had was a name, address, and phone number. After faking the data, the programmer had to jam the ID of the newly created contact into the sales record and send the `UpdateContact` message to the `SaleRecordService`.

Of course, to test anything you had to fire up all the necessary services, one by one, and fire up the message bus, and the BPel server, and ... And then, there were the propagation delays as these messages bounced from service to service, and waited in queue after queue.

And then if you wanted to add a new feature—well, you can imagine the coupling between all those services, and the sheer volume of WSDLs that needed changing, and all the redeployments those changes necessitated...

Hell starts to seem like a nice place by comparison.

There's nothing intrinsically wrong with a software system that is structured around services. The error at W was the premature adoption and enforcement of a suite of tools that promised SoA—that is, the premature adoption of a massive suite of domain object services. The cost of those errors was sheer person-hours—person-hours in droves—flushed down the SoA vortex.

I could go on describing one architectural failure after another. But let's talk about an architectural success instead.

FitNesse

My Son, Micah, and I started work on `FitNesse` in 2001. The idea was to create a simple wiki that wrapped Ward Cunningham's FIT tool for writing acceptance tests.

This was back in the days before Maven "solved" the jar file problem. I was adamant that anything we produced should not require people to download more than one jar file. I called this rule, "Download and Go." This rule drove many of our decisions.

One of the first decisions was to write our own web server, specific to the needs of `FitNesse`. This might sound absurd. Even in 2001 there were plenty of open source web servers that we could have used. Yet writing our own turned out to be a really good decision because a bare-bones web server is a very simple piece of software to write and it allowed us to postpone any web framework decision until much later.[2]

---

2. Many years later we were able to slip the Velocity framework into `FitNesse`.

Another early decision was to avoid thinking about a database. We had MySQL in the back of our minds, but we purposely delayed that decision by employing a design that made the decision irrelevant. That design was simply to put an interface between all data accesses and the data repository itself.

We put the data access methods into an interface named `WikiPage`. Those methods provided all the functionality we needed to find, fetch, and save pages. Of course, we didn't implement those methods at first; we simply stubbed them out while we worked on features that didn't involve fetching and saving the data.

Indeed, for three months we simply worked on translating wiki text into HTML. This didn't require any kind of data storage, so we created a class named `MockWikiPage` that simply left the data access methods stubbed.

Eventually, those stubs became insufficient for the features we wanted to write. We needed real data access, not stubs. So we created a new derivative of `WikiPage` named `InMemoryPage`. This derivative implemented the data access method to manage a hash table of wiki pages, which we kept in RAM.

This allowed us to write feature after feature for a full year. In fact, we got the whole first version of the `FitNesse` program working this way. We could create pages, link to other pages, do all the fancy wiki formatting, and even run tests with FIT. What we couldn't do was save any of our work.

When it came time to implement persistence, we thought again about MySQL, but decided that wasn't necessary in the short term, because it would be really easy to write the hash tables out to flat files. So we implemented `FileSystemWikiPage`, which just moved the functionality out to flat files, and then we continued developing more features.

Three months later, we reached the conclusion that the flat file solution was good enough; we decided to abandon the idea of MySQL altogether. We deferred that decision into nonexistence and never looked back.

That would be the end of the story if it weren't for one of our customers who decided that he needed to put the wiki into MySQL for his own purposes. We showed him the architecture of WikiPages that had allowed us to defer the decision. He came back *a day later* with the whole system working in MySQL. He simply wrote a MySqlWikiPage derivative and got it working.

We used to bundle that option with FitNesse, but nobody else ever used it, so eventually we dropped it. Even the customer who wrote the derivative eventually dropped it.

Early in the development of FitNesse, we drew a *boundary line* between business rules and databases. That line prevented the business rules from knowing anything at all about the database, other than the simple data access methods. That decision allowed us to defer the choice and implementation of the database for well over a year. It allowed us to try the file system option, and it allowed us to change direction when we saw a better solution. Yet it did not prevent, or even impede, moving in the original direction (MySQL) when someone wanted it.

The fact that we did not have a database running for 18 months of development meant that, for 18 months, we did not have schema issues, query issues, database server issues, password issues, connection time issues, and all the other nasty issues that raise their ugly heads when you fire up a database. It also meant that all our tests ran fast, because there was no database to slow them down.

In short, drawing the boundary lines helped us delay and defer decisions, and it ultimately saved us an enormous amount of time and headaches. And that's what a good architecture should do.

WHICH LINES DO YOU DRAW, AND WHEN DO YOU DRAW THEM?

You draw lines between things that matter and things that don't. The GUI doesn't matter to the business rules, so there should be a line between them. The database doesn't matter to the GUI, so there should be a line between them. The database doesn't matter to the business rules, so there should be a line between them.

Some of you may have rejected one or more of those statements, especially the part about the business rules not caring about the database. Many of us have been taught to believe that the database is inextricably connected to the business rules. Some of us have even been convinced that the database is the embodiment of the business rules.

But, as we shall see in another chapter, this idea is misguided. The database is a tool that the business rules can use *indirectly*. The business rules don't need to know about the schema, or the query language, or any of the other details about the database. All the business rules need to know is that there is a set of functions that can be used to fetch or save data. This allows us to put the database behind an interface.

You can see this clearly in Figure 17.1. The `BusinessRules` use the `DatabaseInterface` to load and save data. The `DatabaseAccess` implements the interface and directs the operation of the actual `Database`.

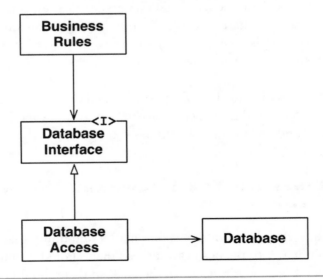

Figure 17.1 The database behind an interface

The classes and interfaces in this diagram are symbolic. In a real application, there would be many business rule classes, many database interface classes, and many database access implementations. All of them, though, would follow roughly the same pattern.

Where is the boundary line? The boundary is drawn across the inheritance relationship, just below the DatabaseInterface (Figure 17.2).

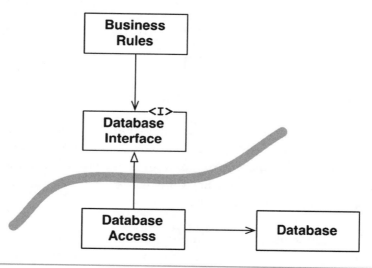

Figure 17.2 The boundary line

Note the two arrows leaving the DatabaseAccess class. Those two arrows point away from the DatabaseAccess class. That means that none of these classes knows that the DatabaseAccess class exists.

Now let's pull back a bit. We'll look at the component that contains many business rules, and the component that contains the database and all its access classes (Figure 17.3).

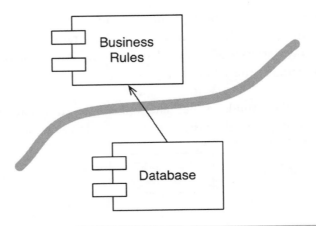

Figure 17.3 The business rules and database components

Note the direction of the arrow. The `Database` knows about the `BusinessRules`. The `BusinessRules` do not know about the `Database`. This implies that the `DatabaseInterface` classes live in the `BusinessRules` component, while the `DatabaseAccess` classes live in the `Database` component.

The direction of this line is important. It shows that the `Database` does not matter to the `BusinessRules`, but the `Database` cannot exist without the `BusinessRules`.

If that seems strange to you, just remember this point: The `Database` component contains the code that translates the calls made by the `BusinessRules` into the query language of the database. It is that translation code that knows about the `BusinessRules`.

Having drawn this boundary line between the two components, and having set the direction of the arrow toward the `BusinessRules`, we can now see that the `BusinessRules` could use *any* kind of database. The `Database` component could be replaced with many different implementations—the `BusinessRules` don't care.

The database could be implemented with Oracle, or MySQL, or Couch, or Datomic, or even flat files. The business rules don't care at all. And that means that the database decision can be deferred and you can focus on getting the business rules written and tested before you have to make the database decision.

WHAT ABOUT INPUT AND OUTPUT?

Developers and customers often get confused about what the system is. They see the GUI, and think that the GUI is the system. They define a system in terms of the GUI, so they believe that they should see the GUI start working immediately. They fail to realize a critically important principle: *The IO is irrelevant.*

This may be hard to grasp at first. We often think about the behavior of the system in terms of the behavior of the IO. Consider a video game, for example. Your experience is dominated by the interface: the screen, the mouse, the buttons, and the sounds. You forget that behind that interface there is a model—a sophisticated set of data structures and functions— driving it. More importantly, that model does not need the interface. It would happily execute its duties, modeling all the events in the game, without the game ever being displayed on the screen. The interface does not matter to the model—the business rules.

And so, once again, we see the GUI and BusinessRules components separated by a boundary line (Figure 17.4). Once again, we see that the less relevant component depends on the more relevant component. The arrows show which component knows about the other and, therefore, which component cares about the other. The GUI cares about the BusinessRules.

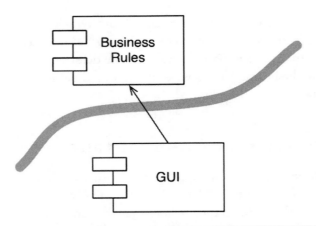

Figure 17.4 The boundary between GUI and BusinessRules components

Having drawn this boundary and this arrow, we can now see that the GUI could be replaced with any other kind of interface—and the BusinessRules would not care.

PLUGIN ARCHITECTURE

Taken together, these two decisions about the database and the GUI create a kind of pattern for the addition of other components. That pattern is the same pattern that is used by systems that allow third-party plugins.

Indeed, the history of software development technology is the story of how to conveniently create plugins to establish a scalable and maintainable system architecture. The core business rules are kept separate from, and independent of, those components that are either optional or that can be implemented in many different forms (Figure 17.5).

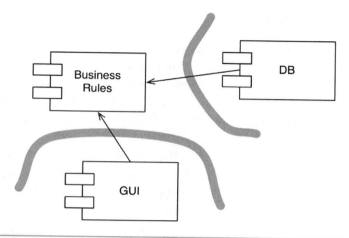

Figure 17.5 Plugging in to the business rules

Because the user interface in this design is considered to be a plugin, we have made it possible to plug in many different kinds of user interfaces. They could be web based, client/server based, SOA based, Console based, or based on any other kind of user interface technology.

The same is true of the database. Since we have chosen to treat it as a plugin, we can replace it with any of the various SQL databases, or a NOSQL database, or a file system-based database, or any other kind of database technology we might deem necessary in the future.

These replacements might not be trivial. If the initial deployment of our system was web-based, then writing the plugin for a client-server UI could be challenging. It is likely that some of the communications between the business rules and the new UI would have to be reworked. Even so, by starting with the presumption of a plugin structure, we have at very least made such a change practical.

THE PLUGIN ARGUMENT

Consider the relationship between ReSharper and Visual Studio. These components are produced by completely different development teams in completely different companies. Indeed, JetBrains, the maker of ReSharper, lives in Russia. Microsoft, of course, resides in Redmond, Washington. It's hard to imagine two development teams that are more separate.

Which team can damage the other? Which team is immune to the other? The dependency structure tells the story (Figure 17.6). The source code of ReSharper depends on the source code of Visual Studio. Thus there is nothing that the ReSharper team can do to disturb the Visual Studio team. But the Visual Studio team could completely disable the ReSharper team if they so desired.

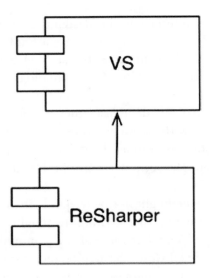

Figure 17.6 ReSharper depends on Visual Studio

That's a deeply asymmetric relationship, and it is one that we desire to have in our own systems. We want certain modules to be immune to others. For example, we don't want the business rules to break when someone changes the format of a web page, or changes the schema of the database. We don't want changes in one part of the system to cause other unrelated parts of the system to break. We don't want our systems to exhibit that kind of fragility.

Arranging our systems into a plugin architecture creates firewalls across which changes cannot propagate. If the GUI plugs in to the business rules, then changes in the GUI cannot affect those business rules.

Boundaries are drawn where there is an *axis of change*. The components on one side of the boundary change at different rates, and for different reasons, than the components on the other side of the boundary.

GUIs change at different times and at different rates than business rules, so there should be a boundary between them. Business rules change at different times and for different reasons than dependency injection frameworks, so there should be a boundary between them.

This is simply the Single Responsibility Principle again. The SRP tells us where to draw our boundaries.

CONCLUSION

To draw boundary lines in a software architecture, you first partition the system into components. Some of those components are core business rules; others are plugins that contain necessary functions that are not directly related to the core business. Then you arrange the code in those components such that the arrows between them point in one direction—toward the core business.

You should recognize this as an application of the Dependency Inversion Principle and the Stable Abstractions Principle. Dependency arrows are arranged to point from lower-level details to higher-level abstractions.

BOUNDARY ANATOMY

The architecture of a system is defined by a set of software components and the boundaries that separate them. Those boundaries come in many different forms. In this chapter we'll look at some of the most common.

BOUNDARY CROSSING

At runtime, a boundary crossing is nothing more than a function on one side of the boundary calling a function on the other side and passing along some data. The trick to creating an appropriate boundary crossing is to manage the source code dependencies.

Why source code? Because when one source code module changes, other source code modules may have to be changed or recompiled, and then redeployed. Managing and building firewalls against this change is what boundaries are all about.

THE DREADED MONOLITH

The simplest and most common of the architectural boundaries has no strict physical representation. It is simply a disciplined segregation of functions and data within a single processor and a single address space. In a previous chapter, I called this the source-level decoupling mode.

From a deployment point of view, this amounts to nothing more than a single executable file—the so-called monolith. This file might be a statically linked C or C++ project, a set of Java class files bound together into an executable jar file, a set of .NET binaries bound into a single .EXE file, and so on.

The fact that the boundaries are not visible during the deployment of a monolith does not mean that they are not present and meaningful. Even when statically linked into a single executable, the ability to independently develop and marshal the various components for final assembly is immensely valuable.

Such architectures almost always depend on some kind of dynamic polymorphism[1] to manage their internal dependencies. This is one of the reasons that object-oriented development has become such an important paradigm in recent decades. Without OO, or an equivalent form of polymorphism, architects must fall back on the dangerous practice of using pointers to functions to achieve the appropriate decoupling. Most architects find prolific use of pointers to functions to be too risky, so they are forced to abandon any kind of component partitioning.

The simplest possible boundary crossing is a function call from a low-level client to a higher-level service. Both the runtime dependency and the compile-time dependency point in the same direction, toward the higher-level component.

In Figure 18.1, the flow of control crosses the boundary from left to right. The `Client` calls function `f()` on the `Service`. It passes along an instance of `Data`. The `<DS>` marker simply indicates a data structure. The `Data` may be passed as a function argument or by some other more elaborate means. Note that the definition of the `Data` is on the *called* side of the boundary.

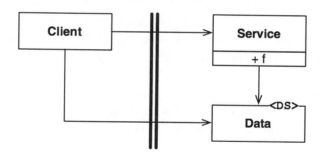

Figure 18.1 Flow of control crosses the boundary from a lower level to a higher level

When a high-level client needs to invoke a lower-level service, dynamic polymorphism is used to invert the dependency against the flow of control. The runtime dependency opposes the compile-time dependency.

---

1. Static polymorphism (e.g., generics or templates) can sometimes be a viable means of dependency management in monolithic systems, especially in languages like C++. However, the decoupling afforded by generics cannot protect you from the need for recompilation and redeployment the way dynamic polymorphism can.

In Figure 18.2, the flow of control crosses the boundary from left to right as before. The high-level `Client` calls the `f()` function of the lower-level `ServiceImpl` through the `Service` interface. Note, however, that all dependencies cross the boundary from right to left *toward the higher-level component*. Note, also, that the definition of the data structure is on the calling side of the boundary.

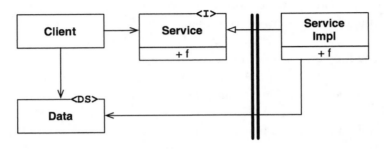

Figure 18.2 Crossing the boundary against the flow of control

Even in a monolithic, statically linked executable, this kind of disciplined partitioning can greatly aid the job of developing, testing, and deploying the project. Teams can work independently of each other on their own components without treading on each other's toes. High-level components remain independent of lower-level details.

Communications between components in a monolith are very fast and inexpensive. They are typically just function calls. Consequently, communications across source-level decoupled boundaries can be very chatty.

Since the deployment of monoliths usually requires compilation and static linking, components in these systems are typically delivered as source code.

DEPLOYMENT COMPONENTS

The simplest physical representation of an architectural boundary is a dynamically linked library like a .Net DLL, a Java jar file, a Ruby Gem, or a UNIX shared library. Deployment does not involve compilation. Instead, the components are delivered in binary, or some equivalent deployable form. This is the deployment-level decoupling mode. The act of deployment is simply the gathering of these deployable units together in some convenient form, such as a WAR file, or even just a directory.

With that one exception, deployment-level components are the same as monoliths. The functions generally all exist in the same processor and address space. The strategies for segregating the components and managing their dependencies are the same.[2]

As with monoliths, communications across deployment component boundaries are just function calls and, therefore, are very inexpensive. There may be a one-time hit for dynamic linking or runtime loading, but communications across these boundaries can still be very chatty.

THREADS

Both monoliths and deployment components can make use of threads. Threads are not architectural boundaries or units of deployment, but rather a way to organize the schedule and order of execution. They may be wholly contained within a component, or spread across many components.

LOCAL PROCESSES

A much stronger physical architectural boundary is the local process. A local process is typically created from the command line or an equivalent system call. Local processes run in the same processor, or in the same set of processors within a multicore, but run in separate address spaces. Memory protection generally prevents such processes from sharing memory, although shared memory partitions are often used.

---

2. Although static polymorphism is not an option in this case.

Most often, local processes communicate with each other using sockets, or some other kind of operating system communications facility such as mailboxes or message queues.

Each local process may be a statically linked monolith, or it may be composed of dynamically linked deployment components. In the former case, several monolithic processes may have the same components compiled and linked into them. In the latter, they may share the same dynamically linked deployment components.

Think of a local process as a kind of uber-component: The process consists of lower-level components that manage their dependencies through dynamic polymorphism.

The segregation strategy between local processes is the same as for monoliths and binary components. Source code dependencies point in the same direction across the boundary, and always toward the higher-level component.

For local processes, this means that the source code of the higher-level processes must not contain the names, or physical addresses, or registry lookup keys of lower-level processes. Remember that the architectural goal is for lower-level processes to be plugins to higher-level processes.

Communication across local process boundaries involve operating system calls, data marshaling and decoding, and interprocess context switches, which are moderately expensive. Chattiness should be carefully limited.

SERVICES

The strongest boundary is a service. A service is a process, generally started from the command line or through an equivalent system call. Services do not depend on their physical location. Two communicating services may, or may not, operate in the same physical processor or multicore. The services assume that all communications take place over the network.

Communications across service boundaries are very slow compared to function calls. Turnaround times can range from tens of milliseconds to seconds. Care must be taken to avoid chatting where possible. Communications at this level must deal with high levels of latency.

Otherwise, the same rules apply to services as apply to local processes. Lower-level services should "plug in" to higher-level services. The source code of higher-level services must not contain any specific physical knowledge (e.g., a URI) of any lower-level service.

CONCLUSION

Most systems, other than monoliths, use more than one boundary strategy. A system that makes use of service boundaries may also have some local process boundaries. Indeed, a service is often just a facade for a set of interacting local processes. A service, or a local process, will almost certainly be either a monolith composed of source code components or a set of dynamically linked deployment components.

This means that the boundaries in a system will often be a mixture of local chatty boundaries and boundaries that are more concerned with latency.

POLICY AND LEVEL

Software systems are statements of policy. Indeed, at its core, that's all a computer program actually is. A computer program is a detailed description of the policy by which inputs are transformed into outputs.

In most nontrivial systems, that policy can be broken down into many different smaller statements of policy. Some of those statements will describe how particular business rules are to be calculated. Others will describe how certain reports are to be formatted. Still others will describe how input data are to be validated.

Part of the art of developing a software architecture is carefully separating those policies from one another, and regrouping them based on the ways that they change. Policies that change for the same reasons, and at the same times, are at the same level and belong together in the same component. Policies that change for different reasons, or at different times, are at different levels and should be separated into different components.

The art of architecture often involves forming the regrouped components into a directed acyclic graph. The nodes of the graph are the components that contain policies at the same level. The directed edges are the dependencies between those components. They connect components that are at different levels.

Those dependencies are source code, compile-time dependencies. In Java, they are `import` statements. In C#, they are `using` statements. In Ruby, they are `require` statements. They are the dependencies that are necessary for the compiler to function.

In a good architecture, the direction of those dependencies is based on the level of the components that they connect. In every case, low-level components are designed so that they depend on high-level components.

LEVEL

A strict definition of "level" is "the distance from the inputs and outputs." The farther a policy is from both the inputs and the outputs of the system, the higher its level. The policies that manage input and output are the lowest-level policies in the system.

The data flow diagram in Figure 19.1 depicts a simple encryption program that reads characters from an input device, translates the characters using a table, and then writes the translated characters to an output device. The data flows are shown as curved solid arrows. The properly designed source code dependencies are shown as straight dashed lines.

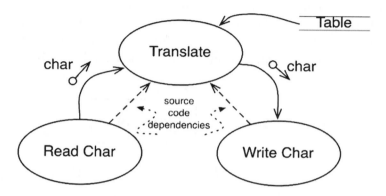

Figure 19.1 A simple encryption program

The `Translate` component is the highest-level component in this system because it is the component that is farthest from the inputs and outputs.[1]

Note that the data flows and the source code dependencies do not always point in the same direction. This, again, is part of the art of software architecture. We want source code dependencies to be decoupled from data flow and *coupled to level*.

It would be easy to create an incorrect architecture by writing the encryption program like this:

```
function encrypt() {
  while(true)
    writeChar(translate(readChar()));
}
```

---

1. Meilir Page-Jones called this component the "Central Transform" in his book *The Practical Guide to Structured Systems Design*, 2nd ed. (Yourdon Press, 1988).

This is incorrect architecture because the high-level `encrypt` function depends on the lower-level `readChar` and `writeChar` functions.

A better architecture for this system is shown in the class diagram in Figure 19.2. Note the dashed border surrounding the `Encrypt` class, and the `CharWriter` and `CharReader` interfaces. All dependencies crossing that border point inward. This unit is the highest-level element in the system.

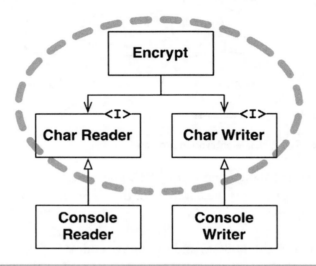

Figure 19.2 Class diagram showing a better architecture for the system

`ConsoleReader` and `ConsoleWriter` are shown here as classes. They are low level because they are close to the inputs and outputs.

Note how this structure decouples the high-level encryption policy from the lower-level input/output policies. This makes the encryption policy usable in a wide range of contexts. When changes are made to the input and output policies, they are not likely to affect the encryption policy.

Recall that policies are grouped into components based on the way that they change. Policies that change for the same reasons and at the same times are grouped together by the SRP and CCP. Higher-level policies—those that are farthest from the inputs and outputs—tend to change less frequently, and for more important reasons, than lower-level policies. Lower-level policies—those that are closest to the inputs and outputs—tend to change frequently, and with more urgency, but for less important reasons.

For example, even in the trivial example of the encryption program, it is far more likely that the IO devices will change than that the encryption algorithm will change. If the encryption algorithm does change, it will likely be for a more substantive reason than a change to one of the IO devices.

Keeping these policies separate, with all source code dependencies pointing in the direction of the higher-level policies, reduces the impact of change. Trivial but urgent changes at the lowest levels of the system have little or no impact on the higher, more important, levels.

Another way to look at this issue is to note that lower-level components should be plugins to the higher-level components. The component diagram in Figure 19.3 shows this arrangement. The `Encryption` component knows nothing of the `IODevices` component; the `IODevices` component depends on the `Encryption` component.

Figure 19.3 Lower-level components should plug in to higher-level components

CONCLUSION

At this point, this discussion of policies has involved a mixture of the Single Responsibility Principle, the Open-Closed Principle, the Common Closure Principle, the Dependency Inversion Principle, the Stable Dependencies Principle, and the Stable Abstractions Principle. Look back and see if you can identify where each principle was used, and why.

20 BUSINESS RULES

If we are going to divide our application into business rules and plugins, we'd better get a good grasp on just what business rules actually are. It turns out there are several different kinds.

Strictly speaking, business rules are rules or procedures that make or save the business money. Very strictly speaking, these rules would make or save the business money, irrespective of whether they were implemented on a computer. They would make or save money even if they were executed manually.

The fact that a bank charges N% interest for a loan is a business rule that makes the bank money. It doesn't matter if a computer program calculates the interest, or if a clerk with an abacus calculates the interest.

We shall call these rules *Critical Business Rules*, because they are critical to the business itself, and would exist even if there were no system to automate them.

Critical Business Rules usually require some data to work with. For example, our loan requires a loan balance, an interest rate, and a payment schedule.

We shall call this data *Critical Business Data*. This is the data that would exist even if the system were not automated.

The critical rules and critical data are inextricably bound, so they are a good candidate for an object. We'll call this kind of object an *Entity*.[1]

ENTITIES

An Entity is an object within our computer system that embodies a small set of critical business rules operating on Critical Business Data. The Entity object either contains the Critical Business Data or has very easy access to that data. The interface of the Entity consists of the functions that implement the Critical Business Rules that operate on that data.

---

1. This is Ivar Jacobson's name for this concept (I. Jacobson et al., *Object Oriented Software Engineering*, Addison-Wesley, 1992).

For example, Figure 20.1 shows what our Loan entity might look like as a class in UML. It has three pieces of Critical Business Data, and presents three related Critical Business Rules at its interface.

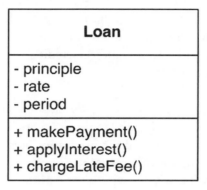

Figure 20.1 Loan entity as a class in UML

When we create this kind of class, we are gathering together the software that implements a concept that is critical to the business, and separating it from every other concern in the automated system we are building. This class stands alone as a representative of the business. It is unsullied with concerns about databases, user interfaces, or third-party frameworks. It could serve the business in any system, irrespective of how that system was presented, or how the data was stored, or how the computers in that system were arranged. The Entity is pure business and *nothing else*.

Some of you may be concerned that I called it a class. Don't be. You don't need to use an object-oriented language to create an Entity. All that is required is that you bind the Critical Business Data and the Critical Business Rules together in a single and separate software module.

USE CASES

Not all business rules are as pure as Entities. Some business rules make or save money for the business by defining and constraining the way that an *automated* system operates. These rules would not be used in a manual environment, because they make sense only as part of an automated system.

For example, imagine an application that is used by bank officers to create a new loan. The bank may decide that it does not want the loan officers to offer loan payment estimates until they have first gathered, and validated, contact information and ensured that the candidate's credit score is 500 or higher. For this reason, the bank may specify that the system will not proceed to the payment estimation screen until the contact information screen has been filled out and verified, and the credit score has been confirmed to be greater than the cutoff.

This is a *use case*.[2] A use case is a description of the way that an automated system is used. It specifies the input to be provided by the user, the output to be returned to the user, and the processing steps involved in producing that output. A use case describes *application-specific* business rules as opposed to the Critical Business Rules within the Entities.

Figure 20.2 shows an example of a use case. Notice that in the last line it mentions the Customer. This is a reference to the Customer entity, which contains the Critical Business Rules that govern the relationship between the bank and its customers.

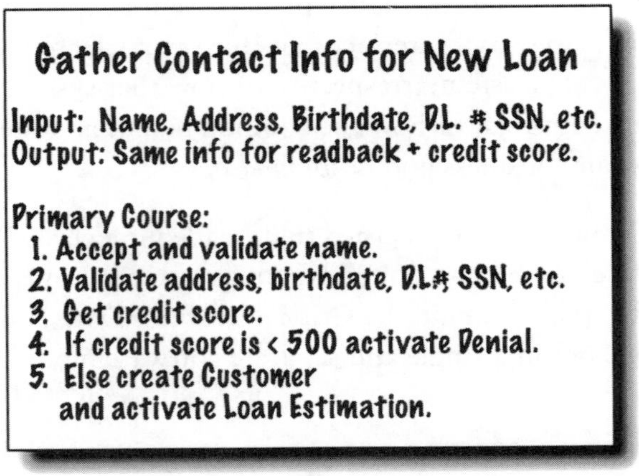

> ## Gather Contact Info for New Loan
>
> Input: Name, Address, Birthdate, D.L. # SSN, etc.
> Output: Same info for readback + credit score.
>
> Primary Course:
> 1. Accept and validate name.
> 2. Validate address, birthdate, D.L.# SSN, etc.
> 3. Get credit score.
> 4. If credit score is < 500 activate Denial.
> 5. Else create Customer
>   and activate Loan Estimation.

Figure 20.2 Example use case

2. Ibid.

Use cases contain the rules that specify how and when the Critical Business Rules within the Entities are invoked. Use cases control the dance of the Entities.

Notice also that the use case does not describe the user interface other than to informally specify the data coming in from that interface, and the data going back out through that interface. From the use case, it is impossible to tell whether the application is delivered on the web, or on a thick client, or on a console, or is a pure service.

This is very important. Use cases do not describe how the system appears to the user. Instead, they describe the application-specific rules that govern the interaction between the users and the Entities. How the data gets in and out of the system is irrelevant to the use cases.

A use case is an object. It has one or more functions that implement the application-specific business rules. It also has data elements that include the input data, the output data, and the references to the appropriate Entities with which it interacts.

Entities have no knowledge of the use cases that control them. This is another example of the direction of the dependencies following the Dependency Inversion Principle. High-level concepts, such as Entities, know nothing of lower-level concepts, such as use cases. Instead, the lower-level use cases know about the higher-level Entities.

Why are Entities high level and use cases lower level? Because use cases are specific to a single application and, therefore, are closer to the inputs and outputs of that system. Entities are generalizations that can be used in many different applications, so they are farther from the inputs and outputs of the system. Use cases depend on Entities; Entities do not depend on use cases.

REQUEST AND RESPONSE MODELS

Use cases expect input data, and they produce output data. However, a well-formed use case object should have no inkling about the way that data is communicated to the user, or to any other component. We certainly don't want the code within the use case class to know about HTML or SQL!

The use case class accepts simple request data structures for its input, and returns simple response data structures as its output. These data structures are not dependent on anything. They do not derive from standard framework interfaces such as `HttpRequest` and `HttpResponse`. They know nothing of the web, nor do they share any of the trappings of whatever user interface might be in place.

This lack of dependencies is critical. If the request and response models are not independent, then the use cases that depend on them will be indirectly bound to whatever dependencies the models carry with them.

You might be tempted to have these data structures contain references to Entity objects. You might think this makes sense because the Entities and the request/response models share so much data. Avoid this temptation! The purpose of these two objects is very different. Over time they will change for very different reasons, so tying them together in any way violates the Common Closure and Single Responsibility Principles. The result would be lots of tramp data, and lots of conditionals in your code.

CONCLUSION

Business rules are the reason a software system exists. They are the core functionality. They carry the code that makes, or saves, money. They are the family jewels.

The business rules should remain pristine, unsullied by baser concerns such as the user interface or database used. Ideally, the code that represents the business rules should be the heart of the system, with lesser concerns being plugged in to them. The business rules should be the most independent and reusable code in the system.

21

SCREAMING ARCHITECTURE

Imagine that you are looking at the blueprints of a building. This document, prepared by an architect, provides the plans for the building. What do these plans tell you?

If the plans you are viewing are for a single-family residence, then you'll likely see a front entrance, a foyer leading to a living room, and perhaps a dining room. There will likely be a kitchen a short distance away, close to the dining room. Perhaps there is a dinette area next to the kitchen, and probably a family room close to that. When you looked at those plans, there would be no question that you were looking at a single family home. The architecture would scream: "HOME."

Now suppose you were looking at the architecture of a library. You would likely see a grand entrance, an area for check-in/out clerks, reading areas, small conference rooms, and gallery after gallery capable of holding bookshelves for all the books in the library. That architecture would scream: "LIBRARY."

So what does the architecture of your application scream? When you look at the top-level directory structure, and the source files in the highest-level package, do they scream "Health Care System," or "Accounting System," or "Inventory Management System"? Or do they scream "Rails," or "Spring/Hibernate," or "ASP"?

THE THEME OF AN ARCHITECTURE

Go back and read Ivar Jacobson's seminal work on software architecture: *Object Oriented Software Engineering*. Notice the subtitle of the book: *A Use Case Driven Approach*. In this book Jacobson makes the point that software architectures are structures that support the use cases of the system. Just as the plans for a house or a library scream about the use cases of those buildings, so should the architecture of a software application scream about the use cases of the application.

Architectures are not (or should not be) about frameworks. Architectures should not be supplied by frameworks. Frameworks are tools to be used, not architectures to be conformed to. If your architecture is based on frameworks, then it cannot be based on your use cases.

THE PURPOSE OF AN ARCHITECTURE

Good architectures are centered on use cases so that architects can safely describe the structures that support those use cases without committing to frameworks, tools, and environments. Again, consider the plans for a house. The first concern of the architect is to make sure that the house is usable—not to ensure that the house is made of bricks. Indeed, the architect takes pains to ensure that the homeowner can make decisions about the exterior material (bricks, stone, or cedar) later, after the plans ensure that the use cases are met.

A good software architecture allows decisions about frameworks, databases, web servers, and other environmental issues and tools to be deferred and delayed. *Frameworks are options to be left open.* A good architecture makes it unnecessary to decide on Rails, or Spring, or Hibernate, or Tomcat, or MySQL, until much later in the project. A good architecture makes it easy to change your mind about those decisions, too. A good architecture emphasizes the use cases and decouples them from peripheral concerns.

BUT WHAT ABOUT THE WEB?

Is the web an architecture? Does the fact that your system is delivered on the web dictate the architecture of your system? Of course not! The web is a delivery mechanism—an IO device—and your application architecture should treat it as such. The fact that your application is delivered over the web is a detail and should not dominate your system structure. Indeed, the decision that your application will be delivered over the web is one that you should defer. Your system architecture should be as ignorant as possible about how it will be delivered. You should be able to deliver it as a console app, or a web app, or a thick client app, or even a web service app, without undue complication or change to the fundamental architecture.

FRAMEWORKS ARE TOOLS, NOT WAYS OF LIFE

Frameworks can be very powerful and very useful. Framework authors often believe very deeply in their frameworks. The examples they write for how to use their frameworks are told from the point of view of a true believer. Other authors who write about the framework also tend to be disciples of the true belief. They show you the way to use the framework. Often they assume an all-encompassing, all-pervading, let-the-framework-do-everything position.

This is not the position you want to take.

Look at each framework with a jaded eye. View it skeptically. Yes, it might help, but at what cost? Ask yourself how you should use it, and how you should protect yourself from it. Think about how you can preserve the use-case emphasis of your architecture. Develop a strategy that prevents the framework from taking over that architecture.

TESTABLE ARCHITECTURES

If your system architecture is all about the use cases, and if you have kept your frameworks at arm's length, then you should be able to unit-test all those use cases without any of the frameworks in place. You shouldn't need the web server running to run your tests. You shouldn't need the database connected to run your tests. Your Entity objects should be plain old objects that have no dependencies on frameworks or databases or other complications. Your use case objects should coordinate your Entity objects. Finally, all of them together should be testable in situ, without any of the complications of frameworks.

CONCLUSION

Your architecture should tell readers about the system, not about the frameworks you used in your system. If you are building a health care system, then when new programmers look at the source repository, their first impression should be, "Oh, this is a heath care system." Those new programmers should be able to learn all the use cases of the system, yet still not know how the system is delivered. They may come to you and say:

"We see some things that look like models—but where are the views and controllers?"

And you should respond:

"Oh, those are details that needn't concern us at the moment. We'll decide about them later."

22

THE CLEAN ARCHITECTURE

Over the last several decades we've seen a whole range of ideas regarding the architecture of systems. These include:

- Hexagonal Architecture (also known as Ports and Adapters), developed by Alistair Cockburn, and adopted by Steve Freeman and Nat Pryce in their wonderful book *Growing Object Oriented Software with Tests*
- DCI from James Coplien and Trygve Reenskaug
- BCE, introduced by Ivar Jacobson from his book *Object Oriented Software Engineering: A Use-Case Driven Approach*

Although these architectures all vary somewhat in their details, they are very similar. They all have the same objective, which is the separation of concerns. They all achieve this separation by dividing the software into layers. Each has at least one layer for business rules, and another layer for user and system interfaces.

Each of these architectures produces systems that have the following characteristics:

- *Independent of frameworks.* The architecture does not depend on the existence of some library of feature-laden software. This allows you to use such frameworks as tools, rather than forcing you to cram your system into their limited constraints.
- *Testable.* The business rules can be tested without the UI, database, web server, or any other external element.
- *Independent of the UI.* The UI can change easily, without changing the rest of the system. A web UI could be replaced with a console UI, for example, without changing the business rules.
- *Independent of the database.* You can swap out Oracle or SQL Server for Mongo, BigTable, CouchDB, or something else. Your business rules are not bound to the database.
- *Independent of any external agency.* In fact, your business rules don't know anything at all about the interfaces to the outside world.

The diagram in Figure 22.1 is an attempt at integrating all these architectures into a single actionable idea.

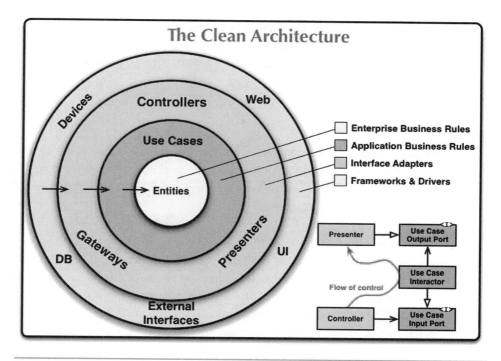

Figure 22.1 The clean architecture

THE DEPENDENCY RULE

The concentric circles in Figure 22.1 represent different areas of software. In general, the further in you go, the higher level the software becomes. The outer circles are mechanisms. The inner circles are policies.

The overriding rule that makes this architecture work is the *Dependency Rule*:

> *Source code dependencies must point only inward, toward higher-level policies.*

Nothing in an inner circle can know anything at all about something in an outer circle. In particular, the name of something declared in an outer circle must not be mentioned by the code in an inner circle. That includes functions, classes, variables, or any other named software entity.

By the same token, data formats declared in an outer circle should not be used by an inner circle, especially if those formats are generated by a framework in an outer circle. We don't want anything in an outer circle to impact the inner circles.

ENTITIES

Entities encapsulate enterprise-wide Critical Business Rules. An entity can be an object with methods, or it can be a set of data structures and functions. It doesn't matter so long as the entities can be used by many different applications in the enterprise.

If you don't have an enterprise and are writing just a single application, then these entities are the business objects of the application. They encapsulate the most general and high-level rules. They are the least likely to change when something external changes. For example, you would not expect these objects to be affected by a change to page navigation or security. No operational change to any particular application should affect the entity layer.

USE CASES

The software in the use cases layer contains *application-specific* business rules. It encapsulates and implements all of the use cases of the system. These use cases orchestrate the flow of data to and from the entities, and direct those entities to use their Critical Business Rules to achieve the goals of the use case.

We do not expect changes in this layer to affect the entities. We also do not expect this layer to be affected by changes to externalities such as the database, the UI, or any of the common frameworks. The use cases layer is isolated from such concerns.

We do, however, expect that changes to the operation of the application will affect the use cases and, therefore, the software in this layer. If the details of a use case change, then some code in this layer will certainly be affected.

INTERFACE ADAPTERS

The software in the interface adapters layer is a set of adapters that convert data from the format most convenient for the use cases and entities, to the format most convenient for some external agency such as the database or the web. It is this layer, for example, that will wholly contain the MVC architecture of a GUI. The presenters, views, and controllers all belong in the interface adapters layer. The models are likely just data structures that are passed from the controllers to the use cases, and then back from the use cases to the presenters and views.

Similarly, data is converted, in this layer, from the form most convenient for entities and use cases, to the form most convenient for whatever persistence framework is being used (i.e., the database). No code inward of this circle should know anything at all about the database. If the database is a SQL database, then all SQL should be restricted to this layer—and in particular to the parts of this layer that have to do with the database.

Also in this layer is any other adapter necessary to convert data from some external form, such as an external service, to the internal form used by the use cases and entities.

FRAMEWORKS AND DRIVERS

The outermost layer of the model in Figure 22.1 is generally composed of frameworks and tools such as the database and the web framework. Generally you don't write much code in this layer, other than glue code that communicates to the next circle inward.

The frameworks and drivers layer is where all the details go. The web is a detail. The database is a detail. We keep these things on the outside where they can do little harm.

ONLY FOUR CIRCLES?

The circles in Figure 22.1 are intended to be schematic: You may find that you need more than just these four. There's no rule that says you must always have just these four. However, the Dependency Rule always applies. Source code dependencies always point inward. As you move inward, the level of abstraction and policy increases. The outermost circle consists of low-level concrete details. As you move inward, the software grows more abstract and encapsulates higher-level policies. The innermost circle is the most general and highest level.

CROSSING BOUNDARIES

At the lower right of the diagram in Figure 22.1 is an example of how we cross the circle boundaries. It shows the controllers and presenters communicating with the use cases in the next layer. Note the flow of control: It begins in the controller, moves through the use case, and then winds up executing in the presenter. Note also the source code dependencies: Each points inward toward the use cases.

We usually resolve this apparent contradiction by using the Dependency Inversion Principle. In a language like Java, for example, we would arrange interfaces and inheritance relationships such that the source code dependencies oppose the flow of control at just the right points across the boundary.

For example, suppose the use case needs to call the presenter. This call must not be direct because that would violate the Dependency Rule: No name in an outer circle can be mentioned by an inner circle. So we have the use case call an interface (shown in Figure 22.1 as "use case output port") in the inner circle, and have the presenter in the outer circle implement it.

The same technique is used to cross all the boundaries in the architectures. We take advantage of dynamic polymorphism to create source code dependencies that oppose the flow of control so that we can conform to the Dependency Rule, no matter which direction the flow of control travels.

Which Data Crosses the Boundaries

Typically the data that crosses the boundaries consists of simple data structures. You can use basic structs or simple data transfer objects if you like. Or the data can simply be arguments in function calls. Or you can pack it into a hashmap, or construct it into an object. The important thing is that isolated, simple data structures are passed across the boundaries. We don't want to cheat and pass Entity objects or database rows. We don't want the data structures to have any kind of dependency that violates the Dependency Rule.

For example, many database frameworks return a convenient data format in response to a query. We might call this a "row structure." We don't want to pass that row structure inward across a boundary. Doing so would violate the Dependency Rule because it would force an inner circle to know something about an outer circle.

Thus, when we pass data across a boundary, it is always in the form that is most convenient for the inner circle.

A Typical Scenario

The diagram in Figure 22.2 shows a typical scenario for a web-based Java system using a database. The web server gathers input data from the user and hands it to the `Controller` on the upper left. The `Controller` packages that data into a plain old Java object and passes this object through the `InputBoundary` to the `UseCaseInteractor`. The `UseCaseInteractor` interprets that data and uses it to control the dance of the `Entities`. It also uses the `DataAccessInterface` to bring the data used by those `Entities` into memory from the `Database`. Upon completion, the `UseCaseInteractor` gathers data from the `Entities` and constructs the `OutputData` as another plain old Java object. The `OutputData` is then passed through the `OutputBoundary` interface to the `Presenter`.

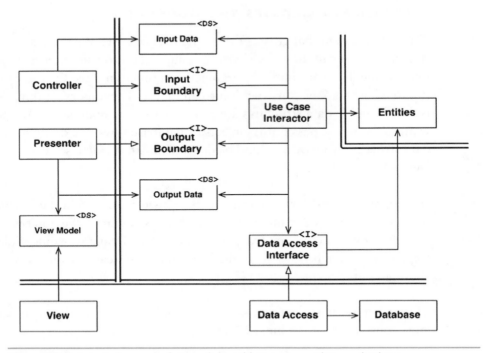

Figure 22.2 A typical scenario for a web-based Java system utilizing a database

The job of the `Presenter` is to repackage the `OutputData` into viewable form as the `ViewModel`, which is yet another plain old Java object. The `ViewModel` contains mostly `Strings` and flags that the `View` uses to display the data. Whereas the `OutputData` may contain `Date` objects, the `Presenter` will load the `ViewModel` with corresponding `Strings` already formatted properly for the user. The same is true of `Currency` objects or any other business-related data. `Button` and `MenuItem` names are placed in the `ViewModel`, as are flags that tell the `View` whether those `Buttons` and `MenuItems` should be gray.

This leaves the `View` with almost nothing to do other than to move the data from the `ViewModel` into the `HTML` page.

Note the directions of the dependencies. All dependencies cross the boundary lines pointing inward, following the Dependency Rule.

CONCLUSION

Conforming to these simple rules is not difficult, and it will save you a lot of headaches going forward. By separating the software into layers and conforming to the Dependency Rule, you will create a system that is intrinsically testable, with all the benefits that implies. When any of the external parts of the system become obsolete, such as the database, or the web framework, you can replace those obsolete elements with a minimum of fuss.

23 PRESENTERS AND HUMBLE OBJECTS

In Chapter 22, we introduced the notion of presenters. Presenters are a form of the *Humble Object* pattern, which helps us identify and protect architectural boundaries. Actually, the Clean Architecture in the last chapter was full of *Humble Object* implementations.

THE HUMBLE OBJECT PATTERN

The *Humble Object* pattern[1] is a design pattern that was originally identified as a way to help unit testers to separate behaviors that are hard to test from behaviors that are easy to test. The idea is very simple: Split the behaviors into two modules or classes. One of those modules is humble; it contains all the hard-to-test behaviors stripped down to their barest essence. The other module contains all the testable behaviors that were stripped out of the humble object.

For example, GUIs are hard to unit test because it is very difficult to write tests that can see the screen and check that the appropriate elements are displayed there. However, most of the behavior of a GUI is, in fact, easy to test. Using the *Humble Object* pattern, we can separate these two kinds of behaviors into two different classes called the Presenter and the View.

PRESENTERS AND VIEWS

The View is the humble object that is hard to test. The code in this object is kept as simple as possible. It moves data into the GUI but does not process that data.

The Presenter is the testable object. Its job is to accept data from the application and format it for presentation so that the View can simply move it to the screen. For example, if the application wants a date displayed in a field, it will hand the Presenter a Date object. The Presenter will then format that

---

1. *xUnit Patterns*, Meszaros, Addison-Wesley, 2007, p. 695.

data into an appropriate string and place it in a simple data structure called the View Model, where the View can find it.

If the application wants to display money on the screen, it might pass a `Currency` object to the Presenter. The Presenter will format that object with the appropriate decimal places and currency markers, creating a string that it can place in the View Model. If that currency value should be turned red if it is negative, then a simple boolean flag in the View model will be set appropriately.

Every button on the screen will have a name. That name will be a string in the View Model, placed there by the presenter. If those buttons should be grayed out, the Presenter will set an appropriate boolean flag in the View model. Every menu item name is a string in the View model, loaded by the Presenter. The names for every radio button, check box, and text field are loaded, by the Presenter, into appropriate strings and booleans in the View model. Tables of numbers that should be displayed on the screen are loaded, by the Presenter, into tables of properly formatted strings in the View model.

Anything and everything that appears on the screen, and that the application has some kind of control over, is represented in the View Model as a string, or a boolean, or an enum. Nothing is left for the View to do other than to load the data from the View Model into the screen. Thus the View is humble.

TESTING AND ARCHITECTURE

It has long been known that testability is an attribute of good architectures. The *Humble Object* pattern is a good example, because the separation of the behaviors into testable and non-testable parts often defines an architectural boundary. The Presenter/View boundary is one of these boundaries, but there are many others.

DATABASE GATEWAYS

Between the use case interactors and the database are the database gateways.[2] These gateways are polymorphic interfaces that contain methods for every create, read, update, or delete operation that can be performed by the application on the database. For example, if the application needs to know the last names of all the users who logged in yesterday, then the `UserGateway` interface will have a method named `getLastNamesOfUsersWhoLoggedInAfter` that takes a `Date` as its argument and returns a list of last names.

Recall that we do not allow SQL in the use cases layer; instead, we use gateway interfaces that have appropriate methods. Those gateways are implemented by classes in the database layer. That implementation is the humble object. It simply uses SQL, or whatever the interface to the database is, to access the data required by each of the methods. The interactors, in contrast, are not humble because they encapsulate application-specific business rules. Although they are not humble, those interactors are *testable*, because the gateways can be replaced with appropriate stubs and test-doubles.

DATA MAPPERS

Going back to the topic of databases, in which layer do you think ORMs like Hibernate belong?

First, let's get something straight: There is no such thing as an object relational mapper (ORM). The reason is simple: Objects are not data structures. At least, they are not data structures from their users' point of view. The users of an object cannot see the data, since it is all private. Those users see only the public methods of that object. So, from the user's point of view, an object is simply a set of operations.

---

2. *Patterns of Enterprise Application Architecture*, Martin Fowler, et. al., Addison-Wesley, 2003, p. 466.

A data structure, in contrast, is a set of public data variables that have no implied behavior. ORMs would be better named "data mappers," because they load data into data structures from relational database tables.

Where should such ORM systems reside? In the database layer of course. Indeed, ORMs form another kind of *Humble Object* boundary between the gateway interfaces and the database.

SERVICE LISTENERS

What about services? If your application must communicate with other services, or if your application provides a set of services, will we find the *Humble Object* pattern creating a service boundary?

Of course! The application will load data into simple data structures and then pass those structures across the boundary to modules that properly format the data and send it to external services. On the input side, the service listeners will receive data from the service interface and format it into a simple data structure that can be used by the application. That data structure is then passed across the service boundary.

CONCLUSION

At each architectural boundary, we are likely to find the *Humble Object* pattern lurking somewhere nearby. The communication across that boundary will almost always involve some kind of simple data structure, and the boundary will frequently divide something that is hard to test from something that is easy to test. The use of this pattern at architectural boundaries vastly increases the testability of the entire system.

P<small>ARTIAL</small> B<small>OUNDARIES</small>

24

Full-fledged architectural boundaries are expensive. They require reciprocal polymorphic `Boundary` interfaces, `Input` and `Output` data structures, and all of the dependency management necessary to isolate the two sides into independently compilable and deployable components. That takes a lot of work. It's also a lot of work to maintain.

In many situations, a good architect might judge that the expense of such a boundary is too high—but might still want to hold a place for such a boundary in case it is needed later.

This kind of anticipatory design is often frowned upon by many in the Agile community as a violation of YAGNI: "You Aren't Going to Need It." Architects, however, sometimes look at the problem and think, "Yeah, but I might." In that case, they may implement a partial boundary.

SKIP THE LAST STEP

One way to construct a partial boundary is to do all the work necessary to create independently compilable and deployable components, and then simply keep them together in the same component. The reciprocal interfaces are there, the input/output data structures are there, and everything is all set up—but we compile and deploy all of them as a single component.

Obviously, this kind of partial boundary requires the same amount of code and preparatory design work as a full boundary. However, it does not require the administration of multiple components. There's no version number tracking or release management burden. That difference should not be taken lightly.

This was the early strategy behind `FitNesse`. The web server component of `FitNesse` was designed to be separable from the wiki and testing part of `FitNesse`. The idea was that we might want to create other web-based applications by using that web component. At the same, we did not want users to have to download two components. Recall that one of our design goals was "*download and go.*" It was our intent that users would download one jar file and execute it without having to hunt for other jar files, work out version compatibilities, and so on.

The story of FitNesse also points out one of the dangers of this approach. Over time, as it became clear that there would never be a need for a separate web component, the separation between the web component and the wiki component began to weaken. Dependencies started to cross the line in the wrong direction. Nowadays, it would be something of a chore to re-separate them.

ONE-DIMENSIONAL BOUNDARIES

The full-fledged architectural boundary uses reciprocal boundary interfaces to maintain isolation in both directions. Maintaining separation in both directions is expensive both in initial setup and in ongoing maintenance.

A simpler structure that serves to hold the place for later extension to a full-fledged boundary is shown in Figure 24.1. It exemplifies the traditional *Strategy* pattern. A ServiceBoundary interface is used by clients and implemented by ServiceImpl classes.

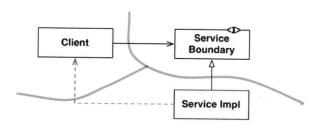

Figure 24.1 The Strategy pattern

It should be clear that this sets the stage for a future architectural boundary. The necessary dependency inversion is in place in an attempt to isolate the Client from the ServiceImpl. It should also be clear that the separation can degrade pretty rapidly, as shown by the nasty dotted arrow in the diagram. Without reciprocal interfaces, nothing prevents this kind of backchannel other than the diligence and discipline of the developers and architects.

FACADES

An even simpler boundary is the *Facade* pattern, illustrated in Figure 24.2. In this case, even the dependency inversion is sacrificed. The boundary is simply defined by the `Facade` class, which lists all the services as methods, and deploys the service calls to classes that the client is not supposed to access.

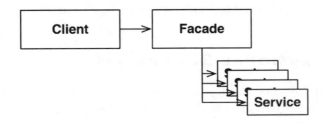

Figure 24.2 The Facade pattern

Note, however, that the `Client` has a transitive dependency on all those service classes. In static languages, a change to the source code in one of the `Service` classes will force the `Client` to recompile. Also, you can imagine how easy backchannels are to create with this structure.

CONCLUSION

We've seen three simple ways to partially implement an architectural boundary. There are, of course, many others. These three strategies are simply offered as examples.

Each of these approaches has its own set of costs and benefits. Each is appropriate, in certain contexts, as a placeholder for an eventual full-fledged boundary. Each can also be degraded if that boundary never materializes.

It is one of the functions of an architect to decide where an architectural boundary might one day exist, and whether to fully or partially implement that boundary.

25 Layers and Boundaries

It is easy to think of systems as being composed of three components: UI, business rules, and database. For some simple systems, this is sufficient. For most systems, though, the number of components is larger than that.

Consider, for example, a simple computer game. It is easy to imagine the three components. The UI handles all messages from the player to the game rules. The game rules store the state of the game in some kind of persistent data structure. But is that all there is?

HUNT THE WUMPUS

Let's put some flesh on these bones. Let's assume that the game is the venerable Hunt the Wumpus adventure game from 1972. This text-based game uses very simple commands like GO EAST and SHOOT WEST. The player enters a command, and the computer responds with what the player sees, smells, hears, and experiences. The player is hunting for a Wumpus in a system of caverns, and must avoid traps, pits, and other dangers lying in wait. If you are interested, the rules of the game are easy to find on the web.

Let's assume that we'll keep the text-based UI, but decouple it from the game rules so that our version can use different languages in different markets. The game rules will communicate with the UI component using a language-independent API, and the UI will translate the API into the appropriate human language.

If the source code dependencies are properly managed, as shown in Figure 25.1, then any number of UI components can reuse the same game rules. The game rules do not know, nor do they care, which human language is being used.

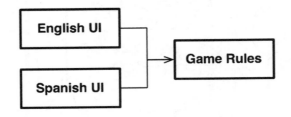

Figure 25.1 Any number of UI components can reuse the game rules

Let's also assume that the state of the game is maintained on some persistent store—perhaps in flash, or perhaps in the cloud, or maybe just in RAM. In any of those cases, we don't want the game rules to know the details. So, again, we'll create an API that the game rules can use to communicate with the data storage component.

We don't want the game rules to know anything about the different kinds of data storage, so the dependencies have to be properly directed following the Dependency Rule, as shown in Figure 25.2.

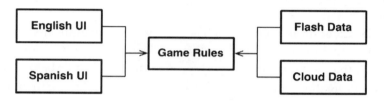

Figure 25.2 Following the Dependency Rule

CLEAN ARCHITECTURE?

It should be clear that we could easily apply the clean architecture approach in this context,[1] with all the use cases, boundaries, entities, and corresponding data structures. But have we really found all the significant architectural boundaries?

For example, language is not the only axis of change for the UI. We also might want to vary the mechanism by which we communicate the text. For example, we might want to use a normal shell window, or text messages, or a chat application. There are many different possibilities.

That means that there is a potential architectural boundary defined by this axis of change. Perhaps we should construct an API that crosses that boundary and isolates the language from the communications mechanism; that idea is illustrated in Figure 25.3.

---

1. It should be just as clear that we would not apply the clean architecture approach to something as trivial as this game. After all, the entire program can probably be written in 200 lines of code or less. In this case, we're using a simple program as a proxy for a much larger system with significant architectural boundaries.

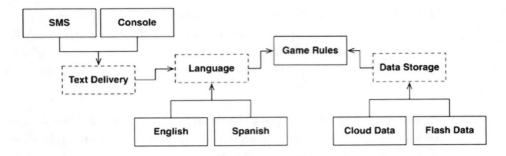

Figure 25.3 The revised diagram

The diagram in Figure 25.3 has gotten a little complicated, but should contain no surprises. The dashed outlines indicate abstract components that define an API that is implemented by the components above or below them. For example, the `Language` API is implemented by `English` and `Spanish`.

`GameRules` communicates with `Language` through an API that `GameRules` defines and `Language` implements. `Language` communicates with `TextDelivery` using an API that `Language` defines but `TextDelivery` implements. The API is defined and owned by the user, rather than by the implementer.

If we were to look inside `GameRules`, we would find polymorphic `Boundary` interfaces used by the code inside `GameRules` and implemented by the code inside the `Language` component. We would also find polymorphic `Boundary` interfaces used by `Language` and implemented by code inside `GameRules`.

If we were to look inside of `Language`, we would find the same thing: Polymorphic `Boundary` interfaces implemented by the code inside `TextDelivery`, and polymorphic `Boundary` interfaces used by `TextDelivery` and implemented by `Language`.

In each case, the API defined by those `Boundary` interfaces is owned by the upstream component.

The variations, such as `English`, `SMS`, and `CloudData`, are provided by polymorphic interfaces defined in the abstract API component, and implemented by the concrete components that serve them. For example, we would expect polymorphic interfaces defined in `Language` to be implemented by `English` and `Spanish`.

We can simplify this diagram by eliminating all the variations and focusing on just the API components. Figure 25.4 shows this diagram.

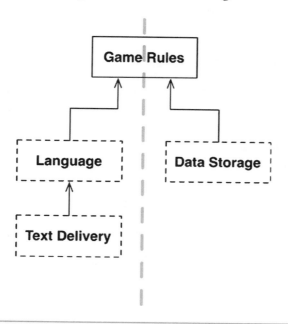

Figure 25.4 Simplified diagram

Notice that the diagram is oriented in Figure 25.4 so that all the arrows point up. This puts `GameRules` at the top. This orientation makes sense because `GameRules` is the component that contains the highest-level policies.

Consider the direction of information flow. All input comes from the user through the `TextDelivery` component at the bottom left. That information rises through the `Language` component, getting translated into commands to `GameRules`. `GameRules` processes the user input and sends appropriate data down to `DataStorage` at the lower right.

`GameRules` then sends output back down to `Language`, which translates the API back to the appropriate language and then delivers that language to the user through `TextDelivery`.

This organization effectively divides the flow of data into two streams.[2] The stream on the left is concerned with communicating with the user, and the stream on the right is concerned with data persistence. Both streams meet at the top[3] at `GameRules`, which is the ultimate processor of the data that goes through both streams.

CROSSING THE STREAMS

Are there always two data streams as in this example? No, not at all. Imagine that we would like to play Hunt the Wumpus on the net with multiple players. In this case, we would need a network component, like that shown in Figure 25.5. This organization divides the data flow into three streams, all controlled by the `GameRules`.

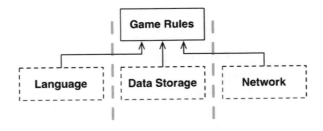

Figure 25.5 Adding a network component

So, as systems become more complex, the component structure may split into many such streams.

---

2. If you are confused by the direction of the arrows, remember that they point in the direction of source code dependencies, not in the direction of data flow.
3. In days long past, we would have called that top component the Central Transform. See *Practical Guide to Structured Systems Design*, 2nd ed., Meilir Page-Jones, 1988.

Splitting the Streams

At this point you may be thinking that all the streams eventually meet at the top in a single component. If only life were so simple! The reality, of course, is much more complex.

Consider the GameRules component for Hunt the Wumpus. Part of the game rules deal with the mechanics of the map. They know how the caverns are connected, and which objects are located in each cavern. They know how to move the player from cavern to cavern, and how to determine the events that the player must deal with.

But there is another set of policies at an even higher level—policies that know the health of the player, and the cost or benefit of a particular event. These policies could cause the player to gradually lose health, or to gain health by discovering food. The lower-level mechanics policy would declare events to this higher-level policy, such as FoundFood or FellInPit. The higher-level policy would then manage the state of the player (as shown in Figure 25.6). Eventually that policy would decide whether the player wins or loses.

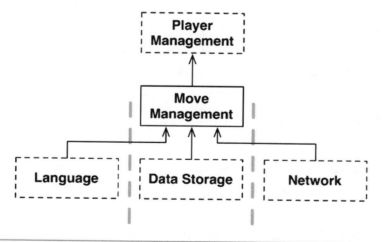

Figure 25.6 The higher-level policy manages the player

Is this an architectural boundary? Do we need an API that separates `MoveManagement` from `PlayerManagement`? Well, let's make this a bit more interesting and add micro-services.

Let's assume that we've got a massive multiplayer version of Hunt the Wumpus. `MoveManagement` is handled locally within the player's computer, but `PlayerManagement` is handled by a server. `PlayerManagement` offers a micro-service API to all the connected `MoveManagement` components.

The diagram in Figure 25.7 depicts this scenario in a somewhat abbreviated fashion. The `Network` elements are a bit more complex than depicted—but you can probably still get the idea. A full-fledged architectural boundary exists between `MoveManagement` and `PlayerManagement` in this case.

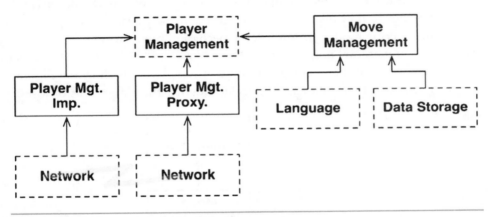

Figure 25.7 Adding a micro-service API

CONCLUSION

What does all this mean? Why have I taken this absurdly simply program, which could be implemented in 200 lines of Kornshell, and extrapolated it out with all these crazy architectural boundaries?

This example is intended to show that architectural boundaries exist everywhere. We, as architects, must be careful to recognize when they are needed. We also have to be aware that such boundaries, when fully implemented, are expensive.

At the same time, we have to recognize that when such boundaries are ignored, they are very expensive to add in later—even in the presence of comprehensive test-suites and refactoring discipline.

So what do we do, we architects? The answer is dissatisfying. On the one hand, some very smart people have told us, over the years, that we should not anticipate the need for abstraction. This is the philosophy of YAGNI: "You aren't going to need it." There is wisdom in this message, since over-engineering is often much worse than under-engineering. On the other hand, when you discover that you truly do need an architectural boundary where none exists, the costs and risks can be very high to add such a boundary.

So there you have it. O Software Architect, you must see the future. You must guess—intelligently. You must weigh the costs and determine where the architectural boundaries lie, and which should be fully implemented, and which should be partially implemented, and which should be ignored.

But this is not a one-time decision. You don't simply decide at the start of a project which boundaries to implement and which to ignore. Rather, you *watch*. You pay attention as the system evolves. You note where boundaries may be required, and then carefully watch for the first inkling of friction because those boundaries don't exist.

At that point, you weigh the costs of implementing those boundaries versus the cost of ignoring them—and you review that decision frequently. Your goal is to implement the boundaries right at the inflection point where the cost of implementing becomes less than the cost of ignoring.

It takes a watchful eye.

THE MAIN COMPONENT

26

KOHNKE

In every system, there is at least one component that creates, coordinates, and oversees the others. I call this component `Main`.

THE ULTIMATE DETAIL

The `Main` component is the ultimate detail—the lowest-level policy. It is the initial entry point of the system. Nothing, other than the operating system, depends on it. Its job is to create all the Factories, Strategies, and other global facilities, and then hand control over to the high-level abstract portions of the system.

It is in this `Main` component that dependencies should be injected by a Dependency Injection framework. Once they are injected into `Main`, `Main` should distribute those dependencies normally, without using the framework.

Think of `Main` as the dirtiest of all the dirty components.

Consider the following `Main` component from a recent version of Hunt the Wumpus. Notice how it loads up all the strings that we don't want the main body of the code to know about.

```
public class Main implements HtwMessageReceiver {
    private static HuntTheWumpus game;
    private static int hitPoints = 10;
    private static final List<String> caverns = new
ArrayList<>();
    private static final String[] environments = new String[]{
        "bright",
        "humid",
        "dry",
        "creepy",
        "ugly",
        "foggy",
        "hot",
```

```java
        "cold",
        "drafty",
        "dreadful"
    };

    private static final String[] shapes = new String[] {
        "round",
        "square",
        "oval",
        "irregular",
        "long",
        "craggy",
        "rough",
        "tall",
        "narrow"
    };

    private static final String[] cavernTypes = new String[] {
        "cavern",
        "room",
        "chamber",
        "catacomb",
        "crevasse",
        "cell",
        "tunnel",
        "passageway",
        "hall",
        "expanse"
    };

    private static final String[] adornments = new String[] {
```

```
    "smelling of sulfur",
     "with engravings on the walls",
     "with a bumpy floor",
     "",
     "littered with garbage",
     "spattered with guano",
     "with piles of Wumpus droppings",
     "with bones scattered around",
     "with a corpse on the floor",
     "that seems to vibrate",
     "that feels stuffy",
     "that fills you with dread"
    };
```

Now here's the `main` function. Notice how it uses the `HtwFactory` to create the game. It passes in the name of the class, `htw.game.HuntTheWumpusFacade`, because that class is even dirtier than `Main`. This prevents changes in that class from causing `Main` to recompile/redeploy.

```
public static void main(String[] args) throws IOException {
    game = HtwFactory.makeGame("htw.game.HuntTheWumpusFacade",
                               new Main());
    createMap();
    BufferedReader br =
      new BufferedReader(new InputStreamReader(System.in));
    game.makeRestCommand().execute();
    while (true) {
      System.out.println(game.getPlayerCavern());
      System.out.println("Health: " + hitPoints + " arrows: " +
                          game.getQuiver());
      HuntTheWumpus.Command c = game.makeRestCommand();
```

```
System.out.println(">");
String command = br.readLine();
if (command.equalsIgnoreCase("e"))
  c = game.makeMoveCommand(EAST);
else if (command.equalsIgnoreCase("w"))
  c = game.makeMoveCommand(WEST);
else if (command.equalsIgnoreCase("n"))
  c = game.makeMoveCommand(NORTH);
else if (command.equalsIgnoreCase("s"))
  c = game.makeMoveCommand(SOUTH);
else if (command.equalsIgnoreCase("r"))
  c = game.makeRestCommand();
else if (command.equalsIgnoreCase("sw"))
  c = game.makeShootCommand(WEST);
else if (command.equalsIgnoreCase("se"))
  c = game.makeShootCommand(EAST);
else if (command.equalsIgnoreCase("sn"))
  c = game.makeShootCommand(NORTH);
else if (command.equalsIgnoreCase("ss"))
  c = game.makeShootCommand(SOUTH);
else if (command.equalsIgnoreCase("q"))
  return;

    c.execute();
  }
}
```

Notice also that main creates the input stream and contains the main loop of the game, interpreting the simple input commands, but then defers all processing to other, higher-level components.

Finally, notice that main creates the map.

```
private static void createMap() {
    int nCaverns = (int) (Math.random() * 30.0 + 10.0);
    while (nCaverns-- > 0)
      caverns.add(makeName());

    for (String cavern : caverns) {
      maybeConnectCavern(cavern, NORTH);
      maybeConnectCavern(cavern, SOUTH);
      maybeConnectCavern(cavern, EAST);
      maybeConnectCavern(cavern, WEST);
    }

    String playerCavern = anyCavern();
    game.setPlayerCavern(playerCavern);
    game.setWumpusCavern(anyOther(playerCavern));
    game.addBatCavern(anyOther(playerCavern));
    game.addBatCavern(anyOther(playerCavern));
    game.addBatCavern(anyOther(playerCavern));

    game.addPitCavern(anyOther(playerCavern));
    game.addPitCavern(anyOther(playerCavern));
    game.addPitCavern(anyOther(playerCavern));

    game.setQuiver(5);
  }

  // much code removed...
}
```

The point is that `Main` is a dirty low-level module in the outermost circle of the clean architecture. It loads everything up for the high level system, and then hands control over to it.

CONCLUSION

Think of `Main` as a plugin to the application—a plugin that sets up the initial conditions and configurations, gathers all the outside resources, and then hands control over to the high-level policy of the application. Since it is a plugin, it is possible to have many `Main` components, one for each configuration of your application.

For example, you could have a `Main` plugin for *Dev*, another for *Test*, and yet another for *Production*. You could also have a `Main` plugin for each country you deploy to, or each jurisdiction, or each customer.

When you think about `Main` as a plugin component, sitting behind an architectural boundary, the problem of configuration becomes a lot easier to solve.

Services: Great and Small

Service-oriented "architectures" and micro-service "architectures" have become very popular of late. The reasons for their current popularity include the following:

- Services seem to be strongly decoupled from each other. As we shall see, this is only partially true.
- Services appear to support independence of development and deployment. Again, as we shall see, this is only partially true.

SERVICE ARCHITECTURE?

First, let's consider the notion that using services, by their nature, is an architecture. This is patently untrue. The architecture of a system is defined by boundaries that separate high-level policy from low-level detail and follow the Dependency Rule. Services that simply separate application behaviors are little more than expensive function calls, and are not necessarily architecturally significant.

This is not to say that all services *should* be architecturally significant. There are often substantial benefits to creating services that separate functionality across processes and platforms—whether they obey the Dependency Rule or not. It's just that services, in and of themselves, do not define an architecture.

A helpful analogy is the organization of functions. The architecture of a monolithic or component-based system is defined by certain function calls that cross architectural boundaries and follow the Dependency Rule. Many other functions in those systems, however, simply separate one behavior from another and are not architecturally significant.

So it is with services. Services are, after all, just function calls across process and/or platform boundaries. Some of those services are architecturally significant, and some aren't. Our interest, in this chapter, is with the former.

SERVICE BENEFITS?

The question mark in the preceding heading indicates that this section is going to challenge the current popular orthodoxy of service architecture. Let's tackle the benefits one at a time.

THE DECOUPLING FALLACY

One of the big supposed benefits of breaking a system up into services is that services are strongly decoupled from each other. After all, each service runs in a different process, or even a different processor; therefore those services do not have access to each other's variables. What's more, the interface of each service must be well defined.

There is certainly some truth to this—but not very much truth. Yes, services are decoupled at the level of individual variables. However, they can still be coupled by shared resources within a processor, or on the network. What's more, they are strongly coupled by the data they share.

For example, if a new field is added to a data record that is passed between services, then every service that operates on the new field must be changed. The services must also strongly agree about the interpretation of the data in that field. Thus those services are strongly coupled to the data record and, therefore, indirectly coupled to each other.

As for interfaces being well defined, that's certainly true—but it is no less true for functions. Service interfaces are no more formal, no more rigorous, and no better defined than function interfaces. Clearly, then, this benefit is something of an illusion.

THE FALLACY OF INDEPENDENT DEVELOPMENT AND DEPLOYMENT

Another of the supposed benefits of services is that they can be owned and operated by a dedicated team. That team can be responsible for writing, maintaining, and operating the service as part of a dev-ops strategy. This independence of development and deployment is presumed to be *scalable*. It is believed that large enterprise systems can be created from dozens, hundreds, or even thousands of independently developable and deployable services. Development, maintenance, and operation of the system can be partitioned between a similar number of independent teams.

There is some truth to this belief—but only some. First, history has shown that large enterprise systems can be built from monoliths and component-based systems as well as service-based systems. Thus services are not the only option for building scalable systems.

Second, the decoupling fallacy means that services cannot always be independently developed, deployed, and operated. To the extent that they are coupled by data or behavior, the development, deployment, and operation must be coordinated.

THE KITTY PROBLEM

As an example of these two fallacies, let's look at our taxi aggregator system again. Remember, this system knows about many taxi providers in a given city, and allows customers to order rides. Let's assume that the customers select taxis based on a number of criteria, such as pickup time, cost, luxury, and driver experience.

We wanted our system to be scalable, so we chose to build it out of lots of little micro-services. We subdivided our development staff into many small teams, each of which is responsible for developing, maintaining, and operating a correspondingly[1] small number of services.

The diagram in Figure 27.1 shows how our fictitious architects arranged services to implement this application. The `TaxiUI` service deals with the customers, who use mobile devices to order taxis. The `TaxiFinder` service examines the inventories of the various `TaxiSuppliers` and determines which taxies are possible candidates for the user. It deposits these into a short-term data record attached to that user. The `TaxiSelector` service takes the user's criteria of cost, time, luxury, and so forth, and chooses an appropriate taxi from among the candidates. It hands that taxi off to the `TaxiDispatcher` service, which orders the appropriate taxi.

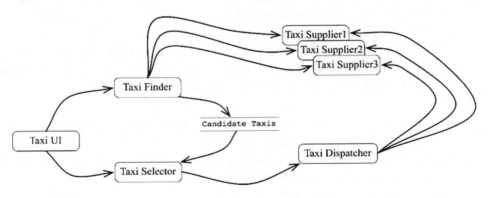

Figure 27.1 Services arranged to implement the taxi aggregator system

---

1. Therefore the number of micro-services will be roughly equal to the number of programmers.

Now let us suppose that this system has been in operation for more than a year. Our staff of developers have been happily developing new features while maintaining and operating all these services.

One bright and cheerful day, the marketing department holds a meeting with the development team. In this meeting, they announce their plans to offer a kitten delivery service to the city. Users can order kittens to be delivered to their homes or to their places of business.

The company will set up several kitten collection points across the city. When a kitten order is placed, a nearby taxi will be selected to collect a kitten from one of those collection points, and then deliver it to the appropriate address.

One of the taxi suppliers has agreed to participate in this program. Others are likely to follow. Still others may decline.

Of course, some drivers may be allergic to cats, so those drivers should never be selected for this service. Also, some customers will undoubtedly have similar allergies, so a vehicle that has been used to deliver kittens within the last 3 days should not be selected for customers who declare such allergies.

Look at that diagram of services. How many of those services will have to change to implement this feature? *All of them.* Clearly, the development and deployment of the kitty feature will have to be very carefully coordinated.

In other words, the services are all coupled, and cannot be independently developed, deployed, and maintained.

This is the problem with cross-cutting concerns. Every software system must face this problem, whether service oriented or not. Functional decompositions, of the kind depicted in the service diagram in Figure 27.1, are very vulnerable to new features that cut across all those functional behaviors.

OBJECTS TO THE RESCUE

How would we have solved this problem in a component-based architecture? Careful consideration of the SOLID design principles would have prompted us to create a set of classes that could be polymorphically extended to handle new features.

The diagram in Figure 27.2 shows the strategy. The classes in this diagram roughly correspond to the services shown in Figure 27.1. However, note the boundaries. Note also that the dependencies follow the Dependency Rule.

Much of the logic of the original services is preserved within the base classes of the object model. However, that portion of the logic that was specific to *rides* has been extracted into a Rides component. The new feature for kittens has been placed into a Kittens component. These two components override the abstract base classes in the original components using a pattern such as *Template Method or Strategy.*

Note again that the two new components, Rides and Kittens, follow the Dependency Rule. Note also that the classes that implement those features are created by factories under the control of the UI.

Clearly, in this scheme, when the Kitty feature is implemented, the TaxiUI must change. But nothing else needs to be changed. Rather, a new jar file, or Gem, or DLL is added to the system and dynamically loaded at runtime.

Thus the Kitty feature is decoupled, and independently developable and deployable.

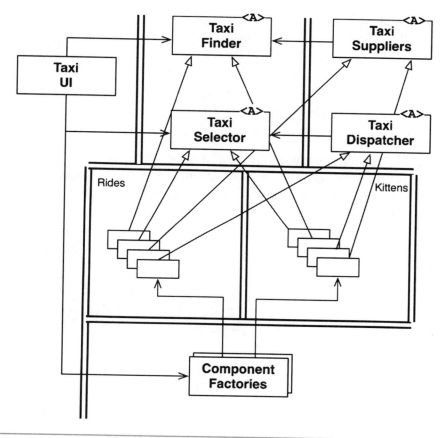

Figure 27.2 Using an object-oriented approach to deal with cross-cutting concerns

COMPONENT-BASED SERVICES

The obvious question is: Can we do that for services? And the answer is, of course: Yes! Services do not need to be little monoliths. Services can, instead, be designed using the SOLID principles, and given a component structure so that new components can be added to them without changing the existing components within the service.

Think of a service in Java as a set of abstract classes in one or more jar files. Think of each new feature or feature extension as another jar file that contains classes that extend the abstract classes in the first jar files. Deploying a new feature then becomes not a matter of redeploying the services, but rather a matter of simply *adding* the new jar files to the load paths of those services. In other words, adding new features conforms to the Open-Closed Principle.

The service diagram in Figure 27.3 shows the structure. The services still exist as before, but each has its own internal component design, allowing new features to be added as new derivative classes. Those derivative classes live within their own components.

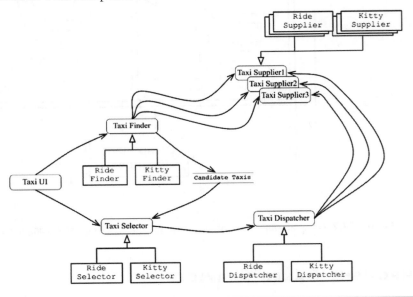

Figure 27.3 Each service has its own internal component design, enabling new features to be added as new derivative classes

CROSS-CUTTING CONCERNS

What we have learned is that architectural boundaries do not fall *between* services. Rather, those boundaries run *through* the services, dividing them into components.

To deal with the cross-cutting concerns that all significant systems face, services must be designed with internal component architectures that follow the Dependency Rule, as shown in the diagram in Figure 27.4. Those services do not define the architectural boundaries of the system; instead, the components within the services do.

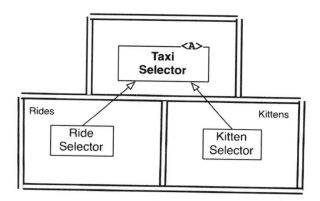

Figure 27.4 Services must be designed with internal component architectures that follow the Dependency Rule

CONCLUSION

As useful as services are to the scalability and develop-ability of a system, they are not, in and of themselves, architecturally significant elements. The architecture of a system is defined by the boundaries drawn within that system, and by the dependencies that cross those boundaries. That architecture is not defined by the physical mechanisms by which elements communicate and execute.

A service might be a single component, completely surrounded by an architectural boundary. Alternatively, a service might be composed of several components separated by architectural boundaries. In rare[2] cases, clients and services may be so coupled as to have no architectural significance whatever.

---

2. We hope they are rare. Unfortunately, experience suggests otherwise.

THE TEST 28 BOUNDARY

Yes, that's right: *The tests are part of the system*, and they participate in the architecture just like every other part of the system does. In some ways, that participation is pretty normal. In other ways, it can be pretty unique.

TESTS AS SYSTEM COMPONENTS

There is a great deal of confusion about tests. Are they part of the system? Are they separate from the system? Which kinds of tests are there? Are unit tests and integration tests different things? What about acceptance tests, functional tests, Cucumber tests, TDD tests, BDD tests, component tests, and so on?

It is not the role of this book to get embroiled in that particular debate, and fortunately it isn't necessary. From an architectural point of view, all tests are the same. Whether they are the tiny little tests created by TDD, or large FitNesse, Cucumber, SpecFlow, or JBehave tests, they are architecturally equivalent.

Tests, by their very nature, follow the Dependency Rule; they are very detailed and concrete; and they always depend inward toward the code being tested. In fact, you can think of the tests as the outermost circle in the architecture. Nothing within the system depends on the tests, and the tests always depend inward on the components of the system.

Tests are also independently deployable. In fact, most of the time they are deployed in test systems, rather than in production systems. So, even in systems where independent deployment is not otherwise necessary, the tests will still be independently deployed.

Tests are the most isolated system component. They are not necessary for system operation. No user depends on them. Their role is to support development, not operation. And yet, they are no less a system component than any other. In fact, in many ways they represent the model that all other system components should follow.

DESIGN FOR TESTABILITY

The extreme isolation of the tests, combined with the fact that they are not usually deployed, often causes developers to think that tests fall outside of the design of the system. This is a catastrophic point of view. Tests that are not well integrated into the design of the system tend to be fragile, and they make the system rigid and difficult to change.

The issue, of course, is coupling. Tests that are strongly coupled to the system must change along with the system. Even the most trivial change to a system component can cause many coupled tests to break or require changes.

This situation can become acute. Changes to common system components can cause hundreds, or even thousands, of tests to break. This is known as the *Fragile Tests Problem*.

It is not hard to see how this can happen. Imagine, for example, a suite of tests that use the GUI to verify business rules. Such tests may start on the login screen and then navigate through the page structure until they can check particular business rules. Any change to the login page, or the navigation structure, can cause an enormous number of tests to break.

Fragile tests often have the perverse effect of making the system rigid. When developers realize that simple changes to the system can cause massive test failures, they may resist making those changes. For example, imagine the conversation between the development team and a marketing team that requests a simple change to the page navigation structure that will cause 1000 tests to break.

The solution is to design for testability. The first rule of software design—whether for testability or for any other reason—is always the same: *Don't depend on volatile things*. GUIs are volatile. Test suites that operate the system through the GUI *must be fragile*. Therefore design the system, and the tests, so that business rules can be tested without using the GUI.

THE TESTING API

The way to accomplish this goal is to create a specific API that the tests can use to verify all the business rules. This API should have superpowers that allow the tests to avoid security constraints, bypass expensive resources (such as databases), and force the system into particular testable states. This API will be a superset of the suite of *interactors* and *interface adapters* that are used by the user interface.

The purpose of the testing API is to decouple the tests from the application. This decoupling encompasses more than just detaching the tests from the UI: The goal is to decouple the *structure* of the tests from the *structure* of the application.

STRUCTURAL COUPLING

Structural coupling is one of the strongest, and most insidious, forms of test coupling. Imagine a test suite that has a test class for every production class, and a set of test methods for every production method. Such a test suite is deeply coupled to the structure of the application.

When one of those production methods or classes changes, a large number of tests must change as well. Consequently, the tests are fragile, and they make the production code rigid.

The role of the testing API is to hide the structure of the application from the tests. This allows the production code to be refactored and evolved in ways that don't affect the tests. It also allows the tests to be refactored and evolved in ways that don't affect the production code.

This separation of evolution is necessary because as time passes, the tests tend to become increasingly more concrete and specific. In contrast, the production code tends to become increasingly more abstract and general. Strong structural coupling prevents—or at least impedes—this necessary evolution, and prevents the production code from being as general, and flexible, as it could be.

SECURITY

The superpowers of the testing API could be dangerous if they were deployed in production systems. If this is a concern, then the testing API, and the dangerous parts of its implementation, should be kept in a separate, independently deployable component.

CONCLUSION

Tests are not outside the system; rather, they are parts of the system that must be well designed if they are to provide the desired benefits of stability and regression. Tests that are not designed as part of the system tend to be fragile and difficult to maintain. Such tests often wind up on the maintenance room floor—discarded because they are too difficult to maintain.

29

CLEAN EMBEDDED ARCHITECTURE

By James Grenning

A while ago I read an article entitled "The Growing Importance of Sustaining Software for the DoD"[1] on Doug Schmidt's blog. Doug made the following claim:

> "Although software does not wear out, firmware and hardware become obsolete, thereby requiring software modifications."

It was a clarifying moment for me. Doug mentioned two terms that I would have thought to be obvious—but maybe not. *Software* is this thing that can have a long useful life, but *firmware* will become obsolete as hardware evolves. If you have spent any time in embedded systems development, you know the hardware is continually evolving and being improved. At the same time, features are added to the new "software," and it continually grows in complexity.

I'd like to add to Doug's statement:

> Although software does not wear out, it can be destroyed from within by unmanaged dependencies on firmware and hardware.

It is not uncommon for embedded software to be denied a potentially long life due to being infected with dependencies on hardware.

I like Doug's definition of firmware, but let's see which other definitions are out there. I found these alternatives:

- "Firmware is held in non-volatile memory devices such as ROM, EPROM, or flash memory." (https://en.wikipedia.org/wiki/Firmware)
- "Firmware is a software program or set of instructions programmed on a hardware device." (https://techterms.com/definition/firmware)
- "Firmware is software that is embedded in a piece of hardware." (https://www.lifewire.com/what-is-firmware-2625881)
- Firmware is "Software (programs or data) that has been written onto read-only memory (ROM)." (http://www.webopedia.com/TERM/F/firmware.html)

---

1. https://insights.sei.cmu.edu/sei_blog/2011/08/the-growing-importance-of-sustaining-software-for-the-dod.html

Doug's statement makes me realize that these accepted definitions of firmware are wrong, or at least obsolete. Firmware does not mean code lives in ROM. It's not firmware because of where it is stored; rather, it is firmware because of what it depends on and how hard it is to change as hardware evolves. Hardware does evolve (pause and look at your for phone for evidence), so we should structure our embedded code with that reality in mind.

I have nothing against firmware, or firmware engineers (I've been known to write some firmware myself). But what we really need is less firmware and more software. Actually, I am disappointed that firmware engineers write so much firmware!

Non-embedded engineers also write firmware! You non-embedded developers essentially write firmware whenever you bury SQL in your code or when you spread platform dependencies throughout your code. Android app developers write firmware when they don't separate their business logic from the Android API.

I've been involved in a lot of efforts where the line between the product code (the software) and the code that interacts with the product's hardware (the firmware) is fuzzy to the point of nonexistence. For example, in the late 1990s I had the fun of helping redesign a communications subsystem that was transitioning from time-division multiplexing (TDM) to voice over IP (VOIP). VOIP is how things are done now, but TDM was considered the state of the art from the 1950s and 1960s, and was widely deployed in the 1980s and 1990s.

Whenever we had a question for the systems engineer about how a call should react to a given situation, he would disappear and a little later emerge with a very detailed answer. "Where did he get that answer?" we asked. "From the current product's code," he'd answer. The tangled legacy code was the spec for the new product! The existing implementation had no separation between TDM and the business logic of making calls. The whole product was hardware/technology dependent from top to bottom and could not be untangled. The whole product had essentially become firmware.

Consider another example: Command messages arrive to this system via serial port. Unsurprisingly, there is a message processor/dispatcher. The message processor knows the format of messages, is able to parse them, and can then dispatch the message to the code that can handle the request. None of this is surprising, except that the message processor/dispatcher resides in the same file as code that interacts with a UART[2] hardware. The message processor is polluted with UART details. The message processor could have been software with a potentially long useful life, but instead it is firmware. The message processor is denied the opportunity to become software—and that is just not right!

I've known and understood the need for separating software from hardware for a long time, but Doug's words clarified how to use the terms *software* and *firmware* in relationship to each other.

For engineers and programmers, the message is clear: Stop writing so much firmware and give your code a chance at a long useful life. Of course, demanding it won't make it so. Let's look at how we can keep embedded software architecture clean to give the software a fighting chance of having a long and useful life.

App-titude Test

Why does so much potential embedded software become firmware? It seems that most of the emphasis is on getting the embedded code to work, and not so much emphasis is placed on structuring it for a long useful life. Kent Beck describes three activities in building software (the quoted text is Kent's words and the italics are my commentary):

1. "First make it work." *You are out of business if it doesn't work.*
2. "Then make it right." *Refactor the code so that you and others can understand it and evolve it as needs change or are better understood.*
3. "Then make it fast." *Refactor the code for "needed" performance.*

Much of the embedded systems software that I see in the wild seems to have been written with "Make it work" in mind—and perhaps also with an

---

2. The hardware device that controls the serial port.

obsession for the "Make it fast" goal, achieved by adding micro-optimizations at every opportunity. In *The Mythical Man-Month*, Fred Brooks suggests we "plan to throw one away." Kent and Fred are giving virtually the same advice: Learn what works, then make a better solution.

Embedded software is not special when it comes to these problems. Most non-embedded apps are built just to work, with little regard to making the code right for a long useful life.

Getting an app to work is what I call the *App-titude test* for a programmer. Programmers, embedded or not, who just concern themselves with getting their app to work are doing their products and employers a disservice. There is much more to programming than just getting an app to work.

As an example of code produced while passing the App-titude test, check out these functions located in one file of a small embedded system:

```
ISR(TIMER1_vect) { ... }
ISR(INT2_vect) { ... }
void btn_Handler(void) { ... }
float calc_RPM(void) { ... }
static char Read_RawData(void) { ... }
void Do_Average(void) { ... }
void Get_Next_Measurement(void) { ... }
void Zero_Sensor_1(void) { ... }
void Zero_Sensor_2(void) { ... }
void Dev_Control(char Activation) { ... }
char Load_FLASH_Setup(void) { ... }
void Save_FLASH_Setup(void) { ... }
void Store_DataSet(void) { ... }
float bytes2float(char bytes[4]) { ... }
void Recall_DataSet(void) { ... }
void Sensor_init(void) { ... }
void uC_Sleep(void) { ... }
```

That list of functions is in the order I found them in the source file. Now I'll separate them and group them by concern:

- Functions that have domain logic

```
float calc_RPM(void) { ... }
void Do_Average(void) { ... }
void Get_Next_Measurement(void) { ... }
void Zero_Sensor_1(void) { ... }
void Zero_Sensor_2(void) { ... }
```

- Functions that set up the hardware platform

```
ISR(TIMER1_vect) { ... }*
ISR(INT2_vect) { ... }
void uC_Sleep(void) { ... }
Functions that react to the on off button press
void btn_Handler(void) { ... }
void Dev_Control(char Activation) { ... }
A Function that can get A/D input readings from the
hardware
static char Read_RawData(void) { ... }
```

- Functions that store values to the persistent storage

```
char Load_FLASH_Setup(void) { ... }
void Save_FLASH_Setup(void) { ... }
void Store_DataSet(void) { ... }
float bytes2float(char bytes[4]) { ... }
void Recall_DataSet(void) { ... }
```

- Function that does not do what its name implies

```
void Sensor_init(void) { ... }
```

Looking at some of the other files in this application, I found many impediments to understanding the code. I also found a file structure that implied that the only way to test any of this code is in the embedded target. Virtually every bit of this code knows it is in a special microprocessor architecture, using "extended" C constructs[3] that tie the code to a particular tool chain and microprocessor. There is no way for this code to have a long useful life unless the product never needs to be moved to a different hardware environment.

This application works: The engineer passed the App-titude test. But the application can't be said to have a clean embedded architecture.

THE TARGET-HARDWARE BOTTLENECK

There are many special concerns that embedded developers have to deal with that non-embedded developers do not—for example, limited memory space, real-time constraints and deadlines, limited IO, unconventional user interfaces, and sensors and connections to the real world. Most of the time the hardware is concurrently developed with the software and firmware. As an engineer developing code for this kind of system, you may have no place to run the code. If that's not bad enough, once you get the hardware, it is likely that the hardware will have its own defects, making software development progress even slower than usual.

Yes, embedded is special. Embedded engineers are special. But embedded development is not *so* special that the principles in this book are not applicable to embedded systems.

One of the special embedded problems is *the target-hardware bottleneck*. When embedded code is structured without applying clean architecture principles and practices, you will often face the scenario in which you can test your code only on the target. If the target is the only place where testing is possible, the target-hardware bottleneck will slow you down.

---

3. Some silicon providers add keywords to the C language to make accessing the registers and IO ports simple from C. Unfortunately, once that is done, the code is no longer C.

A CLEAN EMBEDDED ARCHITECTURE IS A TESTABLE EMBEDDED ARCHITECTURE

Let's see how to apply some of the architectural principles to embedded software and firmware to help you eliminate the target-hardware bottleneck.

Layers

Layering comes in many flavors. Let's start with three layers, as shown in Figure 29.1. At the bottom, there is the hardware. As Doug warns us, due to technology advances and Moore's law, the hardware will change. Parts become obsolete, and new parts use less power or provide better performance or are cheaper. Whatever the reason, as an embedded engineer, I don't want to have a bigger job than is necessary when the inevitable hardware change finally happens.

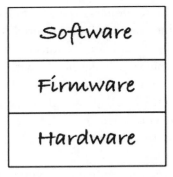

Figure 29.1 Three layers

The separation between hardware and the rest of the system is a given—at least once the hardware is defined (Figure 29.2). Here is where the problems often begin when you are trying to pass the App-titude test. There is nothing that keeps hardware knowledge from polluting all the code. If you are not careful about where you put things and what one module is allowed to know about another module, the code will be very hard to change. I'm not just talking about when the hardware changes, but when the user asks for a change, or when a bug needs to be fixed.

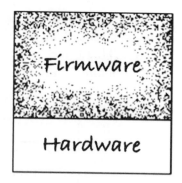

Figure 29.2 Hardware must be separated from the rest of the system

Software and firmware intermingling is an anti-pattern. Code exhibiting this anti-pattern will resist changes. In addition, changes will be dangerous, often leading to unintended consequences. Full regression tests of the whole system will be needed for minor changes. If you have not created externally instrumented tests, expect to get bored with manual tests—and then you can expect new bug reports.

The Hardware Is a Detail

The line between software and firmware is typically not so well defined as the line between code and hardware, as shown in Figure 29.3.

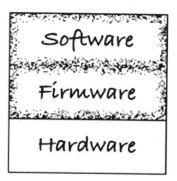

Figure 29.3 The line between software and firmware is a bit fuzzier than the line between code and hardware

One of your jobs as an embedded software developer is to firm up that line. The name of the boundary between the software and the firmware is the hardware abstraction layer (HAL) (Figure 29.4). This is not a new idea: It has been in PCs since the days before Windows.

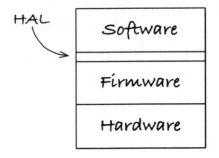

Figure 29.4 The hardware abstraction layer

The HAL exists for the software that sits on top of it, and its API should be tailored to that software's needs. As an example, the firmware can store bytes and arrays of bytes into flash memory. In contrast, the application needs to store and read name/value pairs to some persistence mechanism. The software should not be concerned that the name/value pairs are stored in flash memory, a spinning disk, the cloud, or core memory. The HAL provides a service, and it does not reveal to the software how it does it. The flash implementation is a detail that should be hidden from software.

As another example, an LED is tied to a GPIO bit. The firmware could provide access to the GPIO bits, where a HAL might provide Led_TurnOn(5). That is a pretty low-level hardware abstraction layer. Let's consider raising the level of abstraction from a hardware perspective to the software/product perspective. What is the LED indicating? Suppose that it indicated low battery power. At some level, the firmware (or a board support package) could provide Led_TurnOn(5), while the HAL provides Indicate_LowBattery(). You can see the HAL expressing services needed by the application. You can also see that layers may contain layers. It is more of a repeating fractal pattern than a limited set of predefined layers. The GPIO assignments are details that should be hidden from the software.

Don't Reveal Hardware Details to the User of the HAL

A clean embedded architecture's software is testable *off* the target hardware. A successful HAL provides that seam or set of substitution points that facilitate off-target testing.

The Processor Is a Detail

When your embedded application uses a specialized tool chain, it will often provide header files to <i>help you</i>.[4] These compilers often take liberties with the C language, adding new keywords to access their processor features. The code will look like C, but it is no longer C.

Sometimes vendor-supplied C compilers provide what look like global variables to give access directly to processor registers, IO ports, clock timers, IO bits, interrupt controllers, and other processor functions. It is helpful to get access to these things easily, but realize that any of your code that uses these helpful facilities is no longer C. It won't compile for another processor, or maybe even with a different compiler for the same processor.

I would hate to think that the silicon and tool provider is being cynical, tying your product to the compiler. Let's give the provider the benefit of a doubt by assuming that it is truly trying to help. But now it's up to you to use that help in a way that does not hurt in the future. You will have to limit which files are allowed to know about the C extensions.

Let's look at this header file designed for the ACME family of DSPs—you know, the ones used by Wile E. Coyote:

```
#ifndef _ACME_STD_TYPES
#define _ACME_STD_TYPES
```

---

4. This statement intentionally uses HTML.

```
#if defined(_ACME_X42)
    typedef unsigned int        Uint_32;
    typedef unsigned short      Uint_16;
    typedef unsigned char       Uint_8;

    typedef int                 Int_32;
    typedef short               Int_16;
    typedef char                Int_8;

#elif defined(_ACME_A42)
    typedef unsigned long       Uint_32;
    typedef unsigned int        Uint_16;
    typedef unsigned char       Uint_8;

    typedef long                Int_32;
    typedef int                 Int_16;
    typedef char                Int_8;
#else
    #error <acmetypes.h> is not supported for this environment
#endif


#endif
```

The `acmetypes.h` header file should not be used directly. If you do, your code gets tied to one of the ACME DSPs. You are using an ACME DSP, you say, so what is the harm? You can't compile your code unless you include this header. If you use the header and define _ACME_X42 or _ ACME_A42, your integers will be the wrong size if you try to test your code off-target. If that is not bad enough, one day you'll want to port your application to another processor, and you will have made that task much more difficult by not choosing portability and by not limiting what files know about ACME.

Instead of using `acmetypes.h`, you should try to follow a more standardized path and use `stdint.h`. But what if the target compiler does not provide `stdint.h`? You can write this header file. The `stdint.h` you write for target builds uses the `acmetypes.h` for target compiles like this:

```
#ifndef _STDINT_H_
#define _STDINT_H_

#include <acmetypes.h>

typedef Uint_32 uint32_t;
typedef Uint_16 uint16_t;
typedef Uint_8  uint8_t;

typedef Int_32  int32_t;
typedef Int_16  int16_t;
typedef Int_8   int8_t;

#endif
```

Having your embedded software and firmware use `stdint.h` helps keep your code clean and portable. Certainly, all of the *software* should be processor independent, but not all of the *firmware* can be. This next code snippet takes advantage of special extensions to C that gives your code access to the peripherals in the micro-controller. It's likely your product uses this micro-controller so that you can use its integrated peripherals. This function outputs a line that says "hi" to the serial output port. (This example is based on real code from the wild.)

```
void say_hi()
{
```

```
    IE = 0b11000000;
    SBUF0 = (0x68);
    while(TI_0 == 0);
    TI_0 = 0;
    SBUF0 = (0x69);
    while(TI_0 == 0);
    TI_0 = 0;
    SBUF0 = (0x0a);
    while(TI_0 == 0);
    TI_0 = 0;
    SBUF0 = (0x0d);
    while(TI_0 == 0);
    TI_0 = 0;
    IE = 0b11010000;
}
```

There are lots of problems with this small function. One thing that might jump out at you is the presence of 0b11000000. This binary notation is cool; can C do that? Unfortunately, no. A few other problems relate to this code directly using the custom C extensions:

IE: Interrupt enable bits.

SBUF0: Serial output buffer.

TI_0: Serial transmit buffer empty interrupt. Reading a 1 indicates the buffer is empty.

The uppercase variables actually access micro-controller built-in peripherals. If you want to control interrupts and output characters, you must use these peripherals. Yes, this is convenient—but it's not C.

A clean embedded architecture would use these device access registers directly in very few places and confine them totally to the *firmware*. Anything that knows about these registers becomes *firmware* and is consequently bound to the silicon. Tying code to the processor will hurt you when you want to get code working before you have stable hardware. It will also hurt you when you move your embedded application to a new processor.

If you use a micro-controller like this, your firmware could isolate these low-level functions with some form of a *processor abstraction layer* (PAL). Firmware above the PAL could be tested off-target, making it a little less firm.

The Operating System Is a Detail

A HAL is necessary, but is it sufficient? In bare-metal embedded systems, a HAL may be all you need to keep your code from getting too addicted to the operating environment. But what about embedded systems that use a real-time operating system (RTOS) or some embedded version of Linux or Windows?

To give your embedded code a good chance at a long life, you have to treat the operating system as a detail and protect against OS dependencies.

The software accesses the services of the operating environment through the OS. The OS is a layer separating the software from firmware (Figure 29.5). Using an OS directly can cause problems. For example, what if your RTOS supplier is bought by another company and the royalties go up, or the quality goes down? What if your needs change and your RTOS does not have the capabilities that you now require? You'll have to change lots of code. These won't just be simple syntactical changes due to the new OS's API, but will likely have to adapt semantically to the new OS's different capabilities and primitives.

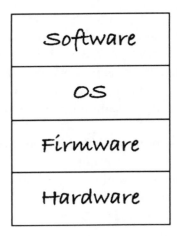

Figure 29.5 Adding in an operating system

A clean embedded architecture isolates software from the operating system, through an *operating system abstraction layer* (OSAL) (Figure 29.6). In some cases, implementing this layer might be as simple as changing the name of a function. In other cases, it might involve wrapping several functions together.

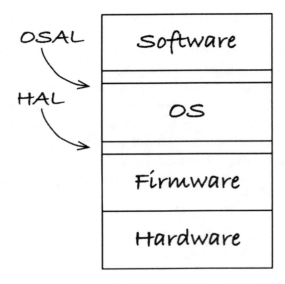

Figure 29.6 The operating system abstraction layer

If you have ever moved your software from one RTOS to another, you know it is painful. If your software depended on an OSAL instead of the OS directly, you would largely be writing a new OSAL that is compatible with the old OSAL. Which would you rather do: modify a bunch of complex existing code, or write new code to a defined interface and behavior? This is not a trick question. I choose the latter.

You might start worrying about code bloat about now. Really, though, the layer becomes the place where much of the duplication around using an OS is isolated. This duplication does not have to impose a big overhead. If you define an OSAL, you can also encourage your applications to have a common structure. You might provide message passing mechanisms, rather than having every thread handcraft its concurrency model.

The OSAL can help provide test points so that the valuable application code in the software layer can be tested off-target and off-OS. A clean embedded architecture's software is testable off the target operating system. A successful OSAL provides that seam or set of substitution points that facilitate off-target testing.

PROGRAMMING TO INTERFACES AND SUBSTITUTABILITY

In addition to adding a HAL and potentially an OSAL inside each of the major layers (software, OS, firmware, and hardware), you can—and should—apply the principles described throughout this book. These principles encourage separation of concerns, programming to interfaces, and substitutability.

The idea of a layered architecture is built on the idea of programming to interfaces. When one module interacts with another though an interface, you can substitute one service provider for another. Many readers will have written their own small version of `printf` for deployment in the target. As long as the interface to your `printf` is the same as the standard version of `printf`, you can override the service one for the other.

One basic rule of thumb is to use header files as interface definitions. When you do so, however, you have to be careful about what goes in the header file. Limit header file contents to function declarations as well as the constants and struct names that are needed by the function.

Don't clutter the interface header files with data structures, constants, and typedefs that are needed by only the implementation. It's not just a matter of clutter: That clutter will lead to unwanted dependencies. Limit the visibility of the implementation details. Expect the implementation details to change. The fewer places where code knows the details, the fewer places where code will have to be tracked down and modified.

A clean embedded architecture is testable within the layers because modules interact through interfaces. Each interface provides that seam or substitution point that facilitates off-target testing.

DRY CONDITIONAL COMPILATION DIRECTIVES

One use of substitutability that is often overlooked relates to how embedded C and C++ programs handle different targets or operating systems. There is a tendency to use conditional compilation to turn on and off segments of code. I recall one especially problematic case where the statement `#ifdef BOARD_V2` was mentioned several thousand times in a telecom application.

This repetition of code violates the Don't Repeat Yourself (DRY) principle.[5] If I see `#ifdef BOARD_V2` once, it's not really a problem. *Six thousand times* is an extreme problem. Conditional compilation identifying the target-hardware's type is often repeated in embedded systems. But what else can we do?

What if there is a hardware abstraction layer? The hardware type would become a detail hidden under the HAL. If the HAL provides a set of interfaces, instead of using conditional compilation, we could use the linker or some form of runtime binding to connect the software to the hardware.

---

5. Hunt and Thomas, *The Pragmatic Programmer*.

CONCLUSION

People who are developing embedded software have a lot to learn from experiences outside of embedded software. If you are an embedded developer who has picked up this book, you will find a wealth of software development wisdom in the words and ideas.

Letting all code become firmware is not good for your product's long-term health. Being able to test only in the target hardware is not good for your product's long-term health. A clean embedded architecture is good for your product's long-term health.

VI DETAILS

THE DATABASE IS A DETAIL

KOHNKE

From an architectural point of view, the database is a non-entity—it is a detail that does not rise to the level of an architectural element. Its relationship to the architecture of a software system is rather like the relationship of a doorknob to the architecture of your home.

I realize that these are fighting words. Believe me, I've had the fight. So let me be clear: I am not talking about the data model. The structure you give to the data within your application is highly significant to the architecture of your system. But the database is not the data model. The database is piece of software. The database is a utility that provides access to the data. From the architecture's point of view, that utility is irrelevant because it's a low-level detail—a mechanism. And a good architect does not allow low-level mechanisms to pollute the system architecture.

RELATIONAL DATABASES

Edgar Codd defined the principles of relational databases in 1970. By the mid-1980s, the relational model had grown to become the dominant form of data storage. There was a good reason for this popularity: The relational model is elegant, disciplined, and robust. It is an excellent data storage and access technology.

But no matter how brilliant, useful, and mathematically sound a technology it is, it is still just a technology. And that means it's a detail.

While relational tables may be convenient for certain forms of data access, there is nothing architecturally significant about arranging data into rows within tables. The use cases of your application should neither know nor care about such matters. Indeed, knowledge of the tabular structure of the data should be restricted to the lowest-level utility functions in the outer circles of the architecture.

Many data access frameworks allow database rows and tables to be passed around the system as objects. Allowing this is an architectural error. It couples the use cases, business rules, and in some cases even the UI to the relational structure of the data.

WHY ARE DATABASE SYSTEMS SO PREVALENT?

Why are software systems and software enterprises dominated by database systems? What accounts for the preeminence of Oracle, MySQL, and SQL Server? In a word: disks.

The rotating magnetic disk was the mainstay of data storage for five decades. Several generations of programmers have known no other form of data storage. Disk technology has grown from huge stacks of massive platters 48 inches in diameter that weighed thousands of pounds and held 20 megabytes, to single thin circles, 3 inches in diameter, that weigh just a few grams and hold a terabyte or more. *It's been a wild ride.* And throughout that ride programmers have been plagued by one fatal trait of disk technology: Disks are *slow*.

On a disk, data is stored within circular tracks. Those tracks are divided into sectors that hold a convenient number of bytes, often 4K. Each platter may have hundreds of tracks, and there can be a dozen or so platters. If you want to read a particular byte off the disk, you have to move the head to the proper track, wait for the disk to rotate to the proper sector, read all 4K of that sector into RAM, and then index into that RAM buffer to get the byte you want. And all that takes time—milliseconds of times.

Milliseconds might not seem like a lot, but a millisecond is a million times longer than the cycle time of most processors. If that data was not on a disk, it could be accessed in nanoseconds, instead of milliseconds.

To mitigate the time delay imposed by disks, you need indexes, caches, and optimized query schemes; and you need some kind of regular means of representing the data so that these indexes, caches, and query schemes know what they are working with. In short, you need a data access and management system. Over the years these systems have split into two distinct kinds: file systems and relational database management systems (RDBMS).

File systems are document based. They provide a natural and convenient way to store whole documents. They work well when you need to save and retrieve a set of documents by name, but they don't offer a lot of help when you're searching the content of those documents. It's easy to find a file named `login.c`, but it's hard, and slow, to find every `.c` file that has a variable named x in it.

Database systems are content based. They provide a natural and convenient way to find records based on their content. They are very good at associating multiple records based on some bit of content that they all share. Unfortunately, they are rather poor at storing and retrieving opaque documents.

Both of these systems organize the data on disk so that it can be stored and retrieved in as efficient a way as possible, given their particular access needs. Each has their own scheme for indexing and arranging the data. In addition, each eventually brings the relevant data into RAM, where it can be quickly manipulated.

WHAT IF THERE WERE NO DISK?

As prevalent as disks once were, they are now a dying breed. Soon they will have gone the way of tape drives, floppy drives, and CDs. They are being replaced by RAM.

Ask yourself this question: When all the disks are gone, and all your data is stored in RAM, how will you organize that data? Will you organize it into tables and access it with SQL? Will you organize it into files and access it through a directory?

Of course not. You'll organize it into linked lists, trees, hash tables, stacks, queues, or any of the other myriad data structures, and you'll access it using pointers or references—because *that's what programmers do*.

In fact, if you think carefully about this issue, you'll realize that this is what you already do. Even though the data is kept in a database or a file system, you read it into RAM and then you reorganize it, for your own convenience, into lists, sets, stacks, queues, trees, or whatever data structure meets your fancy. It is very unlikely that you leave the data in the form of files or tables.

DETAILS

This reality is why I say that the database is a detail. It's just a mechanism we use to move the data back and forth between the surface of the disk and RAM. The database is really nothing more than a big bucket of bits where we store our data on a long-term basis. But we seldom use the data in that form.

Thus, from an architectural viewpoint, we should not care about the form that the data takes while it is on the surface of a rotating magnetic disk. Indeed, we should not acknowledge that the disk exists at all.

BUT WHAT ABOUT PERFORMANCE?

Isn't performance an architectural concern? Of course it is—but when it comes to data storage, it's a concern that can be entirely encapsulated and separated from the business rules. Yes, we need to get the data in and out of the data store quickly, but that's a low-level concern. We can address that concern with low-level data access mechanisms. It has nothing whatsoever to do with the overall architecture of our systems.

ANECDOTE

In the late 1980s, I led a team of software engineers at a startup company that was trying to build and market a network management system that measured the communications integrity of T1 telecommunication lines. The system retrieved data from the devices at the endpoints of those lines, and then ran a series of predictive algorithms to detect and report problems.

We were using UNIX platforms, and we stored our data in simple random access files. We had no need of a relational database because our data had few content-based relationships. It was better kept in trees and linked lists in those random access files. In short, we kept the data in a form that was most convenient to load into RAM where it could be manipulated.

We hired a marketing manager for this startup—a nice and knowledgeable guy. But he immediately told me that we had to have a relational database in the system. It wasn't an option and it wasn't an engineering issue—it was a marketing issue.

This made no sense to me. Why in the world would I want to rearrange my linked lists and trees into a bunch of rows and tables accessed through SQL? Why would I introduce all the overhead and expense of a massive RDBMS when a simple random access file system was more than sufficient? So I fought him, tooth and nail.

We had a hardware engineer at this company who took up the RDBMS chant. He became convinced that our software system needed an RDBMS for technical reasons. He held meetings behind my back with the executives of the company, drawing stick figures on the whiteboard of a house balancing on a pole, and he would ask the executives, "Would you build a house on a pole?" His implied message was that an RDBMS that keeps its tables in random access files was somehow more reliable than the random access files that we were using.

I fought him. I fought the marketing guy. I stuck to my engineering principles in the face of incredible ignorance. I fought, and fought, and fought.

In the end, the hardware developer was promoted over my head to become the software manager. In the end, they put a RDBMS into that poor system. And, in the end, they were absolutely right and I was wrong.

Not for engineering reasons, mind you: I was right about that. I was right to fight against putting an RDBMS into the architectural core of the system. The reason I was wrong was because our customers expected us to have a relational database. They didn't know what they would do with it. They didn't have any realistic way of using the relational data in our system. But it didn't matter: Our customers fully expected an RDBMS. It had become a check box item that all the software purchasers had on their list. There was no engineering rationale—rationality had nothing to do with it. It was an irrational, external, and entirely baseless need, but it was no less real.

Where did that need come from? It originated from the highly effective marketing campaigns employed by the database vendors at the time. They had managed to convince high-level executives that their corporate "data assets" needed protection, and that the database systems they offered were the ideal means of providing that protection.

We see the same kind of marketing campaigns today. The word "enterprise" and the notion of "Service-Oriented Architecture" have much more to do with marketing than with reality.

What *should* I have done in that long-ago scenario? I should have bolted an RDBMS on the side of the system and provided some narrow and safe data access channel to it, while maintaining the random access files in the core of the system. What *did* I do? I quit and became a consultant.

CONCLUSION

The organizational structure of data, the data model, is architecturally significant. The technologies and systems that move data on and off a rotating magnetic surface are not. Relational database systems that force the data to be organized into tables and accessed with SQL have much more to do with the latter than with the former. The data is significant. The database is a detail.

THE WEB IS A DETAIL

Were you a developer in the 1990s? Do you remember how the web changed everything? Do you remember how we looked at our old client–server architectures with disdain in the face of the shiny new technology of The Web?

Actually the web didn't change anything. Or, at least, it shouldn't have. The web is just the latest in a series of oscillations that our industry has gone through since the 1960s. These oscillations move back and forth between putting all the computer power in central servers and putting all computer power out at the terminals.

We've seen several of these oscillations just in the last decade or so since the web became prominent. At first we thought all the computer power would be in server farms, and the browsers would be stupid. Then we started putting applets in the browsers. But we didn't like that, so we moved dynamic content back to the servers. But then we didn't like that, so we invented Web 2.0 and moved lots of processing back into the browser with Ajax and JavaScript. We went so far as to create whole huge applications written to execute in the browsers. And now we're all excited about pulling that JavaScript back into the server with Node.

(Sigh.)

THE ENDLESS PENDULUM

Of course, it would be incorrect to think that those oscillations started with the web. Before the web, there was client–server architecture. Before that, there were central minicomputers with arrays of dumb terminals. Before that, there were mainframes with smart green-screen terminals (that were very much analogous to modern-day browsers). Before that, there were computer rooms and punched cards …

And so the story goes. We can't seem to figure out where we want the computer power. We go back and forth between centralizing it and distributing it. And, I imagine, those oscillations will continue for some time to come.

When you look at it in the overall scope of IT history, the web didn't change anything at all. The web was simply one of many oscillations in a struggle that began before most of us were born and will continue well after most of us have retired.

As architects, though, we have to look at the long term. Those oscillations are just short-term issues that we want to push away from the central core of our business rules.

Let me tell you the story of company Q. Company Q built a very popular personal finance system. It was a desktop app with a very useful GUI. I loved using it.

Then came the web. In its next release, company Q changed the GUI to look, and behave, like a browser. I was thunderstruck! What marketing genius decided that personal finance software, running on a desktop, should have the look and feel of a web browser?

Of course, I hated the new interface. Apparently everyone else did, too—because after a few releases, company Q gradually removed the browser-like feel and turned its personal finance system back into a regular desktop GUI.

Now imagine you were a software architect at Q. Imagine that some marketing genius convinces upper management that the whole UI has to change to look more like the web. What do you do? Or, rather, what should you have done before this point to protect your application from that marketing genius?

You should have decoupled your business rules from your UI. I don't know whether the Q architects had done that. One day I'd love to hear their story. Had I been there at the time, I certainly would have lobbied very hard to isolate the business rules from the GUI, because you never know what the marketing geniuses will do next.

Now consider company A, which makes a lovely smartphone. Recently it released an upgraded version of its "operating system" (it's so strange that we can talk about the operating system inside a phone). Among other things, that "operating system" upgrade completely changed the look and feel of all the applications. Why? Some marketing genius said so, I suppose.

I'm not an expert on the software within that device, so I don't know if that change caused any significant difficulties for the programmers of the apps that run in company A's phone. I do hope the architects at A, and the architects of the apps, keep their UI and business rules isolated from each other, because there are always marketing geniuses out there just waiting to pounce on the next little bit of coupling you create.

THE UPSHOT

The upshot is simply this: The GUI is a detail. The web is a GUI. So the web is a detail. And, as an architect, you want to put details like that behind boundaries that keep them separate from your core business logic.

Think about it this way: *The WEB is an IO device*. In the 1960s, we learned the value of writing applications that were device independent. The motivation for that independence has not changed. The web is not an exception to that rule.

Or is it? The argument can be made that a GUI, like the web, is so unique and rich that it is absurd to pursue a device-independent architecture. When you think about the intricacies of JavaScript validation or drag-and-drop AJAX calls, or any of the plethora of other widgets and gadgets you can put on a web page, it's easy to argue that device independence is impractical.

To some extent, this is true. The interaction between the application and the GUI is "chatty" in ways that are quite specific to the kind of GUI you have. The dance between a browser and a web application is different from the dance between a desktop GUI and its application. Trying to abstract out that dance, the way devices are abstracted out of UNIX, seems unlikely to be possible.

But another boundary between the UI and the application *can* be abstracted. The business logic can be thought of as a suite of use cases, each of which performs some function on behalf of a user. Each use case can be described based on the input data, the processing preformed, and the output data.

At some point in the dance between the UI and the application, the input data can be said to be complete, allowing the use case to be executed. Upon completion, the resultant data can be fed back into the dance between the UI and the application.

The complete input data and the resultant output data can be placed into data structures and used as the input values and output values for a process that executes the use case. With this approach, we can consider each use case to be operating the IO device of the UI in a device-independent manner.

CONCLUSION

This kind of abstraction is not easy, and it will likely take several iterations to get just right. But it is possible. And since the world is full of marketing geniuses, it's not hard to make the case that it's often very necessary.

FRAMEWORKS ARE DETAILS

Frameworks have become quite popular. Generally speaking, this is a good thing. There are many frameworks out there that are free, powerful, and useful.

However, frameworks are not architectures—though some try to be.

FRAMEWORK AUTHORS

Most framework authors offer their work for free because they want to be helpful to the community. They want to give back. This is laudable. However, regardless of their high-minded motives, those authors do not have *your* best interests at heart. They can't, because they don't know you, and they don't know your problems.

Framework authors know their own problems, and the problems of their coworkers and friends. And they write their frameworks to solve *those* problems—not yours.

Of course, your problems will likely overlap with those other problems quite a bit. If this were not the case, frameworks would not be so popular. To the extent that such overlap exists, frameworks can be very useful indeed.

ASYMMETRIC MARRIAGE

The relationship between you and the framework author is extraordinarily asymmetric. You must make a huge commitment to the framework, but the framework author makes no commitment to you whatsoever.

Think about this point carefully. When you use a framework, you read through the documentation that the author of that framework provides. In that documentation, the author, and other users of that framework, advise you on how to integrate your software with the framework. Typically, this means wrapping your architecture around that framework. The author recommends that you derive from the framework's base classes, and import the framework's facilities into your business objects. The author urges you to *couple* your application to the framework as tightly as possible.

For the framework author, coupling to his or her own framework is not a risk. The author *wants* to couple to that framework, because the author has absolute control over that framework.

What's more, the author wants *you* to couple to the framework, because once coupled in this way, it is very hard to break away. Nothing feels more validating to a framework author than a bunch of users willing to inextricably derive from the author's base classes.

In effect, the author is asking you to marry the framework—to make a huge, long-term commitment to that framework. And yet, under no circumstances will the author make a corresponding commitment to you. It's a one-directional marriage. You take on all the risk and burden; the framework author takes on nothing at all.

THE RISKS

What are the risks? Here are just a few for you to consider.

- The architecture of the framework is often not very clean. Frameworks tend to violate he Dependency Rule. They ask you to inherit their code into your business objects—your Entities! They want their framework coupled into that innermost circle. Once in, that framework isn't coming back out. The wedding ring is on your finger; and it's going to stay there.
- The framework may help you with some early features of your application. However, as your product matures, it may outgrow the facilities of the framework. If you've put on that wedding ring, you'll find the framework fighting you more and more as time passes.

- The framework may evolve in a direction that you don't find helpful. You may be stuck upgrading to new versions that don't help you. You may even find old features, which you made use of, disappearing or changing in ways that are difficult for you to keep up with.

- A new and better framework may come along that you wish you could switch to.

THE SOLUTION

What is the solution?

> *Don't marry the framework!*

Oh, you can *use* the framework—just don't couple to it. Keep it at arm's length. Treat the framework as a detail that belongs in one of the outer circles of the architecture. Don't let it into the inner circles.

If the framework wants you to derive your business objects from its base classes, say no! Derive proxies instead, and keep those proxies in components that are *plugins* to your business rules.

Don't let frameworks into your core code. Instead, integrate them into components that plug in to your core code, following the Dependency Rule.

For example, maybe you like Spring. Spring is a good dependency injection framework. Maybe you use Spring to auto-wire your dependencies. That's fine, but you should not sprinkle @autowired annotations all throughout your business objects. Your business objects should not know about Spring.

Instead, you can use Spring to inject dependencies into your Main component. It's OK for Main to know about Spring since Main is the dirtiest, lowest-level component in the architecture.

I Now Pronounce You ...

There are some frameworks that you simply must marry. If you are using C++, for example, you will likely have to marry STL—it's hard to avoid. If you are using Java, you will almost certainly have to marry the standard library.

That's normal—but it should still be a *decision*. You must understand that when you marry a framework to your application, you will be stuck with that framework for the rest of the life cycle of that application. For better or for worse, in sickness and in health, for richer, for poorer, forsaking all others, you *will* be using that framework. This is not a commitment to be entered into lightly.

Conclusion

When faced with a framework, try not to marry it right away. See if there aren't ways to date it for a while before you take the plunge. Keep the framework behind an architectural boundary if at all possible, for as long as possible. Perhaps you can find a way to get the milk without buying the cow.

Case Study: Video Sales

33

VCR TAPES

KOHNKE

Now it's time to put these rules and thoughts about architecture together into a case study. This case study will be short and simple, yet will depict both the process a good architect uses and the decisions that such an architect makes.

THE PRODUCT

For this case study, I've chosen a product with which I am rather intimately familiar: the software for a website that sells videos. Of course, it is reminiscent of cleancoders.com, the site where I sell my software tutorial videos.

The basic idea is trivial. We have a batch of videos we want to sell. We sell them, on the web, to both individuals and businesses. Individuals can pay one price to stream the videos, and another, higher price to download those videos and own them permanently. Business licenses are streaming only, and are purchased in batches that allow quantity discounts.

Individuals typically act as both the viewers and the purchasers. Businesses, in contrast, often have people who buy the videos that other people will watch.

Video authors need to supply their video files, written descriptions, and ancillary files with exams, problems, solutions, source code, and other materials.

Administrators need to add new video series, add and delete videos to and from the series, and establish prices for various licenses.

Our first step in determining the initial architecture of the system is to identify the actors and use cases.

USE CASE ANALYSIS

Figure 33.1 shows a typical use-case analysis.

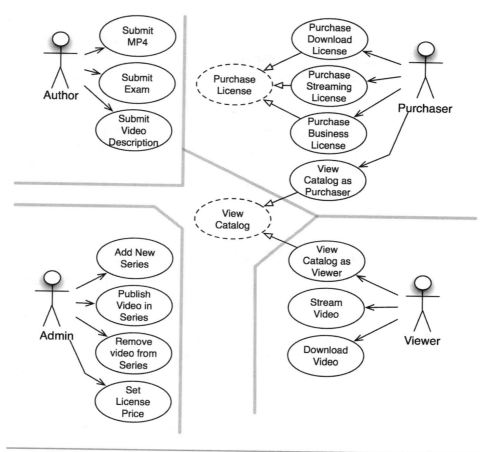

Figure 33.1 A typical use-case analysis

The four main actors are evident. According to the Single Responsibility Principle, these four actors will be the four primary sources of change for the system. Every time some new feature is added, or some existing feature is changed, that step will be taken to serve one of these actors. Therefore we want to partition the system such that a change to one actor does not affect any of the other actors.

The use cases shown in Figure 33.1 are not a complete list. For example, you won't find log-in or log-out use cases. The reason for this omission is simply to manage the size of the problem in this book. If I were to include all the different use cases, then this chapter would have to turn into a book in its own right.

Note the dashed use cases in the center of Figure 33.1. They are *abstract*[1] use cases. An abstract use case is one that sets a general policy that another use case will flesh out. As you can see, the *View Catalog as Viewer* and *View Catalog as Purchaser* use cases both inherit from the *View Catalog* abstract use case.

On the one hand, it was not strictly necessary for me to create that abstraction. I could have left the abstract use case out of the diagram without compromising any of the features of the overall product. On the other hand, these two use cases are *so similar* that I thought it wise to recognize the similarity and find a way to unify it early in the analysis.

COMPONENT ARCHITECTURE

Now that we know the actors and use cases, we can create a preliminary component architecture (Figure 33.2).

The double lines in the drawing represent architectural boundaries as usual. You can see the typical partitioning of views, presenters, interactors, and controllers. You can also see that I've broken each of those categories up by their corresponding actors.

Each of the components in Figure 33.2 represents a potential `.jar` file or `.dll` file. Each of those components will contain the views, presenters, interactors, and controllers that have been allocated to it.

Note the special components for the `Catalog View` and the `Catalog Presenter`. This is how I dealt with the abstract *View Catalog* use case. I assume that those views and presenters will be coded into abstract classes within those components, and that the inheriting components will contain view and presenter classes that will inherit from those abstract classes.

---

1. This is my own notation for "abstract" use cases. It would have been more standard to use a UML stereotype such as <>, but I don't find adhering to such standards very useful nowadays.

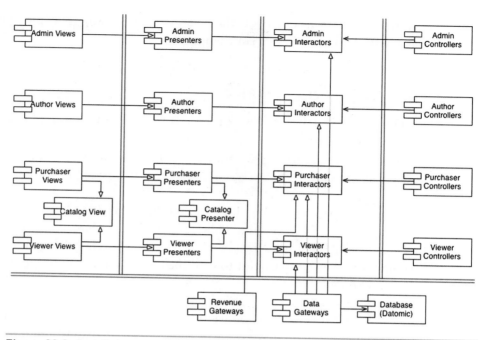

Figure 33.2 A preliminary component architecture

Would I really break the system up into all these components, and deliver them as .jar or .dll files? Yes and no. I would certainly break the compile and build environment up this way, so that I *could* build independent deliverables like that. I would also reserve the right to combine all those deliverables into a smaller number of deliverables if necessary. For example, given the partitioning in Figure 33.2, it would be easy to combine them into five .jar files—one for views, presenters, interactors, controllers, and utilities, respectively. I could then independently deploy the components that are most likely to change independently of each other.

Another possible grouping would be to put the views and presenters together into the same .jar file, and put the interactors, controllers, and utilities in their own .jar file. Still another, even more primitive, grouping would be to create two .jar files, with views and presenters in one file, and everything else in the other.

Keeping these options open will allow us to adapt the way we deploy the system based on how the system changes over time.

DEPENDENCY MANAGEMENT

The flow of control in Figure 33.2 proceeds from right to left. Input occurs at the controllers, and that input is processed into a result by the interactors. The presenters then format the results, and the views display those presentations.

Notice that the arrows do not all flow from the right to the left. In fact, most of them point from left to right. This is because the architecture is following the *Dependency Rule*. All dependencies cross the boundary lines in one direction, and they always point toward the components containing the higher-level policy.

Also notice that the *using* relationships (open arrows) point *with* the flow of control, and that the *inheritance* relationships (closed arrows) point *against* the flow of control. This depicts our use of the Open–Closed Principle to make sure that the dependencies flow in the right direction, and that changes to low-level details do not ripple upward to affect high-level policies.

CONCLUSION

The architecture diagram in Figure 33.2 includes two dimensions of separation. The first is the separation of actors based on the Single Responsibility Principle; the second is the Dependency Rule. The goal of both is to separate components that change for different reasons, and at different rates. The different reasons correspond to the actors; the different rates correspond to the different levels of policy.

Once you have structured the code this way, you can mix and match how you want to actually deploy the system. You can group the components into deployable deliverables in any way that makes sense, and easily change that grouping when conditions change.

THE MISSING CHAPTER

34

By Simon Brown

All of the advice you've read so far will certainly help you design better software, composed of classes and components with well-defined boundaries, clear responsibilities, and controlled dependencies. But it turns out that the devil is in the implementation details, and it's really easy to fall at the last hurdle if you don't give that some thought, too.

Let's imagine that we're building an online book store, and one of the use cases we've been asked to implement is about customers being able to view the status of their orders. Although this is a Java example, the principles apply equally to other programming languages. Let's put the Clean Architecture to one side for a moment and look at a number of approaches to design and code organization.

PACKAGE BY LAYER

The first, and perhaps simplest, design approach is the traditional horizontal layered architecture, where we separate our code based on what it does from a technical perspective. This is often called "package by layer." Figure 34.1 shows what this might look like as a UML class diagram.

In this typical layered architecture, we have one layer for the web code, one layer for our "business logic," and one layer for persistence. In other words, code is sliced horizontally into layers, which are used as a way to group similar types of things. In a "strict layered architecture," layers should depend only on the next adjacent lower layer. In Java, layers are typically implemented as packages. As you can see in Figure 34.1, all of the dependencies between layers (packages) point downward. In this example, we have the following Java types:

- OrdersController: A web controller, something like a Spring MVC controller, that handles requests from the web.

- OrdersService: An interface that defines the "business logic" related to orders.

- OrdersServiceImpl: The implementation of the orders service.[1]

---

1. This is arguably a horrible way to name a class, but as we'll see later, perhaps it doesn't really matter.

- `OrdersRepository`: An interface that defines how we get access to persistent order information.
- `JdbcOrdersRepository`: An implementation of the repository interface.

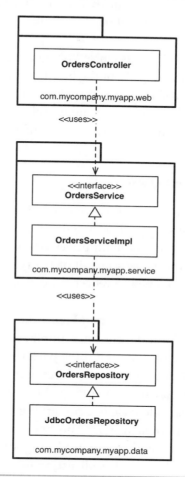

Figure 34.1 Package by layer

In "Presentation Domain Data Layering,"[2] Martin Fowler says that adopting such a layered architecture is a good way to get started. He's not alone. Many of the books, tutorials, training courses, and sample code you'll find will also

---

2. https://martinfowler.com/bliki/PresentationDomainDataLayering.html.

point you down the path of creating a layered architecture. It's a very quick way to get something up and running without a huge amount of complexity. The problem, as Martin points out, is that once your software grows in scale and complexity, you will quickly find that having three large buckets of code isn't sufficient, and you will need to think about modularizing further.

Another problem is that, as Uncle Bob has already said, a layered architecture doesn't scream anything about the business domain. Put the code for two layered architectures, from two very different business domains, side by side and they will likely look eerily similar: web, services, and repositories. There's also another huge problem with layered architectures, but we'll get to that later.

PACKAGE BY FEATURE

Another option for organizing your code is to adopt a "package by feature" style. This is a vertical slicing, based on related features, domain concepts, or aggregate roots (to use domain-driven design terminology). In the typical implementations that I've seen, all of the types are placed into a single Java package, which is named to reflect the concept that is being grouped.

With this approach, as shown in Figure 34.2, we have the same interfaces and classes as before, but they are all placed into a single Java package rather than being split among three packages. This is a very simple refactoring from the "package by layer" style, but the top-level organization of the code now screams something about the business domain. We can now see that this code base has something to do with orders rather than the web, services, and repositories. Another benefit is that it's potentially easier to find all of the code that you need to modify in the event that the "view orders" use case changes. It's all sitting in a single Java package rather than being spread out.[3]

I often see software development teams realize that they have problems with horizontal layering ("package by layer") and switch to vertical layering

---

3. This benefit is much less relevant with the navigation facilities of modern IDEs, but it seems there has been a renaissance moving back to lightweight text editors, for reasons I am clearly too old to understand.

("package by feature") instead. In my opinion, both are suboptimal. If you've read this book so far, you might be thinking that we can do much better—and you're right.

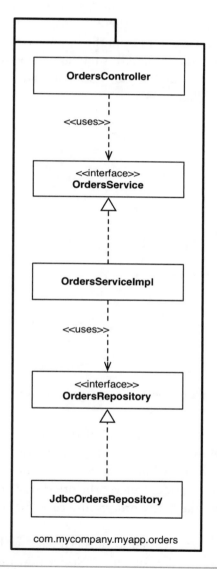

Figure 34.2 Package by feature

PORTS AND ADAPTERS

As Uncle Bob has said, approaches such as "ports and adapters," the "hexagonal architecture," "boundaries, controllers, entities," and so on aim to create architectures where business/domain-focused code is independent and separate from the technical implementation details such as frameworks and databases. To summarize, you often see such code bases being composed of an "inside" (domain) and an "outside" (infrastructure), as suggested in Figure 34.3.

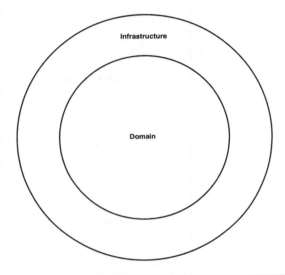

Figure 34.3 A code base with an inside and an outside

The "inside" region contains all of the domain concepts, whereas the "outside" region contains the interactions with the outside world (e.g., UIs, databases, third-party integrations). The major rule here is that the "outside" depends on the "inside"—never the other way around. Figure 34.4 shows a version of how the "view orders" use case might be implemented.

The com.mycompany.myapp.domain package here is the "inside," and the other packages are the "outside." Notice how the dependencies flow toward the "inside." The keen-eyed reader will notice that the OrdersRepository from previous diagrams has been renamed to simply be Orders. This comes from the world of domain-driven design, where the advice is that the naming of everything on the "inside" should be stated in terms of the "ubiquitous domain language." To put that another way, we talk about "orders" when we're having a discussion about the domain, not the "orders repository."

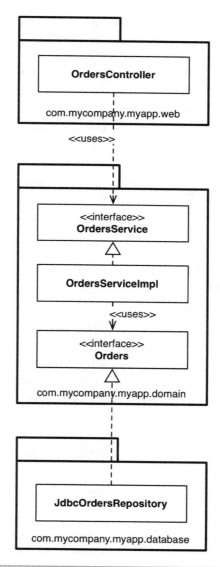

Figure 34.4 View orders use case

It's also worth pointing out that this is a simplified version of what the UML class diagram might look like, because it's missing things like interactors and objects to marshal the data across the dependency boundaries.

PACKAGE BY COMPONENT

Although I agree wholeheartedly with the discussions about SOLID, REP, CCP, and CRP and most of the advice in this book, I come to a slightly different conclusion about how to organize code. So I'm going to present another option here, which I call "package by component." To give you some background, I've spent most of my career building enterprise software, primarily in Java, across a number of different business domains. Those software systems have varied immensely, too. A large number have been web-based, but others have been client–server[4], distributed, message-based, or something else. Although the technologies differed, the common theme was that the architecture for most of these software systems was based on a traditional layered architecture.

I've already mentioned a couple of reasons why layered architectures should be considered bad, but that's not the whole story. The purpose of a layered architecture is to separate code that has the same sort of function. Web stuff is separated from business logic, which is in turn separated from data access. As we saw from the UML class diagram, from an implementation perspective, a layer typically equates to a Java package. From a code accessibility perspective, for the `OrdersController` to be able to have a dependency on the `OrdersService` interface, the `OrdersService` interface needs to be marked as `public`, because they are in different packages. Likewise, the `OrdersRepository` interface needs to be marked as `public` so that it can be seen outside of the repository package, by the `OrdersServiceImpl` class.

---

4. My first job after graduating from university in 1996 was building client–server desktop applications with a technology called PowerBuilder, a super-productive 4GL that exceled at building database-driven applications. A couple of years later, I was building client–server applications with Java, where we had to build our own database connectivity (this was pre-JDBC) and our own GUI toolkits on top of AWT. That's "progress" for you!

In a strict layered architecture, the dependency arrows should always point downward, with layers depending only on the next adjacent lower layer. This comes back to creating a nice, clean, acyclic dependency graph, which is achieved by introducing some rules about how elements in a code base should depend on each other. The big problem here is that we can cheat by introducing some undesirable dependencies, yet still create a nice, acyclic dependency graph.

Suppose that you hire someone new who joins your team, and you give the newcomer another `orders`-related use case to implement. Since the person is new, he wants to make a big impression and get this use case implemented as quickly as possible. After sitting down with a cup of coffee for a few minutes, the newcomer discovers an existing `OrdersController` class, so he decides that's where the code for the new `orders`-related web page should go. But it needs some `orders` data from the database. The newcomer has an epiphany: "Oh, there's an `OrdersRepository` interface already built, too. I can simply dependency-inject the implementation into my controller. Perfect!" After a few more minutes of hacking, the web page is working. But the resulting UML diagram looks like Figure 34.5.

The dependency arrows still point downward, but the `OrdersController` is now additionally bypassing the `OrdersService` for some use cases. This organization is often called a *relaxed layered architecture*, as layers are allowed to skip around their adjacent neighbor(s). In some situations, this is the intended outcome—if you're trying to follow the CQRS[5] pattern, for example. In many other cases, bypassing the business logic layer is undesirable, especially if that business logic is responsible for ensuring authorized access to individual records, for example.

While the new use case works, it's perhaps not implemented in the way that we were expecting. I see this happen a lot with teams that I visit as a consultant, and it's usually revealed when teams start to visualize what their code base really looks like, often for the first time.

---

5. In the *Command Query Responsibility Segregation* pattern, you have separate patterns for updating and reading data.

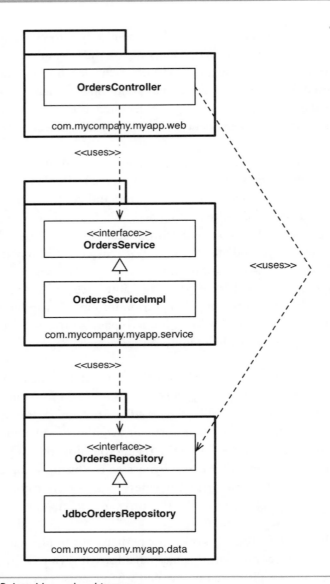

Figure 34.5 Relaxed layered architecture

What we need here is a guideline—an architectural principle—that says something like, "Web controllers should never access repositories directly." The question, of course, is enforcement. Many teams I've met simply say, "We enforce this principle through good discipline and code reviews, because we trust our developers." This confidence is great to hear, but we all know what happens when budgets and deadlines start looming ever closer.

A far smaller number of teams tell me that they use static analysis tools (e.g., NDepend, Structure101, Checkstyle) to check and automatically enforce architecture violations at build time. You may have seen such rules yourself; they usually manifest themselves as regular expressions or wildcard strings that state "types in package **/web should not access types in **/data"; and they are executed after the compilation step.

This approach is a little crude, but it can do the trick, reporting violations of the architecture principles that you've defined as a team and (you hope) failing the build. The problem with both approaches is that they are fallible, and the feedback loop is longer than it should be. If left unchecked, this practice can turn a code base into a "big ball of mud."[6] I'd personally like to use the compiler to enforce my architecture if at all possible.

This brings us to the "package by component" option. It's a hybrid approach to everything we've seen so far, with the goal of bundling all of the responsibilities related to a single coarse-grained component into a single Java package. It's about taking a service-centric view of a software system, which is something we're seeing with micro-service architectures as well. In the same way that ports and adapters treat the web as just another delivery mechanism, "package by component" keeps the user interface separate from these coarse-grained components. Figure 34.6 shows what the "view orders" use case might look like.

In essence, this approach bundles up the "business logic" and persistence code into a single thing, which I'm calling a "component." Uncle Bob presented his definition of "component" earlier in the book, saying:

> Components are the units of deployment. They are the smallest entities that can be deployed as part of a system. In Java, they are jar files.

---

6. http://www.laputan.org/mud/

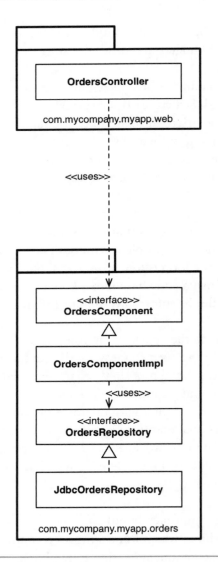

Figure 34.6 View orders use case

My definition of a component is slightly different: "A grouping of related functionality behind a nice clean interface, which resides inside an execution environment like an application." This definition comes from my "C4 software architecture model,"[7] which is a simple hierarchical way to think about the static structures of a software system in terms of containers, components, and classes (or code). It says that a software system is made up of one or more containers (e.g., web applications, mobile apps, stand-alone applications, databases, file systems), each of which contains one or more components, which in turn are implemented by one or more classes (or code). Whether each component resides in a separate jar file is an orthogonal concern.

A key benefit of the "package by component" approach is that if you're writing code that needs to do something with `orders`, there's just one place to go—the `OrdersComponent`. Inside the component, the separation of concerns is still maintained, so the business logic is separate from data persistence, but that's a component implementation detail that consumers don't need to know about. This is akin to what you might end up with if you adopted a micro-services or Service-Oriented Architecture—a separate `OrdersService` that encapsulates everything related to handling orders. The key difference is the decoupling mode. You can think of well-defined components in a monolithic application as being a stepping stone to a micro-services architecture.

THE DEVIL IS IN THE IMPLEMENTATION DETAILS

On the face of it, the four approaches do all look like different ways to organize code and, therefore, could be considered different architectural styles. This perception starts to unravel very quickly if you get the implementation details wrong, though.

Something I see on a regular basis is an overly liberal use of the `public` access modifier in languages such as Java. It's almost as if we, as developers, instinctively use the `public` keyword without thinking. It's in our muscle memory. If you don't believe me, take a look at the code samples for books, tutorials, and open source frameworks on GitHub. This tendency is apparent, regardless of which architectural style a code base is aiming to adopt— horizontal layers, vertical layers, ports and adapters, or something else.

---

7. See https://www.structurizr.com/help/c4 for more information.

Marking all of your types as `public` means you're not taking advantage of the facilities that your programming language provides with regard to encapsulation. In some cases, there's literally nothing preventing somebody from writing some code to instantiate a concrete implementation class directly, violating the intended architecture style.

ORGANIZATION VERSUS ENCAPSULATION

Looking at this issue another way, if you make all types in your Java application `public`, the packages are simply an organization mechanism (a grouping, like folders), rather than being used for encapsulation. Since public types can be used from anywhere in a code base, you can effectively ignore the packages because they provide very little real value. The net result is that if you ignore the packages (because they don't provide any means of encapsulation and hiding), it doesn't really matter which architectural style you're aspiring to create. If we look back at the example UML diagrams, the Java packages become an irrelevant detail if all of the types are marked as `public`. In essence, all four architectural approaches presented earlier in this chapter are exactly the same when we overuse this designation (Figure 34.7).

Take a close look at the arrows between each of the types in Figure 34.7: They're all identical regardless of which architectural approach you're trying to adopt. Conceptually the approaches are very different, but syntactically they are identical. Furthermore, you could argue that when you make all of the types `public`, what you really have are just four ways to describe a traditional horizontally layered architecture. This is a neat trick, and of course nobody would ever make all of their Java types `public`. Except when they do. And I've seen it.

The access modifiers in Java are not perfect,[8] but ignoring them is just asking for trouble. The way Java types are placed into packages can actually make a huge difference to how accessible (or inaccessible) those types can be when

---

8. In Java, for example, although we tend to think of packages as being hierarchical, it's not possible to create access restrictions based on a package and subpackage relationship. Any hierarchy that you create is in the name of those packages, and the directory structure on disk, only.

Java's access modifiers are applied appropriately. If I bring the packages back and mark (by graphically fading) those types where the access modifier can be made more restrictive, the picture becomes pretty interesting (Figure 34.8).

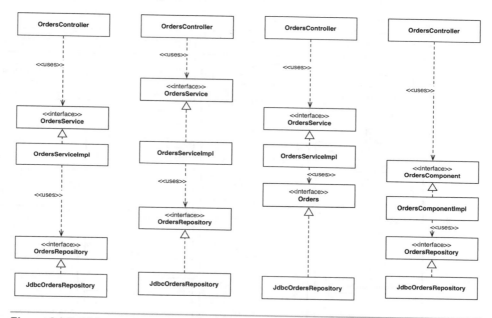

Figure 34.7 All four architectural approaches are the same

Moving from left to right, in the "package by layer" approach, the `OrdersService` and `OrdersRepository` interfaces need to be `public`, because they have inbound dependencies from classes outside of their defining package. In contrast, the implementation classes (`OrdersServiceImpl` and `JdbcOrdersRepository`) can be made more restrictive (package protected). Nobody needs to know about them; they are an implementation detail.

In the "package by feature" approach, the `OrdersController` provides the sole entry point into the package, so everything else can be made package protected. The big caveat here is that nothing else in the code base, outside of this package, can access information related to orders unless they go through the controller. This may or may not be desirable.

In the ports and adapters approach, the `OrdersService` and `Orders` interfaces have inbound dependencies from other packages, so they need to be made `public`. Again, the implementation classes can be made package protected and dependency injected at runtime.

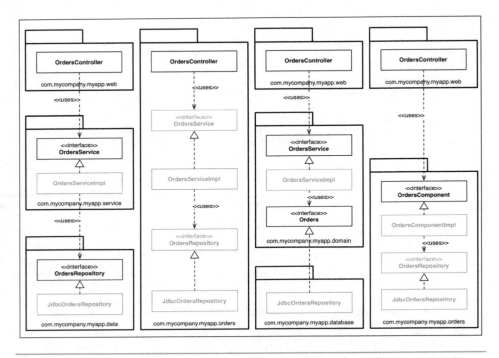

Figure 34.8 Grayed-out types are where the access modifier can be made more restrictive

Finally, in the "package by component" approach, the `OrdersComponent` interface has an inbound dependency from the controller, but everything else can be made package protected. The fewer `public` types you have, the smaller the number of potential dependencies. There's now no way[9] that code outside this package can use the `OrdersRepository` interface or implementation directly, so we can rely on the compiler to enforce this architectural principle. You can do the same thing in .NET with the `internal` keyword, although you would need to create a separate assembly for every component.

9. Unless you cheat and use Java's reflection mechanism, but please don't do that!

Just to be absolutely clear, what I've described here relates to a monolithic application, where all of the code resides in a single source code tree. If you are building such an application (and many people are), I would certainly encourage you to lean on the compiler to enforce your architectural principles, rather than relying on self-discipline and post-compilation tooling.

OTHER DECOUPLING MODES

In addition to the programming language you're using, there are often other ways that you can decouple your source code dependencies. With Java, you have module frameworks like OSGi and the new Java 9 module system. With module systems, when used properly, you can make a distinction between types that are `public` and types that are *published*. For example, you could create an `Orders` module where all of the types are marked as `public`, but publish only a small subset of those types for external consumption. It's been a long time coming, but I'm enthusiastic that the Java 9 module system will give us another tool to build better software, and spark people's interest in design thinking once again.

Another option is to decouple your dependencies at the source code level, by splitting code across *different source code trees*. If we take the ports and adapters example, we could have three source code trees:

- The source code for the business and domain (i.e., everything that is independent of technology and framework choices): `OrdersService`, `OrdersServiceImpl`, and `Orders`
- The source code for the web: `OrdersController`
- The source code for the data persistence: `JdbcOrdersRepository`

The latter two source code trees have a compile-time dependency on the business and domain code, which itself doesn't know anything about the web or the data persistence code. From an implementation perspective, you can do this by configuring separate modules or projects in your build tool (e.g., Maven, Gradle, MSBuild). Ideally you would repeat this pattern, having a separate source code tree for each and every component in your application.

This is very much an idealistic solution, though, because there are real-world performance, complexity, and maintenance issues associated with breaking up your source code in this way.

A simpler approach that some people follow for their ports and adapters code is to have just two source code trees:

• Domain code (the "inside")
• Infrastructure code (the "outside")

This maps on nicely to the diagram (Figure 34.9) that many people use to summarize the ports and adapters architecture, and there is a compile-time dependency from the infrastructure to the domain.

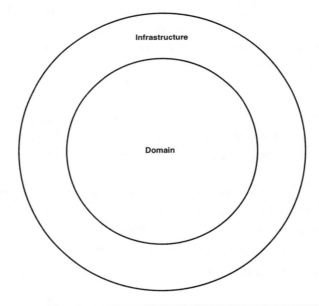

Figure 34.9 Domain and infrastructure code

This approach to organizing source code will also work, but be aware of the potential trade-off. It's what I call the "Périphérique anti-pattern of ports and adapters." The city of Paris, France, has a ring road called the Boulevard Périphérique, which allows you to circumnavigate Paris without entering the complexities of the city. Having all of your infrastructure code in a single source code tree means that it's potentially possible for infrastructure code in one area of your application (e.g., a web controller) to directly call code in another area of your application (e.g., a database repository), without navigating through the domain. This is especially true if you've forgotten to apply appropriate access modifiers to that code.

CONCLUSION: THE MISSING ADVICE

The whole point of this chapter is to highlight that your best design intentions can be destroyed in a flash if you don't consider the intricacies of the implementation strategy. Think about how to map your desired design on to code structures, how to organize that code, and which decoupling modes to apply during runtime and compile-time. Leave options open where applicable, but be pragmatic, and take into consideration the size of your team, their skill level, and the complexity of the solution in conjunction with your time and budgetary constraints. Also think about using your compiler to help you enforce your chosen architectural style, and watch out for coupling in other areas, such as data models. The devil is in the implementation details.

Afterword

My professional career as a software developer began in the 1990s, at a time when the dinosaurs of Big Architecture ruled the world. To get ahead, you had to learn about objects and components, about design patterns, and about the Unified Modeling Language (and its precursors).

Projects—and boy, should we rue the day when we decided to call them that?—started with long design phases, where detailed blueprints for our systems were laid out by "senior" programmers for more "junior" programmers to follow. Which, of course, they didn't. Ever.

And so it was that, after rising to the lofty ranks of "software architect"—and then "lead architect," "chief architect," "Lord Architect of the Privy Council," and all the other highfalutin titles we gave ourselves back in the day—I seemed doomed to spend my days connecting boxes with arrows and coding with PowerPoint, and having barely any impact on the real code itself.

It struck me then that this was nonsense; every line of code contains at least one design decision, and therefore anyone who writes code has a much greater impact on the quality of the software than a PowerPoint jockey like me ever could.

And then, thankfully, the Agile Software Development revolution arrived and put architects like me out of our misery. I'm a programmer. I like programming. And the best way I've found to have a positive impact on code is to write it.

The dinosaurs of Big Architecture—typically to be found wandering the primeval plains of Big Process—were wiped out by the asteroid of Extreme Programming. And it came as a blessed relief.

Development teams were set free to focus on what matters and to concentrate their efforts on things that add value. Instead of waiting weeks or months for a Big Architecture document so they could dutifully ignore it and write the code they were going to write anyway, teams could just agree to a test with their customer, have a quick design session to get their bearings, and then write the code they were going to write anyway.

The Big Architecture dinosaurs were gone, and small, nimble Just-Enough-Design-Up-Front-with-Plenty-of-Refactoring mammals replaced us. Software architecture became responsive.

Well, that was the theory, anyway.

The problem with leaving architecture to programmers is that programmers have to be able to think like architects. It turns out that not all of the stuff we learned during the Big Architecture era was of no value. The way that software is structured can have a profound impact on our ability to keep adapting and evolving it, even in the short term.

Every design decision needs to leave the door open for future changes. Like playing pool, each shot isn't just about sinking that ball; it's also about lining up the next shot. Writing working code that doesn't block future code is a non-trivial skillset. It takes years to master.

And so, the era of Big Architecture gave way to a new era of Fragile Architecture: designs that grew quickly to deliver value sooner, but that made sustaining that pace of innovation very difficult.

It's all very well talking about "embracing change," but if it costs $500 to change a line of code, change ain't happening.

Bob Martin's original papers on OO design principles had a big impact on me as a young software developer. I looked at my code with a fresh perspective, and noticed problems that—until then—never seemed like problems to me.

Now you've seen how it's possible to write code that delivers value today without blocking future value tomorrow; the onus is on you to put in the practice so you can apply these principles to your own code.

Like riding a bicycle, you can't master software design just by reading about it. To get the best from a book like this, you need to get practical. Analyze your code and look for the kinds of problems Bob highlights, then practice refactoring the code to fix these problems. If you're new to the refactoring discipline, then this will be a doubly valuable experience.

Learn how you can incorporate design principles and Clean Architecture into your development processes, so that new code is less likely to cause pain. For example, if you're doing TDD, make a point of having a little design review after passing each test, and clean up as you go. (It's way cheaper than fixing bad designs later.) Perhaps, before you commit code, ask a colleague to review it with you. And look into the possibility of adding a code "quality gate" to your build pipeline as a last line of defense against unclean architecture. (And if you don't have a build pipeline, maybe it's time to create one?)

Most important of all is to talk about Clean Architecture. Talk about it with your team. Talk about it with the wider developer community. Quality is everybody's business, and it's important to reach a consensus about the difference between good and bad architecture.

Be mindful that most software developers are not very architecture-aware, just as I wasn't 25 years ago. More experienced developers clued me into it. Once you've wrapped your head around Clean Architecture, take the time to wrap someone else's head around it. Pay it forward.

While the technology landscape for developers evolves continuously, foundational principles like the ones described here rarely change. I have little doubt that this is a book that's going to stay on your shelf for many years after your copy of *Lean JSON Cloud NoSQL for Dummies* has ended up in a yard sale. I hope it does for your Design Fu what Bob's original papers did for mine.

The real journey starts here.

—*Jason Gorman*
January 26, 2017

VII

APPENDIX

ARCHITECTURE
ARCHAEOLOGY

To unearth the principles of good architecture, let's take a 45-year journey through some of the projects I have worked on since 1970. Some of these projects are interesting from an architectural point of view. Others are interesting because of the lessons learned and because of how they fed into subsequent projects.

This appendix is somewhat autobiographical. I've tried to keep the discussion relevant to the topic of architecture; but, as in anything autobiographical, other factors sometimes intrude. ;-)

UNION ACCOUNTING SYSTEM

In the late 1960s, a company by the name of ASC Tabulating signed a contract with Local 705 of the Teamsters Union to provide an accounting system. The computer ASC chose to implement this system on was a GE Datanet 30, as shown in Figure A.1.

Figure A.1 GE Datanet 30

Courtesy Ed Thelen, ed-thelen.org

As you can see from the picture, this was a huge[1] machine. It filled a room, and the room needed strict environmental controls.

This computer was built in the days before integrated circuits. It was built out of discrete transistors. There were even some vacuum tubes in it (albeit only in the sense amplifiers of the tape drives).

By today's standards the machine was huge, slow, small, and primitive. It had 16K × 18 bits of core, with a cycle time of about 7 microseconds.[2] It filled a big, environmentally controlled room. It had 7 track magnetic tape drives and a disk drive with a capacity of 20 megabytes or so.

That disk was a monster. You can see it in the picture in Figure A.2—but that doesn't quite give you the scale of the beast. The top of that cabinet was over my head. The platters were 36 inches in diameter, and 3/8 of an inch thick. One of the platters is pictured in Figure A.3.

Now count the platters in that first picture. There are more than a dozen. Each one had its own individual seek arm that was driven by pneumatic actuators. You could watch those seek heads move across the platters. The seek time was probably about half a second to a second.

When this beast was turned on, it sounded like a jet engine. The floor would rumble and shake until it got up to speed.[3]

---

1. One of the stories we heard about the particular machine at ASC was that it was shipped in a large semi-trailer truck along with a household of furniture. On the way, the truck hit a bridge at high speed. The computer was fine, but it slid forward and crushed the furniture into splinters.
2. Today we would say that it had a clock rate of 142 kHz.
3. Imagine the mass of that disk. Imagine the kinetic energy! One day we came in and saw little metal shavings dropping out from the button of the cabinet. We called the maintenance man. He advised us to shut the unit down. When he came to repair it, he said that one of the bearings had worn out. Then he told us stories about how these disks, if not repaired, could tear loose from their moorings, plow through concrete block walls, and embed themselves into cars in the parking lot.

MASS RANDOM ACCESS DATA STORAGE UNIT

Figure A.2 The data storage unit with its platters

Courtesy Ed Thelen, ed-thelen.org

The great claim to fame of the Datanet 30 was its capability to drive a large number of asynchronous terminals at relatively high speed. That's exactly what ASC needed.

ASC was based in Lake Bluff, Illinois, 30 miles north of Chicago. The Local 705 office was in downtown Chicago. The union wanted a dozen or so of their data entry clerks to use CRT[4] terminals (Figure A.4) to enter data into the system. They would print reports on ASR35 teletypes (Figure A.5).

---

4. Cathode ray tube: monochrome, green-screen, ASCII displays.

Figure A.3 One platter of that disk: 3/8 inch thick, 36 inches in diameter

Courtesy, Ed Thelen, ed-thelen.org

The CRT terminals ran at 30 characters per second. This was a pretty good rate for the late 1960s because modems were relatively unsophisticated in those days.

ASC leased a dozen or so dedicated phone lines and twice that number of 300 baud modems from the phone company to connect the Datanet 30 to these terminals.

These computers did not come with operating systems. They didn't even come with file systems. What you got was an assembler.

If you needed to store data on the disk, you stored data on the disk. Not in a file. Not in a directory. You figured out which track, platter, and sector to put the data into, and then you operated the disk to put the data there. Yes, that means we wrote our own disk driver.

Figure A.4 Datapoint CRT terminal

Courtesy of Bill Degnan, vintagecomputer.net

The Union Accounting system had three kinds of records: Agents, Employers, and Members. The system was a CRUD system for these records, but also included operations for posting dues, computing changes in the general ledger, and so on.

The original system was written in assembler by a consultant who somehow managed to cram the whole thing into 16K.

As you might imagine, that big Datanet 30 was an expensive machine to operate and maintain. The software consultant who kept the software running was expensive, too. What's more, minicomputers were becoming popular, and were much cheaper.

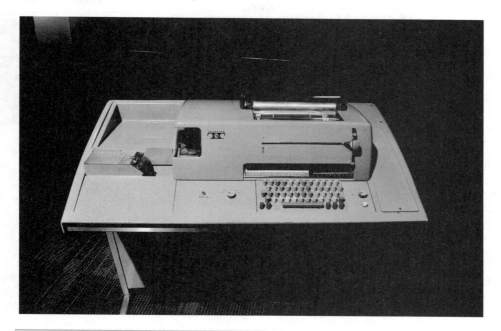

Figure A.5 ASR35 teletype

Joe Mabel, with permission

In 1971, when I was 18 years old, ASC hired me and two of my geeky friends to replace the whole union accounting system with one that was based on a Varian 620/f minicomputer (Figure A.6). The computer was cheap. We were cheap. So it seemed like a good deal for ASC.

The Varian machine had a 16-bit bus and 32K × 16 core memory. It had a cycle time of about 1 microsecond. It was much more powerful than the Datanet 30. It used IBM's wildly successful 2314 disk technology, allowing us to store 30 megabytes on platters that were only 14 inches in diameter and could not explode through concrete block walls!

Of course, we still had no operating system. No file system. No high-level language. All we had was an assembler. But we made do.

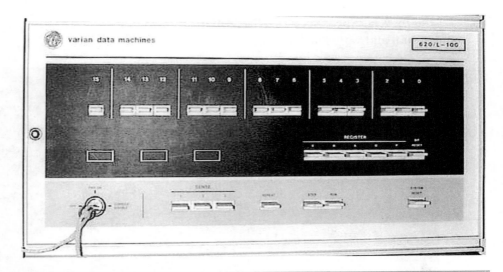

Figure A.6 Varian 620/f minicomputer

The Minicomputer Orphanage

Instead of trying to cram the whole system into 32K, we created an overlay system. Applications would be loaded from disk into a block of memory dedicated to overlays. They would be executed in that memory, and preemptively swapped back out onto disk, with their local RAM, to allow other programs to execute.

Programs would get swapped into the overlay area, execute enough to fill the output buffers, and then get swapped out so that another program could be swapped in.

Of course, when your UI runs at 30 characters per second, your programs spend a lot of time waiting. We had plenty of time to swap the programs in and off the disk to keep all of the terminals running as fast as they could go. Nobody ever complained of response time issues.

We wrote a preemptive supervisor that managed the interrupts and IO. We wrote the applications; we wrote the disk drivers, the terminal drivers, the tape drivers, and everything else in that system. There was not a single bit in that system that we did not write. Though it was a struggle involving far too many 80-hour weeks, we got the beast up and running in a matter of 8 or 9 months.

The architecture of the system was simple (Figure A.7). When an application was started, it would generate output until its particular terminal buffer was full. Then the supervisor would swap the application out, and swap a new application in. The supervisor would continue to dribble out the contents of the terminal buffer at 30 cps until it was nearly empty. Then it would swap the application back in to fill the buffer again.

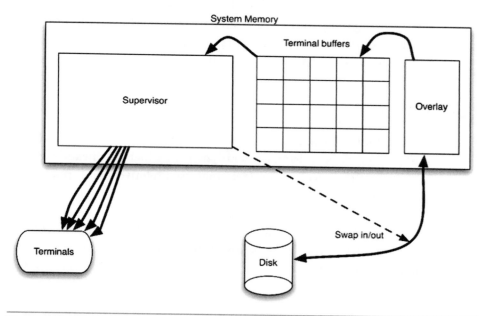

Figure A.7 The system architecture

There are two boundaries in this system. The first is the character output boundary. The applications had no idea that their output was going to a 30-cps terminal. Indeed, the character output was entirely abstract from the applications' point of view. The applications simply passed strings to the supervisor, and the supervisor took care of loading the buffers, sending the characters to the terminals, and swapping the applications in and out of memory.

This boundary was dependency normal—that is, dependencies pointed *with* the flow of control. The applications had compile-time dependencies on the supervisor, and the flow of control passed from the applications to the supervisor. The boundary prevented the applications from knowing which kind of device the output was going to.

The second boundary was dependency inverted. The supervisor could start the applications, but had no compile-time dependencies upon them. The flow of control passed from the supervisor to the applications. The polymorphic interface that inverted the dependency was simply this: Every application was started by jumping to the exact same memory address within the overlay area. The boundary prevented the supervisor from knowing anything about the applications other than the starting point.

LASER TRIM

In 1973, I joined a company in Chicago called Teradyne Applied Systems (TAS). This was a division of Teradyne Inc., which was headquartered in Boston. Our product was a system that used relatively high-powered lasers to trim electronic components to very fine tolerances.

Back in those days, manufacturers would silk-screen electronic components onto ceramic substrates. Those substrates were on the order of 1 inch square. The components were typically resistors—devices that resist the flow of current.

The resistance of a resistor depends on a number of factors, including its composition and its geometry. The wider the resistor, the less resistance it has.

Our system would position the ceramic substrate in a harness that had probes that made contact with the resistors. The system would measure the resistance of the resistors, and then use a laser to burn off parts of the resistor, making it thinner and thinner until it reached the desired resistance value within a tenth of a percent or so.

We sold these systems to manufacturers. We also used some in-house systems to trim relatively small batches for small manufacturers.

The computer was an M365. This was in the days when many companies built their own computers: Teradyne built the M365 and supplied it to all its divisions. The M365 was an enhanced version of a PDP-8—a popular minicomputer of the day.

The M365 controlled the positioning table, which moved the ceramic substrates under the probes. It controlled the measurement system and the laser. The laser was positioned using X-Y mirrors that could rotate under program control. The computer could also control the power setting of the laser.

The development environment of the M365 was relatively primitive. There was no disk. Mass storage was on tape cartridges that looked like old 8-track audio tape cassettes. The tapes and drives were made by Tri-Data.

Like the 8-track audio cassettes of the day, the tape was oriented in a loop. The drive moved the tape in only one direction—there was no rewind! If you wanted to position the tape at the beginning, you had to send it forward to its "load point."

The tape moved at a speed of approximately 1 foot per second. Thus, if the tape loop was 25 feet long, it could take as long as 25 seconds to send it to the load point. For this reason Tridata made cartridges in several lengths, ranging from 10 feet to 100 feet.

The M365 had a button on the front that would load memory with a little bootstrap program and execute it. This program would read the first block of data from the tape, and execute that. Typically this block held a loader that loaded the operating system that lived on the rest of the tape.

The operating system would prompt the user for the name of a program to run. Those programs were stored on the tape, just after the operating system. We would type in the name of the program—for example, the ED-402

Editor—and the operating system would search the tape for that program, load it, and execute it.

The console was an ASCII CRT with green phosphors, 72 characters wide[5] by 24 lines. The characters were all uppercase.

To edit a program, you would load the ED-402 Editor, and then insert the tape that held your source code. You would read one tape block of that source code into memory, and it would be displayed on the screen. The tape block might hold 50 lines of code. You would make your edits by moving the cursor around on the screen and typing in a manner similar to vi. When you were done, you would write that block onto a different tape, and read the next block from the source tape. You kept on doing this until you were done.

There was no scrolling back to previous blocks. You edited your program in a straight line, from beginning to end. Going back to the beginning forced you to finish copying the source code onto the output tape and then start a new editing session on that tape. Perhaps not surprisingly, given these constraints, we printed our programs out on paper, marked all the edits by hand in red ink, and then edited our programs block by block by consulting our markups on the listing.

Once the program was edited, we returned to the OS and invoked the assembler. The assembler read the source code tape, and wrote a binary tape, while also producing a listing on our data products line printer.

The tapes weren't 100% reliable, so we always wrote two tapes at the same time. That way, at least one of them had a high probability of being free of errors.

Our program was approximately 20,000 lines of code, and took nearly 30 minutes to compile. The odds that we would get a tape read error during that time were roughly 1 in 10. If the assembler got a tape error, it would ring the

---

5. The magic number 72 came from Hollerith punched cards, which held 80 characters each. The last 8 characters were "reserved" for sequence numbers in case you dropped the deck.

bell on the console and then start printing a stream of errors on the printer. You could hear this maddening bell all across the lab. You could also hear the cursing of the poor programmer who just learned that the 30-minute compile needed to start over.

The architecture of the program was typical for those days. There was a Master Operating Program, appropriately called "the MOP." Its job was to manage basic IO functions and provide the rudiments of a console "shell." Many of the divisions of Teradyne shared the MOP source code, but each had forked it for its own uses. Consequently, we would send source code updates around to each other in the form of marked-up listings that we would then integrate manually (and very carefully).

A special-purpose utility layer controlled the measurement hardware, the positioning tables, and the laser. The boundary between this layer and the MOP was muddled at best. While the utility layer called the MOP, the MOP had been specifically modified for that layer, and often called back into it. Indeed, we didn't really think of these two as separate layers. To us, it was just some code that we added to the MOP in a highly coupled way.

Next came the isolation layer. This layer provided a virtual machine interface for the application programs, which were written in a completely different domain-specific data-driven language (DSL). The language had operations for moving the laser, moving the table, making cuts, making measurements, and so on. Our customers would write their laser trimming application programs in this language, and the isolation layer would execute them.

This approach was not intended to create a machine-independent laser trim language. Indeed, the language had many idiosyncrasies that were deeply coupled to the layers below. Rather, this approach gave the application programmers a "simpler" language than M356 assembler in which to program their trim jobs.

Trim jobs could be loaded from tape and executed by the system. Essentially, our system was an operating system for trim applications.

The system was written in M365 assembler and compiled in a single compilation unit that produced absolute binary code.

The boundaries in this application were soft at best. Even the boundary between the system code and the applications written in the DSL was not well enforced. There were couplings everywhere.

But that was typical of software in the early 1970s.

ALUMINUM DIE-CAST MONITORING

In the middle of the 1970s, while OPEC was placing an embargo on oil, and gasoline shortages were causing angry drivers to get into fights at gas stations, I began working at Outboard Marine Corporation (OMC). This is the parent company of Johnson Motors and Lawnboy lawnmowers.

OMC maintained a huge facility in Waukegan, Illinois, for creating die-cast aluminum parts for all of the company's motors and products. Aluminum was melted down in huge furnaces, and then carried in large buckets to dozens upon dozens of individually operated aluminum die-cast machines. Each machine had a human operator responsible for setting the molds, cycling the machine, and extracting the newly cast parts. These operators were paid based on how many parts they produced.

I was hired to work on a shop-floor automation project. OMC had purchased an IBM System/7—which was IBM's answer to the minicomputer. They tied this computer to all the die-cast machines on the floor, so that we could count, and time, the cycles of each machine. Our role was to gather all that information and present it on 3270 green-screen displays.

The language was assembler. And, again, every bit of code that executed in this computer was code that we wrote. There was no operating system, no subroutine libraries, and no framework. It was just raw code.

It was also interrupt-driven real-time code. Every time a die-cast machine cycled, we had to update a batch of statistics, and send messages to a great IBM 370 in-the-sky, running a CICS-COBOL program that presented those statistics on the green screens.

I hated this job. Oh, boy, did I. Oh, the *work* was *fun*! But the culture ... Suffice it to say that I was *required* to wear a tie.

Oh, I tried. I really did. But I was clearly unhappy working there, and my colleagues knew it. They knew it because I couldn't remember critical dates or manage to get up early enough to attend important meetings. This was the only programming job I was ever fired from—and I deserved it.

From an architectural point of view, there's not a lot to learn here except for one thing. The System/7 had a very interesting instruction called *set program interrupt* (SPI). This allowed you to trigger an interrupt of the processor, allowing it to handle any other queued lower-priority interrupts. Nowadays, in Java we call this `Thread.yield()`.

4-TEL

In October 1976, having been fired from OMC, I returned to a different division of Teradyne—a division I would stay with for 12 years. The product I worked on was named 4-TEL. Its purpose was to test every telephone line in a telephone service area, every night, and produce a report of all lines requiring repair. It also allowed telephone test personnel to test specific telephone lines in detail.

This system started its life with the same kind of architecture as the Laser Trim system. It was a monolithic application written in assembly language without any significant boundaries. But at the time I joined the company, that was about to change.

The system was used by testers located in a service center (SC). A service center covered many central offices (CO), each of which could handle as many as 10,000 phone lines. The dialing and measurement hardware had to be located inside the CO. So that's where the M365 computers were put. We called those computers the central office line testers (COLTs). Another M365 was placed at the SC; it was called the service area computer (SAC). The SAC had several modems that it could use to dial up the COLTs and communicate at 300 baud (30 cps).

At first, the COLT computers did everything, including all the console communication, menus, and reports. The SAC was just a simple multiplexor that took the output from the COLTs and put it on a screen.

The problem with this setup was that 30 cps is really slow. The testers didn't like watching the characters trickle across the screen, especially since they were only interested in a few key bits of data. Also, in those days, the core memory in the M365 was expensive, and the program was big.

The solution was to separate the part of the software that dialed and measured lines from the part that analyzed the results and printed the reports. The latter would be moved into the SAC, and the former would remain behind in the COLTs. This would allow the COLT to be a smaller machine, with much less memory, and would greatly speed up the response at the terminal, since the reports would be generated in the SAC.

The result was remarkably successful. Screen updates were very fast (once the appropriate COLT had been dialed), and the memory footprint of the COLTs shrank a lot.

The boundary was very clean and highly decoupled. Very short packets of data were exchanged between the SAC and COLT. These packets were a very simple form of DSL, representing primitive commands like "DIAL XXXX" or "MEASURE."

The M365 was loaded from tape. Those tape drives were expensive and weren't very reliable—especially in the industrial environment of a telephone central office. Also, the M365 was an expensive machine relative to the rest of the electronics within the COLT. So we embarked upon a project to replace the M365 with a microcomputer based on an 8085 µprocessor.

The new computer was composed of a processor board that held the 8085, a RAM board that held 32K of RAM, and three ROM boards that held 12K of read-only memory apiece. All these boards fit into the same chassis as the measurement hardware, thereby eliminating the bulky extra chassis that had housed the M365.

The ROM boards held 12 Intel 2708 EPROM (Erasable Programmable Read-Only Memory) chips.[6] Figure A.8 shows an example of such a chip. We loaded those chips with software by inserting them into special devices called PROM burners that were driven by our development environment. The chips could be erased by exposing them to high-intensity ultraviolet light.[7]

My buddy CK and I translated the M365 assembly language program for the COLT into 8085 assembly language. This translation was done by hand and took us about 6 months. The end result was approximately 30K of 8085 code.

Our development environment had 64K of RAM and no ROM, so we could quickly download our compiled binaries into RAM and test them.

Once we got the program working, we switched to using the EPROMs. We burned 30 chips and inserted them into just the right slots in the three ROM boards. Each chip was labeled so we could tell which chip went into which slot.

The 30K program was a single binary, 30K long. To burn the chips, we simply divided that binary image into 30 different 1K segments, and burned each segment onto the appropriately labeled chip.

---

6. Yes, I understand that's an oxymoron.
7. They had a little clear plastic window that allowed you to see the silicon chip inside, and allowed the UV to erase the data.

Figure A.8 EPROM chip

This worked very well, and we began to mass-produce the hardware and deploy the system into the field.

But software is soft.[8] Features needed to be added. Bugs needed to be fixed. And as the installed base grew, the logistics of updating the software by burning 30 chips per installation, and having field service people replace all 30 chips at each site became a nightmare.

There were all kinds of problems. Sometimes chips would be mislabeled, or the labels would fall off. Sometimes the field service engineer would mistakenly replace the wrong chip. Sometimes the field service engineer would

---

8. Yes, I know that when software is burned into ROM, it's called firmware—but even firmware is really still soft.

inadvertently break a pin off one of the new chips. Consequently, the field engineers had to carry extras of all 30 chips with them.

Why did we have to change all 30 chips? Every time we added or removed code from our 30K executable, it changed the addresses in which each instruction was loaded. It also changed the addresses of the subroutines and functions that we called. So every chip was affected, no matter how trivial the change.

One day, my boss came to me and asked me to solve that problem. He said we needed a way to make a change to the firmware without replacing all 30 chips every time. We brainstormed this issue for a while, and then embarked upon the "Vectorization" project. It took me three months.

The idea was beautifully simple. We divided the 30K program into 32 independently compilable source files, each less than 1K. At the beginning of each source file, we told the compiler in which address to load the resulting program (e.g., ORG C400 for the chip that was to be inserted into the C4 position).

Also at the beginning of each source file, we created a simple, fixed-size data structure that contained all the addresses of all the subroutines on that chip. This data structure was 40 bytes long, so it could hold no more than 20 addresses. This meant that no chip could have more than 20 subroutines.

Next, we created a special area in RAM known as the vectors. It contained 32 tables of 40 bytes—exactly enough RAM to hold the pointers at the start of each chip.

Finally, we changed every call to every subroutine on every chip into an indirect call through the appropriate RAM vector.

When our processor booted, it would scan each chip and load the vector table at the start of each chip into the RAM vectors. Then it would jump into the main program.

This worked very well. Now, when we fixed a bug, or added a feature, we could simply recompile one or two chips, and send just those chips to the field service engineers.

We had made the chips *independently deployable*. We had invented polymorphic dispatch. We had invented objects.

This was a plugin architecture, quite literally. We plugged those chips in. We eventually engineered it so that a feature could be installed into our products by plugging the chip with that feature into one of the open chip sockets. The menu control would automatically appear, and the binding into the main application would happen automatically.

Of course, we didn't know about object-oriented principles at the time, and we knew nothing about separating user interface from business rules. But the rudiments were there, and they were very powerful.

One unexpected side benefit of the approach was that we could patch the firmware over a dial-up connection. If we found a bug in the firmware, we could dial up our devices and use the on-board monitor program to alter the RAM vector for the faulty subroutine to point to a bit of empty RAM. Then we'd enter the repaired subroutine into that RAM area, by typing it in machine code, in hexadecimal.

This was a great boon to our field service operation, and to our customers. If they had a problem, they didn't need us to ship new chips and schedule an urgent field service call. The system could be patched, and a new chip could be installed at the next regularly scheduled maintenance visit.

THE SERVICE AREA COMPUTER

The 4-TEL service area computer (SAC) was based on an M365 minicomputer. This system communicated with all the COLTs out in the field, through either dedicated or dial-up modems. It would command those COLTs to measure telephone lines, would receive back the raw results, and would then perform a complex analysis of those results to identify and locate any faults.

DISPATCH DETERMINATION

One of the economic foundations for this system was based on the correct allocation of repair craftsmen. Repair craft were separated, by union rules, into three categories: central office, cable, and drop. CO craftsmen fixed problems inside the central office. Cable craftsmen fixed problems in the cable plant that connected the CO to the customer. Drop craftsmen fixed problems inside the customer's premises, and in the lines connecting the external cable to that premises (the "drop").

When a customer complained about a problem, our system could diagnose that problem and determine which kind of craftsman to dispatch. This saved the phone companies lots of money because incorrect dispatches meant delays for the customer and wasted trips for the craftsmen.

The code that made this dispatch determination was designed and written by someone who was very bright, but a terrible communicator. The process of writing the code has been described as "Three weeks of staring at the ceiling and two days of code pouring out of every orifice of his body—after which he quit."

Nobody understood this code. Every time we tried to add a feature or fix a defect, we broke it in some way. And since it was upon this code that one of the primary economic benefits our system rested, every new defect was deeply embarrassing to the company.

In the end, our management simply told us to lock that code down and never modify it. That code became *officially rigid*.

This experience impressed upon me the value of good, clean code.

ARCHITECTURE

The system was written in 1976 in M365 assembler. It was a single, monolithic program of roughly 60,000 lines. The operating system was a home-grown, nonpreemptive, task-switcher based on polling. We called it MPS for *multiprocessing system*. The M365 computer had no built-in stack, so task-specific variables were kept in a special area of memory and swapped out at every context switch. Shared variables were managed with locks and semaphores. Reentrancy issues and race conditions were constant problems.

There was no isolation of device control logic, or UI logic, from the business rules of the system. For example, modem control code could be found smeared throughout the bulk of the business rules and UI code. There was no attempt to gather it into a module or abstract the interface. The modems were controlled, at the bit level, by code that was scattered everywhere around the system.

The same was true for the terminal UI. Messages and formatting control code were not isolated. They ranged far and wide throughout the 60,000-line code base.

The modem modules we were using were designed to be mounted on PC boards. We bought those units from a third party, and integrated them with other circuitry onto a board that fit into our custom backplane. These units were expensive. So, after a few years, we decided to design our own modems. We, in the software group, begged the hardware designer to use the same bit formats for controlling the new modem. We explained that the modem control code was smeared everywhere, and that our system would have to deal with both kinds of modems in the future. So, we begged and cajoled, "Please make the new modem look just like the old modem from a software control point of view."

But when we got the new modem, the control structured was entirely different. It was not just a little different. It was entirely, and completely, different.

Thanks, hardware engineer.

What were we to do? We were not simply replacing all the old modems with new modems. Instead, we were mixing old and new modems in our systems. The software needed to be able to handle both kinds of modems at the same time. Were we doomed to surround every place in the code that manipulated the modems with flags and special cases? There were hundreds of such places!

In the end, we opted for an even worse solution.

One particular subroutine wrote data to the serial communication bus that was used to control all our devices, including our modems. We modified that subroutine to recognize the bit patterns that were specific to the old modem, and translate them into the bit patterns needed by the new modem.

This was not straightforward. Commands to the modem consisted of sequences of writes to different IO addresses on the serial bus. Our hack had to interpret these commands, in sequence, and translate them into a different sequence using different IO addresses, timings, and bit positions.

We got it to work, but it was the worst hack imaginable. It was because of this fiasco that I learned the value of isolating hardware from business rules, and of abstracting interfaces.

THE GRAND REDESIGN IN THE SKY

By the time the 1980s rolled around, the idea of producing your own minicomputer and your own computer architecture was beginning to fall out of fashion. There were many microcomputers on the market, and getting them to work was cheaper and more standard then continuing to rely on proprietary computer architectures from the late 1960s. That, plus the horrible architecture of the SAC software, induced our technical management to start a complete re-architecture of the SAC system.

The new system was to be written in C using a UNIX O/S on disk, running on an Intel 8086 microcomputer. Our hardware guys started working on the new computer hardware, and a select group of software developers, "The Tiger Team," was commissioned with the rewrite.

I won't bore you with the details of the initial fiasco. Suffice it to say that the first Tiger Team failed entirely after burning two or three man-years on a software project that never delivered anything.

A year or two later, probably 1982, the process was started again. The goal was the total and complete redesign of the SAC in C and UNIX on our own, newly designed, impressively powerful 80286 hardware. We called that computer "Deep Thought."

It took years, then more years, and then even more years. I don't know when the first UNIX-based SAC was finally deployed; I believe I had left the company by then (1988). Indeed, I'm not at all sure it ever was deployed.

Why the delay? In short, it is very difficult for a redesign team to catch up with a large staff of programmers who are actively maintaining the old system. Here's just one example of the difficulties they encountered.

EUROPE

At about the same time that the SAC was being redesigned in C, the company started to expand sales into Europe. They could not wait for the redesigned software to be finished, so of course, they deployed the old M365 systems into Europe.

The problem was that the phone systems in Europe were very different from the phone systems in the United States. The organization of the craft and of the bureaucracies were different as well. So one of our best programmers was sent to the United Kingdom to lead a team of U.K. developers to modify the SAC software to deal with all these European issues.

Of course, no serious attempt was made to integrate these changes into the U.S.-based software. This was long before networks made it feasible to transmit large code bases across the ocean. These U.K. developers simply forked the U.S.-based code and modified it as needed.

This, of course, caused difficulties. Bugs were found on both sides of the Atlantic that needed repair on the other side. But the modules had changed significantly, so it was very difficult to determine whether the fix made in the United States would work in the United Kingdom.

After a few years of heartburn, and the installation of a high-throughput line connecting the U.S. and U.K. offices, a serious attempt was made to integrate these two forks back together again, making the differences a matter of configuration. This effort failed the first, second, and third times it was tried. The two code bases, though remarkably similar, were still too different to reintegrate—especially in the rapidly changing market environment that existed at that time.

Meanwhile, the "Tiger Team," trying to rewrite everything in C and UNIX, realized that it also had to deal with this European/US dichotomy. And, of course, that did nothing to accelerate their progress.

SAC Conclusion

There are many other stories I could tell you about this system, but it's just too depressing for me to continue. Suffice it to say that many of the hard lessons of my software life were learned while immersed in the horrible assembler code of the SAC.

C Language

The 8085 computer hardware that we used in the 4-Tel Micro project gave us a relatively low-cost computing platform for many different projects that could be embedded into industrial environments. We could load it up with 32K of RAM and another 32K of ROM, and we had an extremely flexible and powerful scheme for controlling peripherals. What we did not have was a flexible and convenient language with which to program the machine. The 8085 assembler was simply not fun to write code in.

On top of that, the assembler we were using was written by our own programmers. It ran on our M365 computers, using the cartridge tape operating system described in the "Laser Trim" section.

As fate would have it, our lead *hardware* engineer convinced our CEO that we needed a *real* computer. He didn't actually know what he would do with it, but he had a lot of political clout. So we purchased a PDP-11/60.

I, a lowly software developer at the time, was ecstatic. I knew *precisely* what I wanted to do with that computer. I was determined that this was going to be *my* machine.

When the manuals arrived, many months before the delivery of the machine, I took them home and devoured them. By the time the computer was delivered, I knew how to operate both the hardware and the software at an intimate level—at least, as intimate as home study can make it.

I helped to write the purchase order. In particular, I specified the disk storage that the new computer would have. I decided we should buy two disk drives that could take removable disk packs that held 25 megabytes each.[9]

Fifty megabytes! The number seemed infinite! I remember walking through the halls of the office, late at night, cackling like the Wicked Witch of the West: "Fifty megabytes! Hahahahahahahahahah!"

I had the facilities manager build a little room that would house six VT100 terminals. I decorated it with pictures from space. Our software developers would use this room to write and compile code.

When the machine arrived, I spent several days setting it up, wiring all the terminals, and getting everything to work. It was a joy—a labor of love.

We purchased standard assemblers for the 8085 from Boston Systems Office, and we translated the 4-Tel Micro code into that syntax. We built a cross-compilation system that allowed us to download compiled binaries from the PDP-11 to our 8085 development environments, and ROM burners. And—Bob's your Uncle—it all worked like a champ.

C

But that left us with the problem of still using 8085 assembler. That was not a situation that I was happy with. I had heard that there was this "new"

---

9. RKO7.

language that was heavily used at Bell Labs. They called it "C." So I purchased a copy of *The C Programming Language* by Kernighan and Ritchie. Like the PDP-11 manuals a few months before, I *inhaled* this book.

I was astounded by the simple elegance of this language. It sacrificed none of the power of assembly language, and provided access to that power with a much more convenient syntax. I was sold.

I purchased a C compiler from Whitesmiths, and got it running on the PDP-11. The output of the compiler was assembler syntax that was compatible with the Boston Systems Office 8085 compiler. So we had a pathway to go from C to the 8085 hardware! We were in business.

Now the only problem was convincing a group of embedded assembly language programmers that they should be using C. But that's a nightmare tale for another time …

BOSS

Our 8085 platform had no operating system. My experience with the MPS system of the M365, and the primitive interrupt mechanisms of the IBM System 7, convinced me that we needed a simple task switcher for the 8085. So I conceived of BOSS: Basic Operating System and Scheduler.[10]

The vast majority of BOSS was written in C. It provided the ability to create concurrent tasks. Those tasks were not preemptive—task switching did not take place based on interrupts. Instead, and just like with the MPS system on the M365, tasks were switched based on a simple polling mechanism. The polling happened whenever a task blocked for an event.

The BOSS call to block a task looked like this:

```
block(eventCheckFunction);
```

---

10. This was later renamed as Bob's Only Successful Software.

This call suspended the current task, placed the `eventCheckFunction` in the polling list, and associated it with the newly blocked task. It then waited in the polling loop, calling each of the functions in the polling list until one of them returned `true`. The task associated with that function was then allowed to run.

In other words, as I said before, it was a simple, nonpreemptive task switcher.

This software became the basis for a vast number of projects over the following years. But one of the first was the pCCU.

pCCU

The late 1970s and early 1980s were a tumultuous time for telephone companies. One of the sources of that tumult was the digital revolution.

For the preceding century, the connection between the central switching office and the customer's telephone had been a pair of copper wires. These wires were bundled into cables that spread in a huge network across the countryside. They were sometimes carried on poles, and sometimes buried underground.

Copper is a precious metal, and the phone company had tons (literally tons) of it covering the country. The capital investment was enormous. Much of that capital could be reclaimed by transporting the telephone conversation over digital connections. A single pair of copper wires could carry hundreds of conversations in digital form.

In response, the phone companies embarked upon the process of replacing their old analog central switching equipment with modern digital switches.

Our 4-Tel product tested copper wires, not digital connections. There were still plenty of copper wires in a digital environment, but they were much shorter than before, and they were localized near the customer's telephones. The signal would be carried digitally from the central office to a local distribution point, where it would be converted back to an analog signal and distributed to the customer over standard copper wires. This meant that our measurement device needed to be located out where the copper wires began, but our dialing device needed to remain at the central office. The problem was that all our COLTs embodied both dialing and measurement in the same device. (We could have saved ourselves a fortune had we recognized that obvious architectural boundary a few years earlier!)

Thus we conceived of a new product architecture: the CCU/CMU (the COLT control unit and the COLT measurement unit). The CCU would be located at the central switching office, and would handle the dialing of the phone lines to be tested. The CMU would be located at the local distribution points, and would measure the copper wires that led to the customer's phone.

The problem was that for each CCU, there were many CMUs. The information about which CMU should be used for each phone number was held by the digital switch itself. Thus the CCU had to interrogate the digital switch to determine which CMU to communicate with and control.

We promised the phone companies that we would have this new architecture working in time for their transition. We knew they were months, if not years away, so we did not feel rushed. We also knew that it would take several man-years to develop this new CCU/CMU hardware and software.

THE SCHEDULE TRAP

As time went on, we found that there were always urgent matters that required us to postpone development of the CCU/CMU architecture. We felt safe about this decision because the phone companies were consistently delaying the deployment of digital switches. As we looked at their schedules, we felt confident that we had plenty of time, so we consistently delayed our development.

Then came the day that my boss called me into his office and said: "*One of our customers is deploying a digital switch next month. We have to have a working CCU/CMU by then.*"

I was aghast! How could we possibly do man-years of development in a month? But my boss had a plan …

We did not, in fact, need a full CCU/CMU architecture. The phone company that was deploying the digital switch was tiny. They had only one central office, and only two local distribution points. More importantly, the "local" distribution points were not particularly local. They actually had regular-old analog switches in them that switched to several hundred customers. Better yet, those switches were of a kind that could be dialed by a normal COLT. Better even still, the customer's phone number contained all the information necessary to decide which local distribution point to use. If the phone number had a 5, 6, or 7 in a certain position, it went to distribution point 1; otherwise, it went to distribution point 2.

So, as my boss explained to me, we did not actually need a CCU/CMU. What we needed was a simple computer at the central office connected by modem lines to two standard COLTs at the distribution points. The SAC would communicate with our computer at the central office, and that computer would decode the phone number and then relay the dialing and measurement commands to the COLT at the appropriate distribution point.

Thus was born the pCCU.

This was the first product written in C and using BOSS that was deployed to a customer. It took me about a week to develop. There is no deep architectural significance to this tale, but it makes a nice preface to the next project.

DLU/DRU

In the early 1980s, one of our customers was a telephone company in Texas. They had large geographic areas to cover. In fact, the areas were so large that a single service area required several different offices from which to dispatch craftsmen. Those offices had test craftspeople who needed terminals into our SAC.

You might think that this was a simple problem to solve—but remember that this story takes place in the early 1980s. Remote terminals were not very common. To make matters worse, the hardware of the SAC presumed that all the terminals were local. Our terminals actually sat on a proprietary, high-speed, serial bus.

We had remote terminal capability, but it was based on modems, and in the early 1980s modems were generally limited to 300 bits per second. Our customers were not happy with that slow speed.

High-speed modems were available, but they were very expensive, and they needed to run on "conditioned" permanent connections. Dial-up quality was definitely not good enough.

Our customers demanded a solution. Our response was DLU/DRU.

DLU/DRU stood for "Display Local Unit" and "Display Remote Unit." The DLU was a computer board that plugged into the SAC computer chassis and pretended to be a terminal manager board. Instead of controlling the serial bus for local terminals, however, it took the character stream and multiplexed it over a single 9600-bps conditioned modem link.

The DRU was a box placed at the customer's remote location. It connected to the other end of the 9600-bps link, and had the hardware to control the terminals on our proprietary serial bus. It demultiplexed the characters received from the 9600-bps link and sent them to the appropriate local terminals.

Strange, isn't it? We had to engineer a solution that nowadays is so ubiquitous we never even think about it. But back then ...

We even had to invent our own communications protocol because, in those days, standard communications protocols were not open source shareware. Indeed, this was long before we had any kind of Internet connection.

ARCHITECTURE

The architecture of this system was very simple, but there are some interesting quirks I want to highlight. First, both units used our 8085 technology, and both were written in C and used BOSS. But that's where the similarity ended.

There were two of us on the project. I was the project lead, and Mike Carew was my close associate. I took on the design and coding of the DLU; Mike did the DRU.

The architecture of the DLU was based on a dataflow model. Each task did a small and focused job, and then passed its output to the next task in line, using a queue. Think of a pipes and filters model in UNIX. The architecture was intricate. One task might feed a queue that many others would service. Other tasks would feed a queue that just one task would service.

Think of an assembly line. Each position on the assembly line has a single, simple, highly focused job to perform. Then the product moves to the next position in line. Sometimes the assembly line splits into many lines. Sometimes those lines merge back into a single line. That was the DLU.

Mike's DRU used a remarkably different scheme. He created one task per terminal, and simply did the entire job for that terminal in that task. No queues. No data flow. Just many identical large tasks, each managing its own terminal.

This is the opposite of an assembly line. In this case the analogy is many expert builders, each of whom builds an entire product.

At the time I thought my architecture was superior. Mike, of course, thought his was better. We had many entertaining discussions about this. In the end, of course, both worked quite well. And I was left with the realization that software architectures can be wildly different, yet equally effective.

VRS

As the 1980s progressed, newer and newer technologies appeared. One of those technologies was the computer control of *voice*.

One of the features of the 4-Tel system was the ability of the craftsman to locate a fault in a cable. The procedure was as follows:

- The tester, in the central office, would use our system to determine the approximate distance, in feet, to the fault. This would be accurate to within 20% or so. The tester would dispatch a cable repair craftsman to an appropriate access point near that position.
- The cable repair craftsman, upon arrival, would call the tester and ask to begin the fault location process. The tester would invoke the fault location feature of the 4-Tel system. The system would begin measuring the electronic characteristics of that faulty line, and would print messages on the screen requesting that certain operations be performed, such as opening the cable or shorting the cable.
- The tester would tell the craftsman which operations the system wanted, and the craftsman would tell the tester when the operation was complete. The tester would then tell the system that the operation was complete, and the system would continue with the test.
- After two or three such interactions, the system would calculate a new distance to the fault. The cable craftsman would then drive to that location and begin the process again.

Imagine how much better that would be if the cable craftsmen, up on the pole or standing at a pedestal, could operate the system themselves. And that is exactly what the new voice technologies allowed us to do. The cable craftsmen could call directly into our system, direct the system with touch tones, and listen to the results being read back to them in a pleasant voice.

THE NAME

The company held a little contest to select a name for the new system. One of the most creative of the names suggested was SAM CARP. This stood for

"Still Another Manifestation of Capitalist Avarice Repressing the Proletariat." Needless to say, that wasn't selected.

Another was the Teradyne Interactive Test System. That one was also not selected.

Still another was Service Area Test Access Network. That, too, was not selected.

The winner, in the end, was VRS: Voice Response System.

ARCHITECTURE

I did not work on this system, but I heard about what happened. The story I am going to relate to you is second-hand, but for the most part, I believe it to be correct.

These were the heady days of microcomputers, UNIX operating systems, C, and SQL databases. We were determined to use them all.

From the many database vendors out there, we eventually chose UNIFY. UNIFY was a database system that worked with UNIX, which was perfect for us.

UNIFY also supported a new technology called *Embedded SQL*. This technology allowed us to embed SQL commands, as strings, right into our C code. And so we did—everywhere.

I mean, it was just so cool that you could put your SQL right into your code, anywhere you wanted. And where did we want to? Everywhere! And so there was SQL smeared throughout the body of that code.

Of course, in those days SQL was hardly a solid standard. There were lots of special vendor-specific quirks. So the special SQL and special UNIFY API calls were also smeared throughout the code.

This worked great! The system was a success. The craftsmen used it, and the telephone companies loved it. Life was all smiles.

Then the UNIFY product we were using was cancelled.

Oh. Oh.

So we decided to switch to SyBase. Or was it Ingress? I don't remember. Suffice it to say, we had to search through all that C code, find all the embedded SQL and special API calls, and replace them with corresponding gestures for the new vendor.

After three months of effort or so, we gave up. We couldn't make it work. We were so coupled to UNIFY that there was no serious hope of restructuring the code at any practical expense.

So, we hired a third party to maintain UNIFY for us, based on a maintenance contract. And, of course, the maintenance rates went up year after year after year.

VRS Conclusion

This is one of the ways that I learned that databases are details that should be isolated from the overall business purpose of the system. This is also one of the reasons that I don't like strongly coupling to third-party software systems.

The Electronic Receptionist

In 1983, our company sat at the confluence of computer systems, telecommunications systems, and voice systems. Our CEO thought this might be a fertile position from which to develop new products. To address this goal, he commissioned a team of three (which included me) to conceive, design, and implement a new product for the company.

It didn't take us long to come up with *The Electronic Receptionist* (ER).

The idea was simple. When you called a company, ER would answer and ask you who you wanted to speak with. You would use touch tones to spell the name of that person, and ER would then connect you. The users of ER could dial in and, by using simple touch-tone commands, tell it which phone number the desired person could be reached at, anywhere in the world. In fact, the system could list several alternate numbers.

When you called ER and dialed RMART (my code), ER would call the first number on my list. If I failed to answer and identify myself, it would call the next number, and the next. If I still wasn't reached, ER would record a message from the caller.

ER would then, periodically, try to find me to deliver that message, and any other message left for me by anyone else.

This was the first voice mail system ever, and we[11] held the patent to it.

We built all the hardware for this system—the computer board, the memory board, the voice/telecom boards, everything. The main computer board was *Deep Thought*, the Intel 80286 processor that I mentioned earlier.

The voice boards each supported one telephone line. They consisted of a telephone interface, a voice encoder/decoder, some memory, and an Intel 80186 microcomputer.

The software for the main computer board was written in C. The operating system was MP/M-86, an early command-line–driven, multiprocessing, disk operating system. MP/M was the poor man's UNIX.

The software for the voice boards was written in assembler, and had no operating system. Communication between Deep Thought and the voice boards occurred through shared memory.

The architecture of this system would today be called *service oriented*. Each telephone line was monitored by a listener process running under MP/M.

---

11. Our company held the patent. Our employment contract made it clear that anything we invented belonged to our company. My boss told me: "You sold it to us for one dollar, and we didn't pay you that dollar."

When a call came in, an initial handler process was started and the call was passed to it. As the call proceeded from state to state, the appropriate handler process would be started and take control.

Messages were passed between these services through disk files. The currently running service would determine what the next service should be; would write the necessary state information into a disk file; would issue the command line to start that service; and then would exit.

This was the first time I had built a system like this. Indeed, this was the first time I had been the principal architect of an entire product. Everything having to do with software was mine—and it worked like a champ.

I would not say that the architecture of this system was "clean" in the sense of this book; it was not a "plugin" architecture. However, it definitely showed signs of true boundaries. The services were independently deployable, and lived within their own domain of responsibility. There were high-level processes and low-level processes, and many of the dependencies ran in the right direction.

ER Demise

Unfortunately, the marketing of this product did not go very well. Teradyne was a company that sold test equipment. We did not understand how to break into the office equipment market.

After repeated attempts over two years, our CEO gave up and—unfortunately—dropped the patent application. The patent was picked up by the company that filed three months after we filed; thus we surrendered the entire voice mail and electronic call-forwarding market.

Ouch!

On the other hand, you can't blame me for those annoying machines that now plague our existence.

CRAFT DISPATCH SYSTEM

ER had failed as a product, but we still had all this hardware and software that we could use to enhance our existing product lines. Moreover, our marketing success with VRS convinced us that we should offer a voice response system for interacting with telephone craftsmen that did not depend on our test systems.

Thus was born CDS, the Craft Dispatch System. CDS was essentially ER, but specifically focused on the very narrow domain of managing the deployment of telephone repairmen in the field.

When a problem was discovered in a phone line, a trouble ticket was created in the service center. Trouble tickets were kept in an automated system. When a repairman in the field finished a job, he would call the service center for the next assignment. The service center operator would pull up the next trouble ticket and read it off to the repairman.

We set about to automate that process. Our goal was for the repairman in the field to call into CDS and ask for the next assignment. CDS would consult the trouble ticket system, and read off the results. CDS would keep track of which repairman was assigned to which trouble ticket, and would inform the trouble ticket system of the status of the repair.

There were quite a few interesting features of this system having to do with interacting with the trouble ticket system, the plant management system, and any automated testing systems.

The experience with the service-oriented architecture of ER made me want to try the same idea more aggressively. The state machine for a trouble ticket was much more involved than the state machine for handling a call with ER. I set about to create what would now be called a *micro-service architecture*.

Every state transition of any call, no matter how insignificant, caused the system to start up a new service. Indeed, the state machine was externalized into a text file that the system read. Each event coming into the system from a phone line turned into a transition in that finite state machine. The existing process would start a new process dictated by the state machine to handle that event; then the existing process would either exit or wait on a queue.

This externalized state machine allowed us to change the flow of the application without changing any code (the Open-Closed Principle). We could easily add a new service, independently of any of the others, and wire it into the flow by modifying the text file that contained the state machine. We could even do this while the system was running. In other words we had *hot-swapping* and an effective BPEL (Business Process Execution Language).

The old ER approach of using disk files to communicate between services was too slow for this much more rapid flip-flopping of services, so we invented a shared memory mechanism that we called the 3DBB.[12] The 3DBB allowed data to be accessed by name; the names we used were names assigned to each state machine instance.

The 3DBB was great for storing strings and constants, but couldn't be used for holding complex data structures. The reason for this is technical but easy to understand. Each process in MP/M lived in its own memory partition. Pointers to data in one memory partition had no meaning in another memory partition. As a consequence, the data in the 3DBB could not contain pointers. Strings were fine, but trees, linked lists, or any data structure with pointers would not work.

The trouble tickets in the trouble ticket system came from many different sources. Some were automated, and some were manual. The manual entries were created by operators who were talking to customers about their troubles. As the customers described their problems, the operators would type in their complaints and observations in a structured text stream. It looked something like this:

```
/pno 8475551212 /noise /dropped-calls
```

---

12. Three-Dimensional Black Board. If you were born in the 1950s, you likely get this reference: Drizzle, Drazzle, Druzzle, Drone.

You get the idea. The / character started a new topic. Following the slash was a code, and following the code were parameters. There were *thousands* of codes, and an individual trouble ticket could have dozens of them in the description. Worse, since they were manually entered, they were often misspelled or improperly formatted. They were meant for humans to interpret, not for machines to process.

Our problem was to decode these semi-free-form strings, interpret and fix any errors, and then turn them into voice output so we could read them to the repairman, up on a pole, listening with a handset. This required, among other things, a very flexible parsing and data representation technique. That data representation had to be passed through the 3DBB, which could handle only strings.

And so, on an airplane, flying between customer visits, I invented a scheme that I called FLD: *Field Labeled Data*. Nowadays we would call this XML or JSON. The format was different, but the idea was the same. FLDs were binary trees that associated names with data in a recursive hierarchy. FLDs could be queried by a simple API, and could be translated to and from a convenient string format that was ideal for the 3DBB.

So, micro-services communicating through shared memory analog of sockets using an XML analog—in 1985.

There is nothing new under the Sun.

CLEAR COMMUNICATIONS

In 1988, a group of Teradyne employees left the company to form a startup named Clear Communications. I joined them a few months later. Our mission was to build the software for a system that would monitor the communications quality of T1 lines—the digital lines that carried long-distance communications across the country. The vision was a huge monitor with a map of the United States crisscrossed by T1 lines flashing red if they were degrading.

Remember, graphical user interfaces were brand new in 1988. The Apple Macintosh was only five years old. Windows was a joke back then. But Sun Microsystems was building Sparcstations that had credible X-Windows GUIs. So we went with Sun—and therefore with C and UNIX.

This was a startup. We worked 70 to 80 hours per week. We had the vision. We had the motivation. We had the will. We had the energy. We had the expertise. We had equity. We had dreams of being millionaires. We were full of shit.

The C code poured out of every orifice of our bodies. We slammed it here, and shoved it there. We constructed huge castles in the air. We had processes, and message queues, and grand, superlative architectures. We wrote a full seven-layer ISO communications stack from scratch—right down to the data link layer.

We wrote GUI code. GOOEY CODE! OMG! We wrote GOOOOOEY code.

I personally wrote a 3000-line C function named `gi()`; its name stood for Graphic Interpreter. It was a masterpiece of goo. It was not the only goo I wrote at Clear, but it was my most infamous.

Architecture? Are you joking? This was a startup. We didn't have time for *architecture*. Just code, dammit! *Code for your very lives!*

So we coded. And we coded. And we coded. But, after three years, what we failed to do was sell. Oh, we had an installation or two. But the market was not particularly interested in our grand vision, and our venture capital financiers were getting pretty fed up.

I hated my life at this point. I saw all my effort and dreams crashing down. I had conflicts at work, conflicts at home because of work, and conflicts with myself.

And then I got a phone call that changed everything.

THE SETUP

Two years before that phone call, two things of significance happened.

First, I managed to set up a uucp connection to a nearby company that had a uucp connection to another facility that was connected to the Internet. These connections were dial-up, of course. Our main Sparcstation (the one on my desk) used a 1200-bps modem to call up our uucp host twice per day. This gave us email and Netnews (an early social network where people discussed interesting issues).

Second, Sun released a C++ compiler. I had been interested in C++ and OO since 1983, but compilers were difficult to come by. So when the opportunity presented itself, I changed languages right away. I left the 3000-line C functions behind, and started to write C++ code at Clear. And I learned …

I read books. Of course, I read *The C++ Programming Language* and *The Annotated C++ Reference Manual* (*The ARM*) by Bjarne Stroustrup. I read Rebecca Wirfs-Brock's lovely book on responsibility-driven design: *Designing Object Oriented Software*. I read *OOA* and *OOD* and *OOP* by Peter Coad. I read *Smalltalk-80* by Adele Goldberg. I read *Advanced C++ Programming Styles and Idioms* by James O. Coplien. But perhaps most significantly of all, I read *Object Oriented Design with Applications* by Grady Booch.

What a name! Grady Booch. How could anyone forget a name like that. What's more, he was the *Chief Scientist* at a company called Rational! How I wanted to be a *Chief Scientist*! And so I read his book. And I learned, and I learned, and I learned …

As I learned, I also began debating on Netnews, the way people now debate on Facebook. My debates were about C++ and OO. For two years, I relieved the frustrations that were building at work by debating with hundreds of folks on Usenet about the best language features and the best principles of design. After a while, I even started making a certain amount of sense.

It was in one of those debates that the foundations of the SOLID principles were laid.

And all that debating, and perhaps even some of the sense, got me noticed …

UNCLE BOB

One of the engineers at Clear was a young fellow by the name of Billy Vogel. Billy gave nicknames to everyone. He called me Uncle Bob. I suspect, despite my name being Bob, that he was making an offhand reference to J. R. "Bob" Dobbs (see https://en.wikipedia.org/wiki/File:Bobdobbs.png).

At first I tolerated it. But as the months went by, his incessant chattering of "Uncle Bob, … Uncle Bob," in the context of the pressures and disappointments of the startup, started to wear pretty thin.

And then, one day, the phone rang.

THE PHONE CALL

It was a recruiter. He had gotten my name as someone who knew C++ and object-oriented design. I'm not sure how, but I suspect it had something to do with my Netnews presence.

He said he had an opportunity in Silicon Valley, at a company named Rational. They were looking for help building a CASE[13] tool.

The blood drained from my face. I *knew* what this was. I don't know how I knew, but I *knew*. This was *Grady Booch's* company. I saw before me the opportunity to join forces with *Grady Booch*!

---

13. Computer Aided Software Engineering

ROSE

I joined Rational, as a contract programmer, in 1990. I was working on the ROSE product. This was a tool that allowed programmers to draw Booch diagrams—the diagrams that Grady had written about in *Object-Oriented Analysis and Design with Applications* (Figure A.9 shows an example).

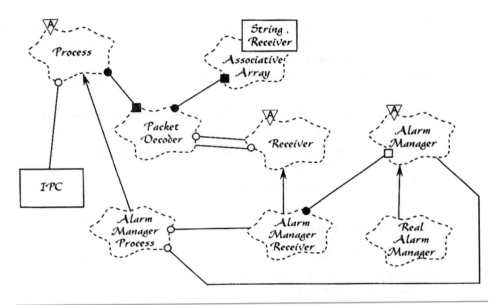

Figure A.9 A Booch diagram

The Booch notation was very powerful. It presaged notations like UML.

ROSE had an architecture—a *real* architecture. It was constructed in true layers, and the dependencies between layers were properly controlled. The architecture made it releasable, developable, and independently deployable.

Oh, it wasn't perfect. There were a lot of things we still didn't understand about architectural principles. We did not, for example, create a true plugin structure.

We also fell for one of the most unfortunate fads of the day—we used a so-called object-oriented database.

But, overall, the experience was a great one. I spent a lovely year and a half working with the Rational team on ROSE. This was one of the most intellectually stimulating experiences of my professional life.

The Debates Continued

Of course, I did not stop debating on Netnews. In fact, I drastically increased my network presence. I started writing articles for *C++ Report*. And, with Grady's help, I started working on my first book: *Designing Object-Oriented C++ Applications Using the Booch Method*.

One thing bothered me. It was perverse, but it was true. No one was calling me "Uncle Bob." I found that I missed it. So I made the mistake of putting "Uncle Bob" in my email and Netnews signatures. And the name stuck. Eventually I realized that it was a pretty good brand.

... By Any Other Name

ROSE was a gigantic C++ application. It was composed of layers, with a strictly enforced dependency rule. That rule is not the rule that I have described in this book. We did *not* point our dependencies toward high-level policies. Rather, we pointed our dependencies in the more traditional direction of flow control. The GUI pointed at the representation, which pointed at the manipulation rules, which pointed at the database. In the end, it was this failure to direct our dependencies toward policy that aided the eventual demise of the product.

The architecture of ROSE was similar to the architecture of a good compiler. The graphical notation was "parsed" into an internal representation; that representation was then manipulated by rules and stored in an object-oriented database.

Object-oriented databases were a relatively new idea, and the OO world was all abuzz with the implications. Every object-oriented programmer wanted to have an object-oriented database in his or her system. The idea was relatively simple, and deeply idealistic. The database stores objects, not tables. The database was supposed to look like RAM. When you accessed an object, it simply appeared in memory. If that object pointed to another object, the other object would appear in memory as soon as you accessed it. It was like magic.

That database was probably our biggest practical mistake. We wanted the magic, but what we got was a big, slow, intrusive, expensive third-party framework that made our lives hell by impeding our progress on just about every level.

That database was not the only mistake we made. The biggest mistake, in fact, was over-architecture. There were many more layers than I have described here, and each had its own brand of communications overhead. This served to significantly reduce the productivity of the team.

Indeed, after many man-years of work, immense struggles, and two tepid releases, the whole tool was scrapped and replaced with a cute little application written by a small team in Wisconsin.

And so I learned that great architectures sometimes lead to great failures. Architecture must be flexible enough to adapt to the size of the problem. Architecting for the enterprise, when all you really need is a cute little desktop tool, is a recipe for failure.

ARCHITECTS REGISTRY EXAM

In the early 1990s, I became a true consultant. I traveled the world teaching people what this new OO thing was. My consulting was focused strongly on the design and architecture of object-oriented systems.

One of my first consulting clients was Educational Testing Service (ETS). It was under contract with the National Council of Architects Registry Board (NCARB) to conduct the registration exams for new architect candidates.

Anyone desiring to be a registered architect (the kind who design buildings) in the United States or Canada must pass the registration exam. This exam involved having the candidate solve a number of architectural problems involving building design. The candidate might be given a set of requirements for a public library, or a restaurant, or a church, and then asked to draw the appropriate architectural diagrams.

The results would be collected and saved until such time as a group of senior architects could be gathered together as jurors, to score the submissions. These gatherings were big, expensive events and were the source of much ambiguity and delay.

NCARB wanted to automate the process by having the candidates take the exams using a computer, and then have another computer do the evaluation and scoring. NCARB asked ETS to develop that software, and ETS hired me to gather a team of developers to produce the product.

ETS had broken the problem down into 18 individual test vignettes. Each would require a CAD-like GUI application that the candidate would use to express his or her solution. A separate scoring application would take in the solutions and produce scores.

My partner, Jim Newkirk, and I realized that these 36 applications had vast amounts of similarity. The 18 GUI apps all used similar gestures and mechanisms. The 18 scoring applications all used the same mathematical techniques. Given these shared elements, Jim and I were determined to develop a reusable framework for all 36 applications. Indeed, we sold this idea to ETS by saying that we'd spend a long time working on the first application, but then the rest would just pop out every few weeks.

At this point you should be face-palming or banging your head on this book. Those of you who are old enough may remember the "reuse" promise of OO. We were all convinced, back then, that if you just wrote good clean object-oriented C++ code, you would just naturally produce lots and lots of reusable code.

So we set about to write the first application—which was the most complicated of the batch. It was called Vignette Grande.

The two of us worked full time on Vignette Grande with an eye toward creating a reusable framework. It took us a year. At the end of that year we had 45,000 lines of framework code and 6000 lines of application code. We delivered this product to ETS, and they contracted with us to write the other 17 applications post-haste.

So Jim and I recruited a team of three other developers and we began to work on the next few vignettes.

But something went wrong. We found that the reusable framework we had created was not particularly reusable. It did not fit well into the new applications being written. There were subtle frictions that just didn't work.

This was deeply discouraging, but we believed we knew what to do about it. We went to ETS and told them that there would be a delay—that the 45,000-line framework needed to be rewritten, or at least readjusted. We told them that it would take a while longer to get that done.

I don't need to tell you that ETS was not particularly happy with this news.

So we began again. We set the old framework aside and began writing four new vignettes simultaneously. We would borrow ideas and code from the old framework but rework them so that they fit into all four without modification. This effort took another year. It produced another 45,000-line framework, plus four vignettes that were on the order of 3000 to 6000 lines each.

Needless to say, the relationship between the GUI applications and the framework followed the Dependency Rule. The vignettes were plugins to the framework. All the high-level GUI policy was in the framework. The vignette code was just glue.

The relationship between the scoring applications and the framework was a bit more complex. The high-level scoring policy was in the vignette. The scoring framework plugged into the scoring vignette.

Of course, both of these applications were statically linked C++ applications, so the notion of plugin was nowhere in our minds. And yet, the way the dependencies ran was consistent with the Dependency Rule.

Having delivered those four applications, we began on the next four. And this time they started popping out the back end every few weeks, just as we had predicted. The delay had cost us nearly a year on our schedule, so we hired another programmer to speed the process along.

We met our dates and our commitments. Our customer was happy. We were happy. Life was good.

But we learned a good lesson: You can't make a reusable framework until you first make a usable framework. Reusable frameworks require that you build them in concert with *several* reusing applications.

CONCLUSION

As I said at the start, this appendix is somewhat autobiographical. I've hit the high points of the projects that I felt had an architectural impact. And, of course, I mentioned a few episodes that were not exactly relevant to the technical content of this book, but were significant nonetheless.

Of course, this was a partial history. There were many other projects that I worked on over the decades. I also purposely stopped this history in the early 1990s—because I have another book to write about the events of the late 1990s.

My hope is that you enjoyed this little trip down my memory lane; and that you were able to learn some things along the way.

INDEX

Register Your Product at informit.com/register

Access additional benefits and **save 35%** on your next purchase

- Automatically receive a coupon for 35% off your next purchase, valid for 30 days. Look for your code in your InformIT cart or the Manage Codes section of your account page.

- Download available product updates.

- Access bonus material if available.

- Check the box to hear from us and receive exclusive offers on new editions and related products.

InformIT.com—The Trusted Technology Learning Source

InformIT is the online home of information technology brands at Pearson, the world's foremost education company. At InformIT.com, you can:

- Shop our books, eBooks, software, and video training
- Take advantage of our special offers and promotions (informit.com/promotions)
- Sign up for special offers and content newsletter (informit.com/newsletters)
- Access thousands of free chapters and video lessons

Connect with InformIT—Visit informit.com/community